Study Guide for

Human
Information
Processing

SECOND EDITION

Study Guide for

Human
Information
Processing

SECOND EDITION

LINDSAY · NORMAN

ROSS BOTT
ALLEN MUNRO

University of California, San Diego

ACADEMIC PRESS, INC. New York San Francisco London
A Subsidiary of Harcourt Brace Jovanovich, Publishers

ACADEMIC PRESS, INC.
111 Fifth Avenue, New York, New York 10003

United Kingdom Edition published by
ACADEMIC PRESS, INC. (LONDON) LTD.
24/28 Oval Road, London NW1

ISBN 0–12–450962–2

PRINTED IN THE UNITED STATES OF AMERICA

Preface

This study guide is designed to accompany Lindsay and Norman's HUMAN INFORMATION PROCESSING (abbreviated "HIP"). Problems and questions range from ones that are relatively easy to several that are somewhat difficult. This variation is intentional; the easy exercises explain and demonstrate the principles introduced in HIP, and the harder problems challenge you to apply those principles to new areas.

Much of this study guide relies on the process of model building to review and expand on the principles in the text. Models will be proposed to explain experimental results. By using models our goal is to help you develop the ability to find truly significant patterns of results. This ability involves a critical attitude toward any experiment. A critical approach will lead you to examine the method carefully for flaws and search for alternative interpretations and explanations for the results. It also involves the knack of devising a clear experiment for testing a theory; for drawing a correspondence between two seemingly unrelated results or patterns; and finally, for sifting out a general trend from an array of results.

For many of the models that are proposed, we will conduct a joint search with you to discover the fatal flaws in the models. For others, you will be asked to design an experiment to test the model further. We encourage you to propose models of your own, and to design experiments to test them.

We believe that the model building approach will strengthen your basic knowledge in psychology. You will master the important terms presented in HIP by using them extensively. You will find that you have less memorizing to do because these concepts will fit into a meaningful picture. As a result, it is our hope that the insights and information that you acquire through using this study guide will stay with you for a long time.

Acknowledgments

Many people helped us in various ways to write this study guide. Don Norman helped us to get started on this project, gave advice, helped us to test the chapters in his class, and lent encouragement. We benefited from the experience and teaching materials developed in earlier versions of a self-paced introductory course by many graduate students and faculty members at the University of California, San Diego. We especially thank Mark Eisenstadt, Don Gentner, Dedre Gentner, Art Graesser, Rob Hoffman, Kris Hooper, Jim Levin, Pam Munro, Steve Palmer, Dave Rumelhart, and Al Stevens.

We also thank the students in the courses who made valuable comments on and suggestions for this study guide.

Contents

1. HUMAN PERCEPTION   1

2. THE VISUAL SYSTEM   13

3. THE DIMENSIONS OF VISION   23

4. THE AUDITORY SYSTEM   31

5. THE DIMENSIONS OF SOUND   49

6. NEURAL INFORMATION PROCESSING   73

7. PATTERN RECOGNITION AND ATTENTION   95

8. THE MEMORY SYSTEMS   115

9. USING MEMORY   127

10. THE REPRESENTATION OF KNOWLEDGE   141

11. THE NEURAL BASIS OF MEMORY   155

12. LANGUAGE   173

13. LEARNING AND COGNITIVE DEVELOPMENT   191

14. PROBLEM SOLVING AND DECISION MAKING   203

15. THE MECHANISMS OF THOUGHT   229

16. SOCIAL INTERACTIONS   243

17. STRESS AND EMOTION   255

    ANSWERS   261

1 Human perception

PRETEST

1. A system which uses internal patterns stored in memory to identify patterns in the outside world is a _____.

2. The dalmatian dog is an example of a _____ image.

3. There are two general types of processing in the interpretation of visual input. They are _____ and _____ processing.

4. In "The Slave Market with Disappearing Bust of Voltaire" there are two _____, both of which are meaningful interpretations.

5. The conversations you are not listening to at a party become part of the _____.

6. A "fork intersection" implies that all three surfaces belong to the same body. This is an example of a _____.

7. Contextual information is primarily used by _____ driven processing.

8. The McCollough effect provides strong evidence for the existence of _____ detectors.

9. Color aftereffects suggest the existence of _____ systems in the visual pathway.

10. How will a stabilized visual image disappear? _____ _____

1. template system;   2. degraded;   3. data-driven and conceptually driven;   4. competing organizations;   5. background;   6. rule;   7. conceptually;   8. line; 9. antagonistic;   10. in meaningful parts

---

INTRODUCTION

Pretend that the scene in front of you is presented on a huge color television screen. If you have ever looked closely at a TV screen, you have probably noticed that the picture is actually not continuous at all, but consists of thousands of closely spaced dots. Each dot is identical to the next one except for differences in color. Thus all that is really in front of you is a huge, orderly collection of dots. Yet when you look at a TV screen from a reasonable distance, you do not see dots--you automatically see and identify objects, shapes and movements. Now you might argue that the scene in front of you really is not a TV screen, that the process we just described occurs only when we watch television. But the first step of our visual system really is like a television camera: Light patterns from the outside world pass through the eye and form images on the retina at the back of the eye. The retina is made up of millions of light detector cells, each of which measures how much light and what color light is shining just on that cell, and passes that information on toward the brain. All the eye knows about the outside visual world is what these millions of tiny dot-shaped light detectors tell it. Thus, as far as the brain knows, the outside world is simply lots of different colored dots--a television screen.

Therefore, our analogy still holds; our neural system somehow has the ability to take a huge set of dots of light and automatically "see" or interpret them as a group of objects organized in a meaningful way. Much of experimental psychology is directly or indirectly related to attempting to describe exactly how our brain performs this "magic," which is called "perception."

The difficulty with discovering how perception works is that the process is normally so automatic and fast that we are not aware of it in ourselves; nor can we observe it in other people. One way to make the perceptual process more visible is to trick it into making mistakes. For this reason, experimenters give it scenes that are difficult to interpret or present it with sets of objects that have no meaningful relationship. A second approach is to stretch the perceptual process to the limits of its abilities, by giving it scenes where much of the information is taken away or presented for a very short time. (For example, in our television analogy, one could randomly delete dots from the picture.)

The major purpose of Chapter 1 of Human Information Processing (HIP) is to provide some evidence about the abilities and limitations of our perceptual system, so that we can learn something about this system. Chapters 2, 3, 4, 5, and 7 of HIP will take this body of evidence and try to build models of parts of our perceptual system, but for now we must collect the evidence. Most of the experimental tests in this chapter you can try on yourself, and it is well worth the time it takes to do them.

This chapter does not propose a theory of perception. However, the experimental information points toward several underlying principles, including the crucial role of context in recognition; the fact that sensory information is always interpreted or given a meaning; the necessity of using features in perception; the natural separation of a pattern into figure and background; and the importance of rules in perception. These principles will have to be explained by any theory or model of how the perceptual system works. Many models will fail because they cannot explain all the incredible capabilities of the human perceptual system. For this chapter, though, your task is to understand these principles, and, given some piece of evidence, to explain what principle it supports and how.

The process of proposing a model of perception and testing it, modifying it, and retesting it, is demonstrated in this chapter for a simple model--the template system. It is useful to spend some time studying this process of modeling, for it will be repeated many times in the upcoming chapters; in a sense, it is the basis of all science.

TEMPLATE SYSTEM ON TRIAL

Imagine you have a large collection of black shapes printed on white paper. Each of these shapes is one of five different kinds, and you have a set of five cardboard sheets with one of the five patterns cut out of the middle of each. You are going to classify the black shapes into five piles by taking each shape in turn and trying cardboard sheets on top of it until you find a case where no white paper shows. This is a template system of sorts (call it TSC); thus, the components of it should be analogous to the parts of the first simple template system suggested in Chapter 1 of HIP as a basis for human perception (call this second system TSP). Your task is to find the parts which correspond in the two systems:

1   What are the templates of the TSC called? _____

2 What parts correspond to this in the TSP? _____

_____

3   In the TSC, what are the patterns to be matched? _____

_____

     The act of your seeing whether any white shows in the TSC corresponds to what

4 process in the TSP? _____

     The act of your finding a cardboard pattern where no white shows in the TSC is

5 analogous to what in the TSP? _____

     One point on which the two example template systems differ is that, whereas in

the TSC one matches each of the cardboard templates to the unknown shape consecu-

6 tively, in the TSP _____

     According to HIP the simple template system for perception fails for two reasons.

Examples of each reason are given below. In each case, name the general problem

referred to:

7   (i) Recognizing the same person from two different distances _____

_____

8   (ii) Turn this page upside down and you can still read it _____

_____

When you see a letter right in front of you, the image of that letter will project

on approximately the middle of the retina. What do you think happens when you see

9 a letter out of the corner of your eye? _____

_____ . From this, name a third reason why this simple system

10 will not work. _____

     Therefore, we need some way of "standardizing" input patterns, that is, making

each <u>A</u> that is seen look the same as all the others, before it is tested against

the templates. To solve our three problems we need three different standardization

operations: adjust the size, orientation, and location. Although it is fairly

clear what each of these operations means, it is far more difficult to set up

methods that really work. For example, in order to standardize the orientation, one

might adjust each letter such that the longer of the two dimensions is aligned with

the vertical. But suppose that some of the letters are actually wider than they are

tall. For instance, if we are trying to recognize the lowercase alphabet, consider

<u>m</u>. Then this alignment operation is going to make <u>m</u> sideways. Can you think of a
11 way of getting around this without changing our alignment operation? _____
_____ Suppose we have gotten
around this, however unsatisfactorily, or take an alphabet where this problem does
not occur, e.g., the capital letters. Then we have aligned the longer dimension
with the vertical, but how do we know whether it is right-side up or upside down?
For instance, <u>A</u> could just as easily be aligned ∀ as right side up. And in the first
case a template <u>A</u> would not match it at all.

This problem with the orientation operation has a very similar analogue in the
other two operations. All three of these problems are variations of the following
quandary or paradox: *In order to know how to analyze what an input is, you have to
know what the input is before you start*. This paradox crops up repeatedly in
psychology, especially perception, and is perhaps one of the most important pitfalls
to be aware of in any theory--it is too easy for a model to be intuitively clear, but
not to work unless what it is supposed to find out, is already known. Keep this
principle in the back of your mind when you study the many models introduced in this
book.

In addition to those already named, there is, in fact, another problem with our
standardizing template system, and this is perhaps the clincher. Consider each <u>A</u>
in Figure 1.1.

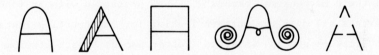

Figure 1.1

You would probably agree that each of these letters can be recognized as <u>A</u>, yet no
reasonable amount of standardization could adjust them to look like our template <u>A</u>.

A Possible Objection: Take the fourth <u>A</u> in Figure 1.1. Suppose we apply a standardization that eliminates the spirals on the legs and changes the curve into a slanted
point. Then this <u>A</u> would look like our standard <u>A</u>. Similarly, we could find
standardizations for each of the others. Explain how this falls into the paradox
12 trap. _____
_____
_____

Another Possible Objection: Why not have templates for each <u>A</u>, such that if some pattern matched any one of these, then it would be called an <u>A</u>? Why is this not

13 a solution? (<u>Hint</u>: consider an <u>A</u> you have never seen before.) _____

_____

Also, even with the <u>A</u> one already knows, one could imagine this method being ex-

14 tremely cumbersome. Why? _____

_____

   If we as humans are not using templates to recognize the letters in Figure 1.1 as <u>A</u>'s, then what are we doing? One way of approaching this is by asking first, "What do those <u>A</u>'s have in common--what distinguishes them from being any other letter or from just being funny-looking patterns?" List anything you see in common

15 in these <u>A</u>'s. _____

_____

_____

   What you listed could probably be called "features," which, in the case of letters, are small parts of a letter that identify it as being a particular one, no matter what variations are found in the rest of the letter. Perhaps we can construct a perceptual system based on these. We need to find a list of features such that some subset of this list will uniquely characterize each letter of the alphabet. Suppose that inside the brain we had a mechanism in charge of each feature (we will call these mechanisms "demons"). When presented with an input pattern, each demon searches all over the pattern looking for and counting instances of its feature. All these "feature demons" shout to "letter demons," each of whom knows what and how many features are in its letter, and the demon that finds the best match for its features "yells" the loudest...but we are getting ahead of the story--this is the "pandemonium system" of Chapter 7.

OUT OF CONTEXT

   It can be shown that in many ways the human perceptual system will almost always interpret things in context. HIP gives many examples of this, a few of which will be considered here, but first let us take the case shown in Figure 1.2.

Figure 1.2

The middle characters in each of the two words are identical, yet the perceptual
system almost automatically interprets the first character as H and the second as A.
Suppose we proposed that, when one reads, each character is analyzed in isolation.
How could you explain that what happened in the words in Figure 1.2 would then be

16 impossible? _____

_____

_____

Consider the painting, "Les Promenades d'Euclide," in Figure 1-24 of HIP. The
phenomenon here is very much like that of Figure 1.2 here. Draw a correspondence
between the two situations. That is, specify what in the picture corresponds to the
two middle characters in the sentence, and show how context acts in an analogous way.

17 _____

_____

_____

_____

In each of these cases, we have two identical pieces of input information, yet
the pieces are interpreted in two quite different ways. Let us take the first
example, THE CAT, again, and analyze it in a different way to see if we can explain
what is happening. When we considered a pattern-recognition system for individual
letters, we rejected a template system for a system probably based on features. Using
this model as a first step, it is possible to list the stages that must be gone
through in understanding the word THE (see Figure 1.3).

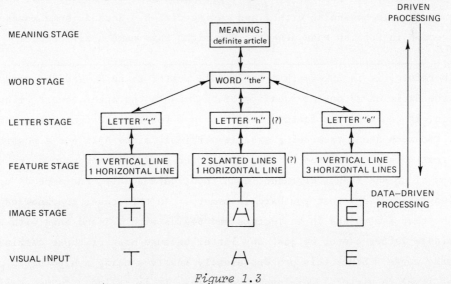

Figure 1.3

The order of these stages as shown in Figure 1.3 cannot be changed: In order to know
that the *letters* are T, H, and E, one needs to know at least some of the features
that make up the letters. Can you give a reason why all the features would not need

18   to be known? _____

_____

Similarly, in order to identify the *word* as THE, one needs to know at least some of
the letters, and so on. Call this ordered process a *data-driven process*, since the
process must begin from the bottom stage with the input data.

It is possible to alter this inevitable flow of information up through the
stages: For example, since the features of the middle character do not clearly
determine the choice of one letter, the processing of that letter in the letter
stage is held up (as indicated by the question marks in Figure 1.3), whereas the
processing of the T and E are completed. Then when the word stage "hears" about the
T and E, it can guess that a likely choice for the word is THE. Can you suggest

19   some other possible words? _____ What
assumptions are you making in suggesting these? (<u>Hint</u>: Why didn't you consider

20   TSE, which is a Chinese word?) _____

21   (<u>Hint</u>: Why didn't you consider THERE?) _____

Why does THE seem more likely than the other possible words, such as TOE or
TIE? First, when we read a phrase such as THE CAT, we expect it to make sense as a
phrase, and not simply to be a list of words, such as TOE CAT, or TIE CAT. Thus,
in processing a noun phrase, one expects it to begin with an article, and THE is
the only article beginning with T and ending with E. Second, some words are just

22   more common in English than others. Why might this make a difference? _____

_____

Therefore, it is likely that the middle letter is an H, and the word stage can
bias the decision as to the identity of the middle character toward being H: For
example, it can tell the feature stage to look for two straight lines, and not to
worry too much about them being exactly vertical, since A is not a possibility.
Note that this process--the biasing of a lower decision--moves *down* the stages
instead of up and is not dependent upon input data at all, but depends upon prior
knowledge--knowledge that you have in memory. In this case, the knowledge is that if
we know that a word has three letters and begins with a T and ends with an E, then
the middle letter cannot be just any letter because most of those combinations would
not make words. Since this process usually involves using a hypothesis at a
higher level to direct lower-level processing, it is called a *conceptually driven*

process. In the last two paragraphs, there was a second example of conceptually

23 driven processing. Can you point out what it was? _____

_____

_____

Can you devise a sentence where conceptually driven processing would operate

one stage higher up, i.e., where the meaning of the rest of a sentence would determine

24 which of two possible meanings would be chosen for an ambiguous word? _____

_____

_____

Consider the painting by Salvador Dali in Figure 1-11 of HIP. Think about what

is happening to your perception of the parts of the picture as you switch from one

interpretation to another. Not all parts of the picture fit equally well into both

interpretations, and when you see the painting in one way, the things that do not

readily fit seem to move into the background. How would you explain this in terms

25 of conceptually driven and data-driven processing? _____

_____

_____

_____

_____

The "two slaves" interpretation seems slightly more prominent than the "bust of

Voltaire" view. In terms of these two types of processing, why might this be so?

26 _____

_____

Listen to some song that you don't know well, preferably by a singer who blurs

his or her words slightly, and for which you can also get a written version (which

you haven't looked at). Without looking at the score, try to pick out each word in

the song. Do you notice that most of the areas for which the words are unclear come

27 in phrases and not just single words? Explain. _____

_____

Now listen to the song while reading the score. Why do the words seem so much clearer

28 even though the singer is not blurring them any less than before? _____

_____

_____

EXPECTATIONS AND RULES

In Figure 1.4, the drawing of a group of blocks,

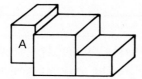

Figure 1.4

draw what you would think the full shape of the block labeled **A** should be:

29

Yet it would be perfectly consistent with Figure 1.4 if block **A** were shaped like any
of the blocks in Figure 1.5. What would you say your expectations as to the shape
30 of the block were based upon? _____

_____

_____

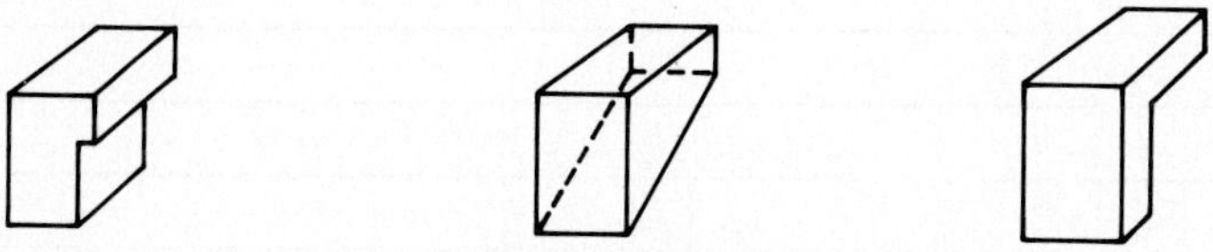

Figure 1.5

When Guzman developed his block-analyzing program, the rules for analyzing line
drawings that he settled upon were in a sense no more than expectations like you
had, and many of the rules could fail in certain situations, much as your expectations
might have been incorrect. The only difference between his "rules" and your
"expectations" is that rules tend to be explicitly written and followed, whereas
expectations are almost always unconsciously followed. Expectations are simply
implicit rules. The reason such rules work at all, and why you have any expectations,
is that, in general, they are correct--events in the world are usually quite repetitive and, therefore, predictable. This repetitiveness and the fact that humans can
notice it is absolutely crucia; without it there almost surely would be no intelligence.

In recognizing THE from the pattern in Figure 1.6, one is utilizing rules.
31 What rule or rules? _____

_____

T⊣E

Figure 1.6

If that pattern were found in a piece of prose, what additional rule is one

32   following? _____

INTERPRETING

In HIP it is stated that sensory information must be interpreted and organized. Now it is clear that this is a useful process when an input (say a picture) has meaning, for an interpretation then is just the finding of that meaning. But when a picture or some other input has no meaning, we still try to interpret or organize

33   it. Give an example. _____
_____. Why do you think we still attempt to interpret? This is an extremely difficult question and psychologists do not yet have a full answer, but it is still worthwhile to ponder.

ANTAGONISTIC SYSTEMS

Most of the experiments presented in the last several pages of Chapter 1 of HIP can be explained by two systems in opposition to each other--when one system gets tired the opposing one takes over temporarily. In Table 1.1, several light patterns are listed. Suppose that each of these patterns is presented for a sufficient amount of time to produce an aftereffect. For each, specify the system of neural detectors that is being exhausted, the antagonistic system, what aftereffect will be seen, and what background must be looked at in order to see this aftereffect:

	Light pattern	Exhausted system	Antagonistic system	Aftereffect and background
34	Bright red light			
35	Waterfall			

Table 1.1

Light pattern	Exhausted system	Antagonistic system	Aftereffect and background
36	Vertical yellow stripes			
37	Bright blue light			
38	Horizontal green stripes moving upward			
39	Rotating spiral moving inward			
40	Vertical green stripes			

Table 1.1 (cont.)

41   It is proposed that antagonistic systems are used in perceiving complementary colors. Why or how would one ever see white, then? _____

_____

42 Suppose one exposes a subject to bright red light for several minutes. The subject is then shown a large green patch on a screen. Use what you know of antagonistic systems to predict what will be seen. _____

_____

43   Both complementary colors and opposite motions are handled by antagonistic systems. Why not horizontal and vertical orientations also? _____

_____

44 If horizontal and vertical were handled by antagonistic systems (but remember that they are not!), what would be the aftereffect, for example, of horizontal green lines? _____

_____

2 The visual system

PRETEST

1. Log (1,000,000) = _____

2. The physical factor that is most important in determining the brightness of a light is _____.

3. What psychological dimension is the physical dimension *wavelength* most closely correlated with? _____

4. Name the principal parts of the eye._____

_____

5. What property do retinal ganglion cells and bipolar cells have in common, in opposition to amacrine cells and horizontal cells? _____

_____

6. What are the two types of receptor cells in the human eye? _____ and _____

7. Does being cross-eyed imply trouble with convergence or with focusing?

_____

8. What is a saccade? _____

9. What part of the retina is most sensitive to lights of extremely low intensity? _____

10. How much pattern analysis is accomplished at the optic chiasma? _____

_____

1. 6; 2. intensity; 3. color; 4. cornea, aqueous humor, pupil, lens, vitreous humor, retina; 5. They pass information upward toward the brain, rather than mediate between units at the retinal level; 6. rods, cones; 7. convergence; 8. a ballistic eye movement followed by a fixation; 9. the area surrounding (but not in) the fovea; 10. none

---

INTRODUCTION

It is very easy to take seeing for granted. If, however, we consider in detail what the visual system must accomplish in order for light energy impinging on the eye to be understood as visual sensations and perceptions, we should be very impressed. The eye gets to work with light energy of various wavelengths in various intensities, and we see shape, color, movement, objects, and events. As you study Chapters 2 and 3, you should keep in mind the size of the leap that the eye and brain make in constructing the experiences of *seeing* on the basis of the changes in location and intensity of light on the retina.

Light

Light is described in terms of its wavelength and intensity. Wavelength is measured in nanometers. What is the unit of measurement for light intensity?

1 _____

The range of intensities of light which can be perceived by the human eye is enormous: one millionth of a candela/meter^2 can just barely be detected by the dark-adapted human eye, and as much as one million candela/meter^2 can be viewed without pain. This great range of intensities is very cumbersome when one uses units such as candela/meter^2. Just getting the entire range of perceivable intensities onto a graph can be a problem. Suppose, for example that we want to measure the sensitivity of the human eye. We do this by dark-adapting subjects and then flashing lights of various intensities and seeing whether the subjects can detect the lights. Figure 2.1 represents the probability that a dark-adapted subject will detect a light of a given intensity. The scale has microcandela/meter^2 gradations. (A microcandela/meter^2 is one millionth of a candela/meter^2.) Obviously, this graph shows the results for only a small part of the lower end of the visible range of light. Imagine that we wish to represent the results of the experiment for the entire intensity range.

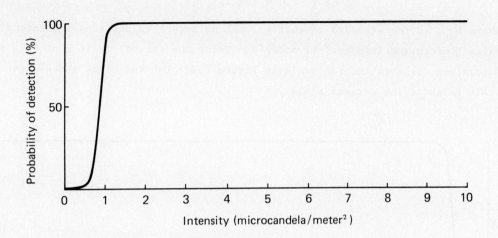

Figure 2.1

How many times longer than the above graph (in Figure 2.1) would such a graph have

2   to be? _____

Obviously, the making of such graphs would prove very inconvenient. One way to
represent the phenomenon of interest over the whole range of human vision is
to make use of a logarithmic scale of light intensities. Figure 2.2 represents the
same light detection experiment that Figure 2.1 does. But the x axis in Figure 2.2
is a *log* scale of light intensity. This type of scale has two advantages. First,
it permits us to use an expanded scale at the lower end of the intensity range,
without committing ourselves to a graph 10 times as long. Second, it allows us to
represent the probability of detection of a light along the entire range of visible
light intensities using much less graph paper than if we had continued the graph of
Figure 2.1.

How many times longer than the graph in Figure 2.2 would a graph have to be to

3   include the entire range of visible nonpainful light intensities? _____

_____

Decibels are simply a type of logarithmic scale. If we wish to express the
intensity of some light in decibels (dB), we must compare that intensity to some
standard intensity. To express some intensity I in decibels, multiply by 10 the
log of the ratio of that intensity and the standard intensity:

$$\text{dB of I = 10 x } \log(I/I_{std}),$$

where I_{std} is the standard intensity. Let us accept as our standard intensity the value 1 microcandela/meter^2 (1 mcd/m^2). Using the decibel scale that this standard determines, relabel the log scale in Figure 2.2. Use the blank spaces under the log scale to enter the decibel scale.

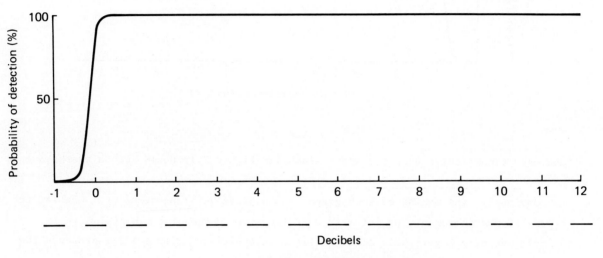

Figure 2.2

THE PARTS OF THE EYE

Figure 2.3 represents a cutaway view of the eye. What are the names of the numbered parts of the eye?

5 _____

6 _____

7 _____

8 _____

9 _____

10 _____

11 _____

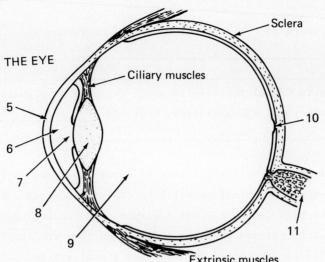

THE EYE

Figure 2.3

Which two parts of the eye are primarily responsible for the focusing of the

12   image? _____ and _____

13   List three functional defects in the design of the human lens. _____

_____

_____

The pupil is capable of considerable changes in size. A fully dilated pupil has

16 times the area of a fully constricted pupil. Assume that this means that a fully

dilated pupil can admit 16 times as much light as the smallest diameter pupil. Re-

call the possible range of perceivable light intensities. How many decibels are in

14 this range? _____   Do the changes in pupil size account for the range

15 of perceivable intensities? _____ Explain. _____

_____

16   What is convergence? _____

Which muscles are responsible for convergence? _____

17   What is focusing (in the eye)? _____

Which muscles are responsible for focusing? _____

THE RETINA

The visual pigment in rod cells is called *rhodopsin*. What is its more common

18 name? _____ What happens to its color when

19 it is exposed to light? _____

Do lights of different wavelengths but equal intensities bleach rhodopsin to

20 the same extent? _____

21 Explain the relationships of retinene and vitamin A to rhodopsin. _____

_____

_____

What kind of changes in visual sensitivity would result from a small amount of

22 bleaching of the eye's total rhodopsin (say 4 or 5%)? _____

_____

Different organisms need different kinds of visual systems. A nocturnal hunter
needs good night vision. A diurnal animal like the pigeon needs a system that
functions well in the high intensities of daylight. In humans, two visual systems
have considerable functional independence even though they are combined in each eye.
For each of the following attributes of the human visual system, mark an X in the
appropriate column to indicate whether that attribute holds for Visual System A
(the system whose receptive elements are cones) or for Visual System B (the system
with rod receptors). If an attribute is shared by <u>both</u> systems, put an X in <u>both</u>
columns.

		Visual System A (cone)	Visual System B (rod)
23	Night vision		
24	Frequency discrimination		
25	Maximum acuity (ability to resolve small objects)		
26	Peripheral vision		
27	Visual pigment in receptors		
28	Maximum sensitivity (detection of dim intensity)		
29	Central vision		
30	Rhodopsin		
31	Foveal vision		

Now let us briefly review the neurological organization of the retina. The term
"vertical organization" is used to refer to the sequence of cells that pass signals
from the recepts to the central nervous system. The types of cells that relay

32 signals from the receptors toward the brain are rods or cones ⟶ _____

⟶ _____ .

The term "horizontal organization" refers to those cells that mediate interactions between cells at the same level in the vertical organization. What are the

two types of cells which are responsible for horizontal organization on the retina?

33 _____ and _____

34   A fiber of the optic nerve is actually part of what kind of cell? _____

THE NEUROANATOMY OF VISION

Where does visual analysis of pattern information begin in the visual system:
at the retina, the optic chiasma, the lateral geniculate nucleus, or the cortex?

35 _____

36   Why does each eye have a blind spot? _____

_____

Does light striking the retina first hit ganglion cells, bipolar cells, or

37 receptors (rods and cones)? _____

From what type of cells do the fibers that cross at the optic chiasma come?

38 _____

An object in the right half of the visual field is focused on which side of the

39 retina of the left eye? _____ On which side of the retina

of the right eye? _____ As a result of the regrouping of fibers

at the optic chiasma, which hemisphere of the brain gets the visual information

40 about this object? _____

EYE MOVEMENTS

Four or five times every second, the eyes make a quick jump, causing an abrupt
change in the visual image focused on the retina. What are these types of movements

41 called? _____ Once one of the eye movements has begun,

its course is not altered. What is the general term for this type of movement?

42 _____ (Hint: This adjective can be applied to other

types of movement that are uncontrolled once initiated, such as the movement of a

cannon ball once it is fired.) In view of the fact that over 50% of the visual

cortex seems to be devoted to the analysis of only the central 10% of the visual

43 field, give a functional explanation for this type of eye movement. _____

_____

_____

WHERE DOES INFORMATION GO FROM THE RETINA?

Suppose that a new species of one-eyed mammal has just been discovered. A group

of neuroanatomists is studying the visual system of this creature. Figure 2.4
represents the layout of this visual system when viewed from above.

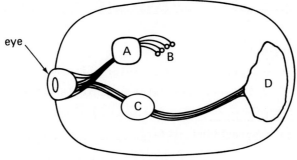

Figure 2.4

The brain structures labeled A-D are thought to be the major centers for relaying
and analyzing visual information. Soon after leaving the eye, the optic nerve splits
into two separate channels. The neuroanatomists have conducted a number of experiments to try to understand the functions of the brain structures on these two
channels. To try to understand the functions of structures A and D, they removed
either one or the other of them from different experimental animals of the species.
At first all of the animals seemed to be equally affected--they all seemed to be
blind. More careful observations soon revealed, however, that the animals that
were missing structure D were still able to orient toward moving objects. That is,
their eyes and head would turn toward the objects when they were moved. However,
these animals could not be trained to make different responses to differently pattern-
ed objects, either moving or stationary. Those animals which had lost structure A
were not capable of this orientation response. In view of this evidence, what
44   human brain structure is most analogous to structure A? _____

Those animals from which structure A had been removed were found still to be
capable of learning to discriminate between visual patterns, so long as the experimental tasks did not require that the animals be able to locate the patterns that
were to be discriminated. On the basis of this evidence, let us assume that
structure D might be analogous to the visual cortex. If this is so, what human brain
45   structure is most analogous to structure C? _____

In Figure 2.4 a number of nerve fibers are depicted which run from structure A
to the collection of nerve bundles labeled B. When individual groups of these
nerves are stimulated electrically in living animals, they move their eyes and
sometimes their heads, as though they were looking at something. Does this evidence

serve to confirm or disconfirm your hypothesis about the human brain structure which
46 is analogous to structure A? _____ Explain. _____

_____

_____

Do you think it likely that Figure 2.4 is a complete representation of the flow of
47 visual information? _____ Explain. _____

_____

_____

3 The dimensions of vision

PRETEST

Write the psychological dimension which most closely corresponds to each of the following physical dimensions of light:

1. wavelength _____

2. intensity _____

3. purity _____

4. The fact that a dark surrounding border will cause a gray patch of a given intensity to appear brighter than will a white surrounding border is an example of _____.

5. The visual system seems to have detectors for recognizing parallel bars with specific spacings. The term for this type of visual analysis is _____ _____.

6. If a violet light and a green light have exactly the same intensity, will they appear equally bright? _____

7. What type of receptor in the retina participates in the perception of color? _____

8. True or False: "The pigment in rods, rhodopsin, does not absorb light equally well across the whole of the visual spectrum." _____

9. The rate at which a flickering light appears to be continuous is called the _____ frequency.

10. If two different wavelengths of light are mixed together, do we usually see both colors, just the higher or the lower wavelength, or a new color? _____ _____

1. color;   2. brightness;   3. saturation;   4. brightness contrast;   5. spatial
frequency analysis;   6. no (the green light will be brighter);   7. cone;   8. True;
9. critical flicker;   10. a new color

THE PERCEPTION OF BRIGHTNESS

   Imagine that you have a specially treated piece of clear transparent film so that
portions of it are no longer transparent. Figure 3.1 shows that the film can be
considered to have three parts (although lines y and z are not actually drawn on the
film). The area from edge x to y has had a uniformly dense concentration of tiny
black particles embedded in it. As a result, very little light can now penetrate
this section of the film. The area from z to edge w has not been altered; thus,
most of the light that strikes the film there passes through. The section of film
from y to z has had a continuously varying concentration of particles embedded in it,
starting from a dense concentration at y, with gradually fewer particles to the right,
until there are virtually none in the film just to the left of z.

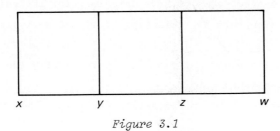

Figure 3.1

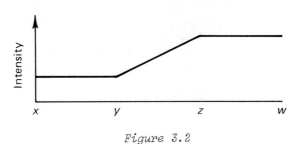

Figure 3.2

   Figure 3.2 shows the intensity of the light passed by the film when it is illuminated from behind by a white light. The intensity of the light is least in the area

from x to y, greatest between z and w, and increases continuously from y to z.

1   Sketch directly on Figure 3.2 a curve showing the *perceived brightness* of the film when it is viewed under these conditions.

What is the term for these areas of perceived brightness and perceived darkness
2 which do not reflect real intensities? _____

In a Gothic novel you are reading, the heroine becomes trapped in the abandoned dungeon of an ancient castle at midnight. Her flashlight soon burns out, and the author tells you that "she then experienced the most intense blackness she had ever seen." Assume that, in fact, she had never been in a place with as little light. Do you think that she had never seen anything blacker than whatever she
3 happened to be looking at in the dungeon? _____ Under what circumstances can something appear blacker than it does when no light falls on it at all? _____

_____

Suppose you are looking at a sheet of white paper on a white background, under good indoor illumination. Without changing the illumination, what could you do to
4 make the sheet of paper brighter? _____

Sometimes raising the general illumination can make an object appear darker.
5 Under what conditions is this the case? _____

_____

What is the name of the psychological process which accounts for the phenomena dealt
6 with in questions 3-5? _____

Recall the experiments on brightness and depth discussed in Chapter 3 of HIP, in which a flat object, shaped in such a way that it appears to be lying on the table is, in fact, standing perpendicular to the table. If this object is closer to the observer than the overhead light, the side facing the observer will be in shadow. It is thus a less intense source of reflected light for the observer than similar objects that are actually lying on the table. How does this object appear
7 to the observer, relative to the similar objects? _____

_____ How can the display be changed to result in more
8 accurate brightness judgments on the part of the observer? _____

_____

VISUAL ADAPTATION

Figure 3.3 shows two dark-adaptation curves. An ophthalmologist shows you the two curves, claiming they came from two interesting patients. The patient with Curve 1 seems to have no peripheral vision, whereas the patient with Curve 2 cannot

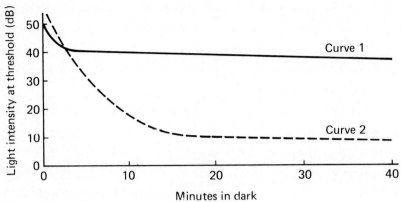

Figure 3.3

read or perform any other task that calls for a very high degree of foveal acuity.
Might these patients' problems be attributable to receptor deficiencies? How?

9 _____

_____

How good do you think their performances would be in a color identification task?

10 _____

_____

     Now imagine that the two curves are actually from the same individual, but that
they were obtained under different conditions. One of the curves was obtained with
a monochromatic blue test light, the other with a monochromatic red test light.

11 Which was which? _____

     Now imagine that you learn that the two curves are not only from the same indi-
vidual, but that the test lights were white light in both conditions. However, the
test lights were presented to different parts of the retina in the different

12 conditions. Where for Curve 1? _____ Where for Curve 2?

_____

     One day, as you begin a hike in the mountains, you pass through a field of red
and blue flowers. You notice that the effect is colorful, and that the red flowers
are brighter than the blue in the mid-morning sun. That evening, as you pass
through the same field at dusk while returning, you realize that the blue flowers

13 are now distinctly brighter than the red. Why? _____

_____

Take a look at the equibrightness contours in Figure 3-17 of HIP. Note the shift
to the right in the higher brightness curves in that figure. Relate this phenomenon

14 to your explanation for the change in brightness of the red and blue flowers. _____

_____

_____

     You decide to replicate the dark-adaptation experiment which results in the
classic curve shown in Figure 3-14 of HIP. You and your subject spend a few minutes
in the experimental booth, which is illuminated by a 60-W bulb, while you check out
your equipment. Then you turn out the light and begin presenting the test lights.
When you plot your results, you find that your curve looks much like Figure 3-14
with the first eight minutes missing. That is, your subject began by being able to
see a test light which was 40 dB over the standard 10^{-6} candela/meter^2; required a
test light of about this brightness for about three minutes; then suddenly began to
see dimmer and dimmer test lights, leveling out at about 25 minutes or so. Why
15 did you get these results? _____

_____

_____

TEMPORAL CHARACTERISTICS OF VISION

     Congratulations! You have just been granted sole rights to the distribution of
Hollywood movies on the planet Betelgeuse VII. You should probably be aware that
the visual response time of the Betelgeusians is a bit quicker than ours. The
visual response to a flashed light (of, say, medium brightness) does not usually
persist longer than 10 msec. in their receptive cells or their "ganglion" cells.
16 How will they perceive normal movies projected with normal projectors? _____

_____

About how many times as many flashes per second will you have to project for them?
17 (Give a general range.) _____
Assuming that their visual systems are similar to ours in most other respects, can
you think of some change you might make in the intensity of the projector light which
18 would help reduce the flicker problem? _____
Obviously, it would be very difficult or impossible to construct movie frames showing
intermediate stages of action to insert between the existing frames of already
19 existing movies. Can you think of some other way to help reduce flicker? _____

_____

COLOR VISION

     To assist you in preparing answers to the next three questions, you should refer to the color circle in Figure 3-19 of HIP.

What monochromatic light would you mix with a light of 470 nanometers to get a

20 colorless gray or white? _____

You meet a couple of color technicians who claim that with the appropriate
mixes of three monochromatic lights, they can produce any colors at any desired
hue or saturation. The wavelengths they use are 570, 470, and 660 nanometers.

21 Do you believe their claims with respect to hue? _____ Do you believe
their claims with respect to saturation? _____ What wavelength and
saturation of monochromatic light would you like to have them try to match to make

22 the most effective counterdemonstration? _____

Imagine an experiment in which subjects are asked to judge the saturation of two
colors. One color is a saturated red, the other a saturated green. Subjects are
instructed as follows:

"Rate on a scale of one to five how <u>red</u> (in the first case) or how <u>green</u> (in the
second case) each of these colors is."

Subjects are asked to do this task under three different conditions, involving three
different adaptation lights.

<u>Condition A</u>: Subjects are first exposed to <u>white</u> light of intermediate intensity
for 5 minutes, then are shown the two colors and asked to rate their saturation.

<u>Condition B</u>: Subjects are first exposed to a <u>green</u> light of intermediate intensity
for about 5 minutes, then are shown the two colors and asked to rate their
saturation.

<u>Condition C</u>: Subjects are first exposed to <u>red</u> light of intermediate intensity for
5 minutes, then are shown the two colors and asked to rate their saturation.

Subjects are not aware that they are being asked to rate the saturation of exactly
the same red and green stimuli in each of these three conditions. Fill in the
letters A, B, and C to show under which conditions the <u>red</u> stimulus will receive
highest, lowest, and intermediate ratings of saturation.

	Highest *saturation*	*Intermediate* *saturation*	*Lowest* *saturation*
23	_____	_____	_____

Now indicate under which conditions the <u>green</u> stimulus will receive highest, lowest, and intermediate ratings of saturation.

	Highest *saturation*	*Intermediate* *saturation*	*Lowest* *saturation*
24	_____	_____	_____

What is the name of the psychological process that accounts for these results?

25 _____

26 The phenomenon of spatially induced supersaturation could be used to augment the above results. What changes would you make in the test stimuli to bring this about? _____

_____

27 You have a yellow rectangle that you would like to make appear more yellow. How can you make use of the phenomenon of spatially induced color to achieve this result?

_____

28 A student in your class believes that it is possible to duplicate all the spectral colors by mixing various quantities of only <u>two</u> monochromatic lights. This student claims to have found perfect matches (in <u>hue</u>, saturation aside) to the colors of the spectrum using one light of 578 nanometers and one light of 440 nanometers. You check the equipment and find that it is all in order. But when the student shows you some of the matches, you are surprised to discover that many of the matches seem to you to be radically disparate in hue. For example, the student has combined the two colors to produce a "red"--to you it looks like a desaturated 630 nanometers. Yet the student is using this mixture to match a <u>greenish</u> spectral color of about 520 nanometers. You say, "Wait, those aren't the same," and the student replies, "Of course not; the mixture isn't as saturated as the spectral color." What do you think explains this radical difference in your perceptions? _____

_____

Actually, most people with color vision handicaps have less extreme symptoms. That is, they need three monochromatic lights to match all the spectral colors in hue, as do other people. The difference is that they require different <u>proportions</u> of these lights for the matches. One theory to account for these differences (which is apparently incorrect) is that these people have less than the normal amount of one

29 of the photochemical pigments. Can you think of an alternative explanation? _____

_____

_____

4 The auditory system

1. Sound is produced when portions of air are periodically compressed and decompressed. The rate at which these pressure changes occur is called the _____ of sound. This is measured in _____ per second or _____.

2. Any two sounds can also differ in the degree to which the air is compressed and decompressed, or the _____, and this is measured in _____.

3. The frequency range of sounds which a normal human ear can hear is about _____ to _____.

4. A waveform can be broken down into a set of waves which add together to form the original wave. This process is called _____.

5. The middle ear bones are located between the _____ and the _____.

6. An important membrane coiled within the cochlea is the _____ _____. It converts pressure changes in the incompressible liquid within the cochlea into a bulge or _____ wave along the membrane.

7. This bulge is largest near the _____ for high frequency sounds and largest near the _____ for low frequencies.

8. _____ cells are attached to the basilar membrane and are part of a structure called the _____ on top of the membrane.

9. A tuning curve can be obtained by inserting a _____ into a ganglion in the auditory nerve. It measures the _____ of the neuron as one varies the frequency.

10. For a constant frequency, the neurons encode increased intensity by _____ the response rate while maintaining synchrony.

1. frequency, cycles, hertz; 2. amplitude, dynes per square centimeter; 3. 20 Hz, 20,000 Hz; 4. Fourier analysis; 5. eardrum, oval window; 6. basilar membrane, traveling; 7. base, apex; 8. Hair, Organ of Corti; 9. microelectrode, firing rate; 10. increasing

---

INTRODUCTION

From the time a sound wave reaches the outside of the ear to when that particular sound "registers" in the cortex of the brain, the sound takes many different forms or *codes*. There is an analogy to this process in the sending of a message by way of a Mailgram. When you call Western Union, your message begins as sound waves. It is then translated into electrical signals in the telephone receiver so that it can be sent by wires to the Western Union station. There, the telegraph operator's telephone receiver translates it back into sound so that the telegraph operator can hear it. The operator then translates it into telegraphic code, which is transmitted as electrical signals across wires to the city where you want to send the message. There, a teletype machine translates it into a typed message, which is mailed to your friend. In this example, each of the following was a "code" of the message you were sending: sound waves, electrical signals, telegraphic code, and printed type. Each transformation during the sending of a Mailgram is necessary in order for the message to carry through the next step. For example, sound waves will not carry through wires, so they must be changed to a code that can be expressed in electrical signals, which can then be carried through wires.

As you read this chapter, pay particular attention to how the information contained in the sound wave reaching the ear is coded and recoded into different forms as it passes along the auditory pathway to the brain. Study those parts of the ear that make these transformations. There are portions of the theory of the auditory pathway in which the physics of the transformations becomes extremely complicated, as, for example, when the traveling wave is generated on the basilar membrane. You need not worry about these physics details. However, you should understand the basic ideas of these transformations and the parts of the ear involved along the auditory pathway.

In addition, experimental evidence is given for some of the crucial codings along the pathway. It is useful to observe how the experiments are chosen to provide tests of the proposed models.

RECODINGS OF THE SOUND WAVE ALONG THE AUDITORY PATHWAY

In some sense one can view the whole auditory pathway as simply a sequence of transformations of sound information into various codes until it is finally coded as a set of neural impulses inside the cortex. Furthermore, one can order the parts of the ear in terms of where they contribute to this sequence. In the left-hand column of Table 4.1 are listed the sequence of codes and the transformations between these codes along the auditory pathway. The arrows in that column represent the transformations: for example, a transformation occurs which changes the code, "sound waves," into the code, "vibration of skin."

Your task is: (i) Specify what ear parts carry each of these codes. For instance, in the Mailgram example, the part of the chain which carries the electrical code of the sound waves are the telephone wires between your home and the Western Union office. These parts involved should go in the second column below, to the right of each code, in the boxes labeled "Parts." (ii) For each transformation between encodings, draw a brief sketch of the parts involved in the transformation and indicate exactly where it occurs. This sketch should be drawn in the second column, across from each of the transformation arrows. Note that some of the parts involved here in the transformation will also have been used to carry the code. The first boxes have been filled in as an example.

	Codes and Transformations between Codes		
1	sound wave	Parts: *outer ear auditory canal*	*sound waves* *auditory canal*))))))))))))) *vibration of eardrum*
2		Diagram of Transformation:	
3	vibration of skin	Parts:	
4		Diagram of Transformation:	
5	vibration of bone	Parts:	
6		Diagram of Transformation:	

Table 4.1

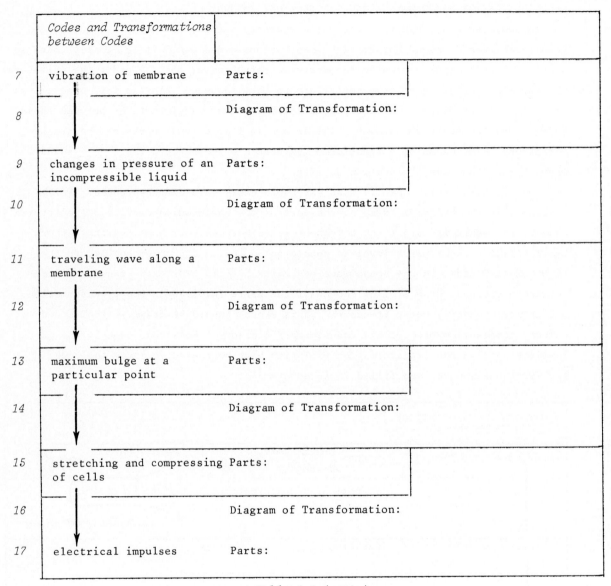

	Codes and Transformations between Codes	
7	vibration of membrane	Parts:
8		Diagram of Transformation:
9	changes in pressure of an incompressible liquid	Parts:
10		Diagram of Transformation:
11	traveling wave along a membrane	Parts:
12		Diagram of Transformation:
13	maximum bulge at a particular point	Parts:
14		Diagram of Transformation:
15	stretching and compressing of cells	Parts:
16		Diagram of Transformation:
17	electrical impulses	Parts:

Table 4.1 (cont.)

The way the auditory pathway is constructed is certainly not the only way (nor the simplest way) that one could have transformed sound waves into neural impulses, but many of the parts are more sensible than they might seem at first glance. The questions that follow are directed to why the pathway might have evolved as it did:

Why not make the eardrum out of bone? (It would certainly be less susceptible

18   to injury and more durable.) _____

_____

A condition which in fact does occur with age is hardening of the eardrums. If
you have answered the previous question correctly, you will know why those so
afflicted tend to be hard of hearing.

      Why have two windows of the cochlea, that is, why not have just the oval window?
19   _____

_____

_____

      Why not get rid of the three bones in the middle ear completely and have the
eardrum take the place of the oval window--they are both membranes that vibrate to the
sound waves anyway. (<u>Hint</u>: The oval window cannot vibrate as much as the eardrum.)
20   _____

_____

_____

21   Why not have the basilar membrane the same width and stiffness from the base to
the apex? _____

_____

_____

Suppose it were. What do you think various frequencies of tones might sound like
22   then? _____
      The vibrations of the oval window alternately push in and pull out the incom-
pressible fluid inside the cochlea. HIP states that these pressure changes travel
almost instantaneously to the round window. A question that may have occurred to you
is, if this is so, why shouldn't the traveling wave generated on the basilar membrane
move instantaneously also, and not realtively slowly as it does? The physics here are
quite complicated, but one way to imagine it is: When the oval window pushes on the
liquid, it is as though one drops a rock into a pool of water, where the "pool of
water" in this case is the basilar membrane. After the initial impact of the rock,
ripples will move slowly out from the point of impact. The traveling wave on the
basilar membrane is like a ripple.

WEIGHING THE EVIDENCE
      There are at least three ways of testing various theories about the auditory
system. One is simply to cut up bodies to see if proposed parts are there. Besides

being messy, this technique can be uninformative when we are concerned with minute electrical connections or with complex physiological events. The other two ways are somewhat more elegant: (I) Many theories make predictions about what humans should hear when presented with particular combinations of tones or sounds. One can present combinations to subjects and ask what they hear. (II) One can use electrodes inserted into the ear and brain of animals and record the activity of individual neurons.

For the statements below you will be asked to sketch very briefly experiments (from HIP or of your own) of type I or II which give evidence for or against the statement:

Humans do a rough *Fourier analysis* of incoming sounds. Give one of each type
23   of experiment. (I) _____

_____

24   (II) _____

_____

25   Neurons in the auditory nerve have a *critical frequency*. _____

_____

_____

Neurons in the auditory nerve seem to be responding to the motion of the basilar membrane in a localized area. By localized area we mean a situation as sketched in Figure 4.1 for each neuron:

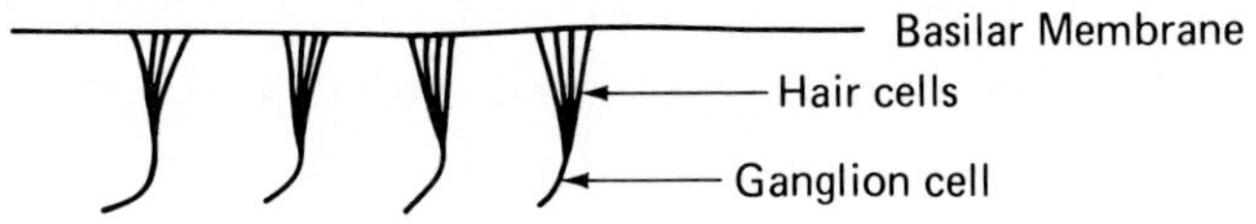

Figure 4.1

26   (II) _____

_____

Suppose neurons were hooked up to hair cells as shown in Figure 4.2.

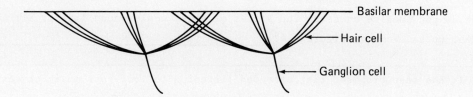

Figure 4.2

If you did the same experiment that you proposed in the previous question, draw the tuning curve that you would expect in Figure 4.3.

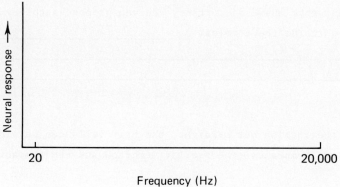

Figure 4.3

Suppose neurons were hooked up to hair cells which were spread fairly evenly all along the basilar membrane, i.e., as shown in Figure 4.4.

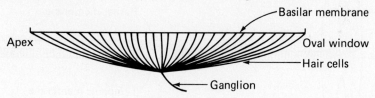

Figure 4.4

Draw the tuning curve that you would expect in Figure 4.5.

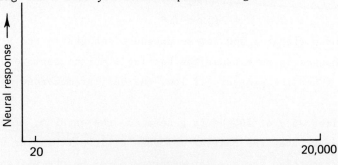

Figure 4.5

What do you imagine an ascending series of tones would sound like if all neurons were
29   hooked up as shown in Figure 4.4? _____

_____

      It has been proposed that extended listening to loud rock music causes extremely
impaired hearing at higher frequencies. Can you think of a simple experiment of
30   type II to test whether this is true? _____

_____

_____

If this claim about rock music is correct, can you propose a theory about what
31   might be happening inside the cochlea? _____

_____

_____

PERIODICITY THEORY
      If one rolls the cochlea out straight, the hair cells can be pictured as being
extended between two membranes--the basilar membrane and the tympanic membrane
(see Figure 4.6).

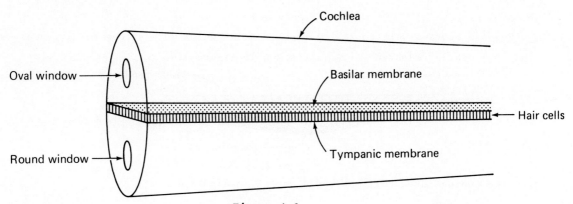

Figure 4.6

When the oval window vibrates and causes pressure changes in the fluid in the cochlea,
these pressure changes in turn cause the basilar membrane to move up and down in the
32   form of a wave. (When the pressure is low, the basilar membrane moves _____,
etc.)

      Now, when a frequency of 500 Hz is generated, the eardrum, middle ear bones,
oval window, and thus even the basilar membrane will be vibrating up and down 500
times a second. Each time the basilar membrane moves up the distance between the
two membranes changes (see Figure 4.7).

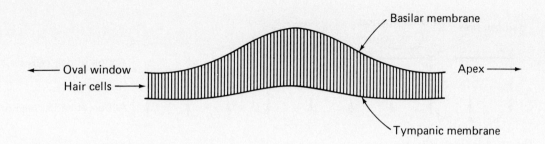

Oval window

Hair cells

Basilar membrane

Apex

Tympanic membrane

Figure 4.7

(Although the tympanic membrane also moves up, it does not move as much.) Thus the
hair cells, since they are attached to both membranes, are stretched. Stretching a
hair cell causes chemical changes inside the cell which in turn initiate an electrical
neural impulse--in a sense, stretching "irritates" the hair cells. When the basilar
membrane moves down, the hair cells are compressed, but compression does not initiate
any neural impulses.

Thus, since the basilar membrane is moving up and down 500 times a second, 500
impulses a second will be generated, each one in synchrony with the upward movements
of the basilar membrane, and thus the oval window, eardrum, and therefore the sound
wave itself. That the neural impulses of the neurons in the auditory system tend to
be synchronous with the sound wave is called the *periodicity theory* of hearing.

Consider a hair cell that has just been stretched and has fired a neural impulse.
Since firing necessitated chemical changes inside the cell, in order to ready itself
for the next stretching and firing it must "undo" these changes. Sometimes this
reverse process takes longer than the time it has until the next upward movement
33 of the basilar membrane, especially at higher frequencies. (Why higher? _____
_____)

Thus, even though it is stretched, it cannot fire. The time this reverse process
takes is called a *refractory period*, and, in general, the length of a particular
hair cell's refractory period is fairly constant. The situation can be diagrammed
as shown in Figure 4.8. Therefore, if a cell's refractory period is as long as
shown in Figure 4.8, the cell will fire to every other upward movement of the
basilar membrane, i.e., 250 times a second.

HIP states that given a frequency of 500 Hz one could find cells firing at rates
of 250 Hz, 125 Hz, and even 62.5 Hz. In the space below Figure 4.8 draw a diagram
like the one in that figure for a cell with a refractory period which would cause it
to fire at 125 Hz in response to a 500 Hz tone:

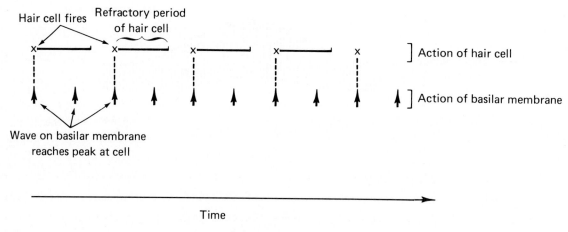

Figure 4.8

34

35 Could one find a cell which responds at 166.7 Hz to the same tone? _____
    If you are at all unsure, it is helpful to sketch a diagram like those above. Could
36 one find one firing at 400 Hz to this tone? _____ At 1000 Hz? _____
37
38 Why or why not? _____

    _____

    _____

    Consider again the cell that fires at 125 Hz. How fast would you expect it to
39 fire to a 250 Hz tone? _____ How small must the refractory
    period be (in seconds or milliseconds) in order to fire at 500 Hz to a 500 Hz tone?

40 _____

It is stated in HIP that when the intensity of a tone increases, the neuron will fire at a higher rate, still keeping in synchrony with the sound wave. How could this happen? Suppose a hair cell is firing at 400 Hz in response to a 2400 Hz tone as shown in Figure 4.9.

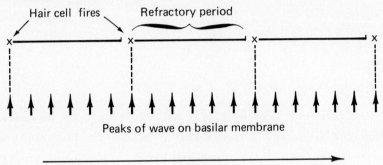

Figure 4.9

A higher intensity tone, although moving the basilar membrane at the same rate, moves it higher, stretching the hair cells more. This can shorten its refractory period--it is as though the cell was not really ready to fire but it has been stretched so much that it is irritated enough to fire anyway. Suppose the refractory period is shortened as shown in Figure 4.10.

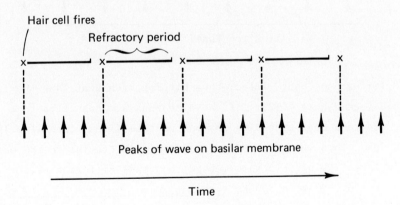

Figure 4.10

41   At what rate will the cell now fire? _____ Notice that it is still in synchrony with the sound wave. On the next page draw a diagram showing that, if the intensity is even greater, the cell could fire at 800 Hz:

42

Suppose there are only neurons firing at 250 Hz to a 500 Hz tone. How does the brain know that the frequency is actually 500 Hz and not just 250? When there are many neurons firing at 250 Hz (as there are here), the "Law of Averages" causes the right message to be given: Some of the neurons will be firing like the neuron on the schedule shown in Figure 4.11. But since there are many neurons, some will

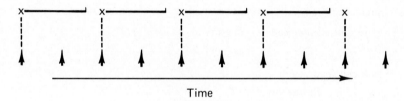

Time

Figure 4.11

have started firing one "beat" later, thus hitting each beat that the first group of neurons missed (see Figure 4.12). If these neurons are connected to a "master neuron" that counts a beat each time any one of them fires, then it will count 500 beats, or 500 Hz. This so-called *volley principle* is crucial to the working of the periodicity theory. Using this same method, how many different sets of neurons are
43   there firing at 166.7 Hz to a 500 Hz tone? _____

Neurons are not totally consistent, and every now and then the refractory period of a neuron will be much longer than the usual, and it will "miss a beat." From the last paragraph, can you explain why the brain does not think the frequency
44   has suddenly dropped? _____

_____

_____

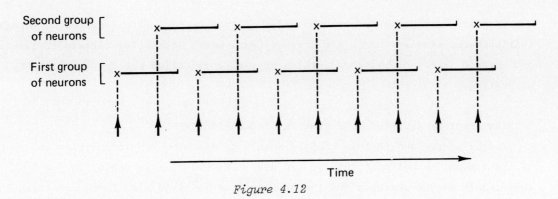

Figure 4.12

THE DUPLICITY THEORY OF HEARING

At the beginning of this chapter we considered a chain of transformations of a sound wave into vibrations of the eardrum and so on, until the sound wave was transformed to a particular place on the basilar membrane depending on the frequency. This encoding of sound frequency in terms of place is appropriately called the *place theory* of hearing.

In this last section we have considered a different chain of transformations in which the frequency of a sound wave is finally encoded in terms of the frequency of firing of neurons. Can you list the set of codes used in this second chain?

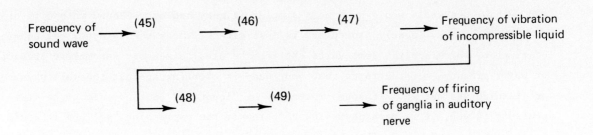

Figure 4.13

Thus the brain has two different ways in which to determine the frequency of a tone: It can check which neurons are firing under a particular "bulge" of the basilar membrane, or it can check the rate of firing of neurons in general under the basilar membrane. Some psychologists have tried to argue that one or the other of these methods is sufficient to explain hearing, and parts of Chapter 5 of HIP

consider evidence presented on both sides of this battle. It is currently thought
that both theories are partially correct (each works better for certain frequencies
and certain pieces of evidence); this compromise is called the *duplicity theory*
of hearing.

A BRIEF STUDY OF DECIBELS WITH SOME PRACTICAL PROBLEMS

Decibels are used in this chapter mostly to describe the intensities and range
of the various sounds that the ear can hear. However, it is useful to feel
comfortable around decibels and the computations involved with them, for today they
are commonly used in a wide number of fields. Perhaps you have come across one or
more statements like the following:

"The signal-to-noise ratio of this receiver is 70 dB."
"The noise pollution level around the San Diego airport is sometimes so heavy
(near 120 dB) that rattling and breaking of windows have become common occurrences."
"This turntable has a rated wow and flutter of less than -50 dB."

In this section we will attempt to familiarize you with several of the many forms
and uses of decibels, and in the relationship between decibels and sound intensity.
An attempt will be made to make the explanations very simple. If you have a
strong math background, you may want to read the first couple of paragraphs and
then jump directly to the problems.

As far as being needed to describe sound, decibels need never have been invented,
and perhaps the world would have been simpler if they had not. Sound intensity or
pressure (or, very loosely, loudness) is most directly measured in dynes per square
centimeter, which are the same units that can be used to measure barometric pressure,
or water pressure, or the force that your hand is exerting against the wall when you
are leaning against it. If sound intensity or "loudness" does not seem much like
pressure to you, it is perhaps useful to think of the expression "so loud it could
puncture your eardrums." There is one major disadvantage with only using dynes per
square centimeter to measure sound intensity: The range of intensities that the
human ear can hear is so large that one would have to deal with both small fractions
(for example, .00025 dynes/cm^2) and up into the billions of dynes per square
centimeter. It would be less cumbersome if one could consider a much smaller range.
Enter decibels.

Decibels cannot be used to measure sound pressure directly; instead one sound
is some number of decibels greater or less than some base or standard sound. Let

us take as our base sound intensity .0002 dynes/cm^2, which is commonly used as a base for decibels in most cases having to do with hearing. Since this is also very close to the threshold of hearing for a middle frequency (1000 Hz), one can imagine decibels to be roughly decibels above what can be barely heard.

Our purpose in introducing decibels was to reduce the range of a fraction to several billion to something manageable, say -200 to 200. One easy way of doing this is by using decibels to count how many "10 times" a sound is from the base sound. For example, if a sound has an intensity of .002 dynes/cm^2, then it is one "10 times" greater than our standard base. Similarly, .02 dynes/cm^2 is two "10 times" (or 100 times) greater than our base. By the same method, how many "10 times" is 2 dynes/cm^2

50   greater than our standard base? _____ How many is 2000 dynes/cm^2? _____
51   It should be easy to convince yourself that another way to compute the number of "10 times" if you are not already doing so is to take the ratio of the sound to the base sound, and then count the number of zeros in your answer, that is:

$$\frac{2 \text{ dynes/cm}^2}{.0002 \text{ dynes/cm}^2} = 10,000$$

which has 4 zeros and thus 4 "10 times." Call this number the number of "bels," that is, 2 dynes/cm^2 is 4 bels with respect to our base intensity. Decibels (or deci-bels) is just 10x number of bels, i.e., 2 dynes/cm^2 is 40 decibels with respect to our base. Use this method to compute the number of decibels that the following intensities are with respect to the base?

52   .002 dynes/cm^2 _____
53   .2 dynes/cm^2 _____
54   20 dynes/cm^2 _____
55   200,000 dynes/cm^2 _____

This procedure will not always work, i.e., suppose the intensity is not an even number of "10 times" greater than the base? You then need tables to find the exact number of bels or decibels, but it is not too hard to get a rough estimate, for example, 3 dynes/cm^2 does not work out evenly, but it is between 2 dynes/cm^2, which is 40 decibels, and 20 dynes/cm^2, which is 50 decibels. Thus 3 dynes/cm^2 is between 40 and 50 decibels. Since 3 is closer to 2, the answer is probably closer to 40, probably around 41 decibels. Although you will never be asked to compute a problem that does not come out evenly, try to find rough estimates (like "between 40 and 50") for the sound intensities below:

56   .1 dynes/cm^2 _____

57   15 dynes/cm^2 _____

58   105 dynes/cm^2 _____

By doing the process in reverse, given a sound intensity of a certain number of decibels with respect to a base intensity, one can compute the pressure of that sound. For example, if a sound is 60 decibels with respect to our standard base of .0002 dynes/cm^2, then that is 6 bels, or 6 "10 times" greater than .0002 dynes/cm^2. Therefore we multiply our base by 10 times, six times in a row, and get 200 dynes/ cm^2. Try the following problems:

59   80 decibels (base .0002 dynes/cm^2)   _____

60   100 decibels (base .0002 dynes/cm^2)   _____

61   0 decibels (base .0002 dynes/cm^2)   _____

62   0 decibels (base .01 dynes/cm^2)   _____

63   30 decibels (base 1 dyne/cm^2)   _____

One final problem--suppose that the sound intensity is less than the base intensity? For example, with a base of .0002 dynes/cm^2, what is the number of decibels of a sound of pressure .00002 dynes/cm^2? A pressure of .002 is 10 decibels; one of .0002 is 0 decibels--thus a pressure of .00002 dynes/cm^2 must be -10 decibels. To summarize, if the ratio of the sound to the base sound is less than 1, count the number of "10 times" it takes to bring the ratio up to 1 and that gives you the number of -bels. As usual, multiply by 10 to get the number of decibels. Try the following

64   .000002 dynes/cm^2 _____

65   .000000002 dynes/cm^2 _____

66   .2 dynes/cm^2 _____

67   -30 decibels (base .0002 dynes/cm^2)   _____

68   -50 decibels (base .0002 dynes/cm^2)   _____

69   -60 decibels (base 10 dynes/cm^2)   _____

If you are still with us at this point, you now know just about all there is to know about decibels and their computation. A way of summarizing all the methods that we have covered is in the following equation:

$$dB = 10 \times \log_{10}\left(\frac{I}{I_{base}}\right)$$

Below are a few problems which use decibels in a wider range of applications.

DECIBEL PROBLEMS

1. Suppose that a recent study indicated that the noise level next to the Santa Monica Freeway in Los Angeles during afternoon rush hour has risen from 80 to 100 dB in the last 15 years. What was the Santa Monica Freeway noise level at the

70 time of the study? _____ What assumption are you making in

71 giving this answer? _____

_____ By how many times has the noise level increased in the

72 last 15 years? _____

2. The Perfek-Sound Corporation has announced a new top-of-the-line receiver. Among its other glowing characteristics is a signal-to-noise ratio of 70 dB. How many times greater is the sound intensity of the signal than the sound intensity of

73 the noise? _____ Assuming that this ratio remains approximately constant at all volumes, what will happen to the noise level as you

74 increase the volume and thus the signal intensity?_____

_____ If the sound intensity of

the music you are listening to (the signal) is 200 dynes/cm^2, what is the sound

75 intensity of the hiss (the noise)? _____ Do you

76 think this is audible? _____ Why? _____

77 _____

If the hiss is barely audible (say .0002 dynes/cm^2), what sound intensity must the

78 music be at (in dynes per square centimeter)? _____ But surely for a large party one is going to play at a sound level higher than this. Suppose you play the music at 110 dB using the receiver. What is the noise level in

79 decibels? _____ From Table 4.1 of HIP, what sound would this

80 be about equivalent to? _____.

Can you think of any reason why the hiss might not be as perceptible as one might

81 imagine it should be? _____

_____

3. John has aspirations to form a jazz-rock band in 2 or 3 months and wants to spend considerable time practicing beforehand on his guitar. The only obstacle to this is the sound level and everyone else in the neighborhood. He has an old wood shack behind his house, but in its present state practicing there would not help the noise level at all. However, he decides that it has possibilities for becoming

a reasonable studio given the right soundproofing and so he starts to work. He buys
and installs some insulation that guarantees a 20 dB reduction in sound level. Next
he finds a store that can supply as much sound baffle board as he needs, with each
layer (covering the inside of the shack) reducing the sound level by 100 times. He
estimates that the sound level of his guitar should be no more than 100 decibels.
If he wants to reduce the sound intensity outside of the shack to 40 dB, how many
layers should he put in? (Remember the insulation that is already installed.)

82 _____ Unfortunately, when he begins to practice
with his new-formed band, he finds that he has not counted on the sound level of
the additional instruments. If the ratio of the sound level of his guitar to that
of his whole band is −30 dB, what is the sound intensity outside the shack when

83 the whole band practices? _____

5 The dimensions of sound

PRETEST

    1. The physical variable corresponding to the psychological variable of loudness is _____. Another important determiner of the loudness of a tone is the _____.

    2. The importance of frequency in determining loudness can be seen by observing that the _____ contours are not horizontal straight lines.

    3. Human hearing is sharpest at about _____ Hz, and is less sensitive below 100 Hz or above 8000 Hz.

    4. A 30 dB increase in the intensity of a tone increases it by _____ times.

    5. Loudness is measured in _____. When the loudness of a tone is doubled, its intensity is increased by _____ dB.

    6. Psychological pitch is measured in _____ whereas musical pitch is measured in _____.

    7. Two tones of different frequencies are played through a loudspeaker. You are able to tell that they are of different frequencies, but if the difference is made any smaller you are unable to tell them apart. The difference between these two frequencies is called a _____.

    8. Displacus, a medical condition where the same tone has different pitches when played to each of the two ears, supports the _____ theory of frequency perception.

    9. A goldfish is able to hear although it does not have a basilar membrane. Which theory of frequency perception does this support? _____

    10. The compromise between place theory and periodicity theory which proposes that each contributes to one's perception of the frequency of a tone and each has a limited range of operation is called the _____.

1. intensity, frequency; 2. equiloudness; 3. 4000 Hz; 4. 1000; 5. sones, 10;
6. mels, octaves; 7. jnd; 8. place; 9. periodicity; 10. duplicity theory

---

INTRODUCTION

Chapter 5 further elaborates on the theory of the auditory pathway, which was introduced in the previous chapter. To explain this theory, the chapter uses two groups of experimental results--one on perception of sound intensity and another on perception of frequency. Some of the questions that follow will present the results of hypothetical experiments and will ask you to use the theory of the auditory pathway to explain these results.

This chapter discusses the relative roles of *place* and *periodicity* theories in hearing. Before we can choose between the theories, we must find decisive experiments--ones that, depending upon the result, may enable us to decide in favor of one theory or the other. This often means finding odd systems, such as the gold-fish hearing system, or defective systems, like that found in the medical condition called *diplacus*. It is important to remember that both theories are partially right, and both contribute to our understanding.

In reading this chapter, it is useful to study the role of the basilar membrane and the hair cells in the auditory pathway. Also, an understanding of Figure 5-2 in HIP is necessary in order to explain several experimental results.

SOUND INTENSITY AND PERCEIVED LOUDNESS

Figure 5.1 is exactly the same as Figure 5-2 in HIP. Pick any one of the lines *1* in the diagram and describe in your own words exactly what it represents. _____

_____

_____

_____

_____

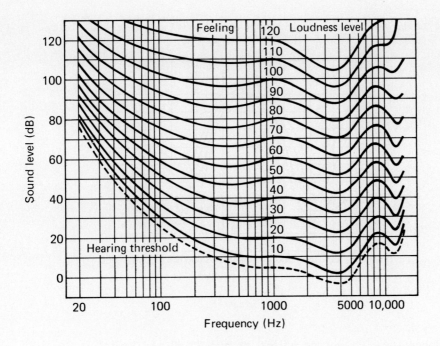

Figure 5.1

In what follows, you will be given pairs of tones of particular sound levels and
frequencies. You are to choose which tone (A or B) would be perceived to be
louder by a person with normal hearing. For example, if you are given:

    (A) 40 Hz, 70 dB   (B) 110 Hz, 60 dB   _____

you would choose (B), because even though (A) is physically more intense, (B) is on
the 60 dB perceived equiloudness contour while (A) is on the 40 dB contour, so (B)
is perceived louder. Try these:

2	(A) 100 Hz, 30 dB	(B) 1000 Hz, 20 dB	_____
3	(A) 110 Hz, 60 dB	(B) 5000 Hz, 90 dB	_____
4	(A) 30 Hz, 30 dB	(B) 10000 Hz, 20 dB	_____
5	(A) 20 Hz, 100 dB	(B) 1000 Hz, 40 dB	_____
6	(A) 30 Hz, 110 dB	(B) 1000 Hz, 110 dB	_____
7	(A) 120 Hz, 70 dB	(B) 8000 Hz, 70 dB	_____
8	(A) 60 Hz, 72 dB	(B) 4000 Hz, 40 dB	_____
9	(A) 20 Hz, 80 dB	(B) 3500 Hz, 19 dB	_____

Robert has noticed that music sounds dull and monotone to him and wonders whether
his hearing is different from that of other people. He goes to a clinic and they run

a series of tests to find his equiloudness contours. These are plotted in Figure 5.2.

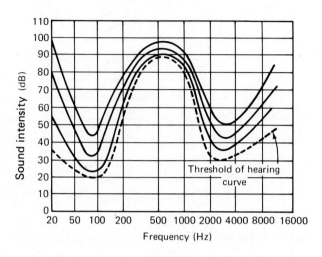

Figure 5.2

10 What does Robert hear if a tone of 900 Hz and 75 dB is played? _____
_____ Suppose one took a tone of a
constant intensity of 60 dB and gradually increased the frequency from 20 Hz to
11 10000 Hz. What would Robert perceive as happening to the loudness of the tone? _____

_____

_____

Can you describe briefly what music must sound like to Robert? Take for example a
12 symphony played at 70 dB and describe how he would hear various instruments. _____

_____

_____

_____

_____

LOUDNESS COMPENSATORS

    Turn to Figure 5.1. Notice that between 1000 and 8000 Hz, although the equi-
loudness contours are quite curved, they are almost parallel to each other, i.e., the
distance between any two contours is constant all along the contours. Thus complex
music with frequencies only in the range between 1000 and 8000 Hz will sound balanced
no matter what intensity it is played at. For example, consider two sounds in music
played at 80 dB, one at 1000 Hz and one at 7000 Hz. By examining the equiloudness

13 contours, can you describe how they are related in loudness? _____

_____ Now take the same two sounds in

14 music played at 40 dB. How are they related in loudness? _____

_____

15 Similarly, at 80 dB a 1000 Hz tone is about 10 dB _____ (louder or

softer) than a 4000 Hz tone, and this same difference also holds approximately at

50 dB.

   The point of this long argument is that if music confined itself to the 1000 to

8000 Hz range, then loudness compensators would be unnecessary. This is because the

16 purpose of loudness compensators is _____

_____

_____

and in this range the music would stay in about the same balance at any intensity.

   Unfortunately, almost no music is limited to this range, and especially uses the

frequencies between 30 and 1000 Hz. (You may want to look at Figure 5-3 of HIP for

the ranges of various instruments.) Notice that in this range the equiloudness

contours are not at all parallel, becoming closer as one moves into the lower

frequencies. Thus music will not have the same balance in this range when played at

17 different intensities. For example, at 80 dB a 1000 Hz sound is _____ dB

18 louder than a 30 Hz sound, whereas at 50 dB the 1000 Hz sound is _____ dB

louder. Thus one needs a loudness compensator such that, when the volume from

concert levels (about 80 dB) is decreased to home levels, the compensator will

19 _____ the intensity of lower frequency sounds so that the

balance between loudnesses of medium and low frequencies is the same as played

originally. The problem below is an application of this principle:

   The Bay City Rockers have agreed to play at a rock extravaganza at Shea Stadium

in New York and have brought along their huge array of speakers and massive ampli-

fiers so that there will be no trouble hearing them in even the highest bleacher

seats. Our concern here, though, is with the people who have waited overnight and

gotten choice seats only two feet away from the stage. The Bay City Rockers must

turn up their sound system so that the people in the upper deck hear a reasonable

sound level, say 80 dB. Since most people will be at this distance (or a little

closer), the Rockers would like their music to sound correctly balanced for them.

Our front-row-sitters, however, will now hear the same music at at least 110 dB.

How will the loudness of the music be balanced for them (i) between 1000 and 8000 Hz?

20 _____ (ii) between 30 and 1000 Hz? (<u>Hint</u>: You

21 have already considered how the balance changes between 80 and 50 dB. Try this same
method on 80 and 110 dB.) _____

_____

Given that the front-row-sitters are going to hear the music at 110 dB and that
the music is balanced at 80 dB, suppose you could build a loudness compensator to
make the music balanced for them. What would be the characteristics of this
22 compensator? (careful) _____

_____

_____

Suppose that the Bay City Rockers decided to do this. Can you foresee any problems?
23 (Suppose you were sitting in the bleachers.) _____

_____

_____

You can't please everybody.

You may have been disturbed by the fact that, in HIP, loudness compensators are
supposed to boost (or raise the intensity of) both low and high frequencies.
Although the high frequencies do not need boosting because of the equiloudness
contours (as we have seen), there is another problem (mentioned in HIP) that occurs
24 when music is played at lower than concert intensities. What is this problem? _____

_____

_____

And this problem is minimized by boosting somewhat the high frequencies.

MASKING

Suppose that in 1982 a rare species of monkey is found with an unusually keen
sense of hearing. It is decided that the monkey will be named the "dog monkey"
because of its hearing and its faint resemblance to a German Shepherd. In order to
find out why this monkey's hearing is so sharp, a team of neurologists does an
extensive analysis of its auditory system. They find that most of the basic
characteristics are very similar to human auditory parts and operation. When a
threshold of hearing curve is taken, it is found that the monkey's threshold is a
constant 10 dB from 20 Hz to 20,000 Hz. At what frequency is this monkey's hearing
25 the most acute relative to humans? _____ Is there a
26 frequency range where human hearing is better than this monkey's? _____
The only place where the two systems really vary is in the operation of the

basilar membrane where, although it is slightly different, the system is quite orderly: A pure tone of a particular frequency and loudness produces a maximum bulge at a particular point on the membrane. For example, if one imagines the basilar membrane unrolled, the bulge for a tone of 500 Hz and 50 dB could be pictured as shown in Figure 5.3.

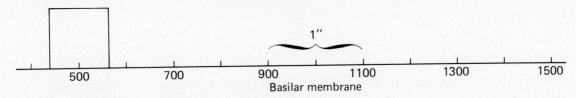

Figure 5.3

Can you name two differences between the operation of this monkey's basilar membrane

27 and the human basilar membrane? (i) _____

_____

28 (ii) _____

_____

To compare this last tone with waves produced by other ones, tones of 500 Hz and 80 dB and of 1000 Hz and 50 dB are added to Figure 5.4.

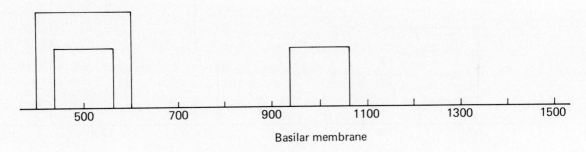

Figure 5.4

Thus each wave is centered at its frequency and is 1/8 inch taller for each 10 dB of its intensity. (You are going to need a ruler for the next two pages.) On Figure 5.5 draw the following three frequencies on the basilar membrane: 600 Hz, 30 dB; 900 Hz, 10 dB; 1500 Hz, 100 dB.

29

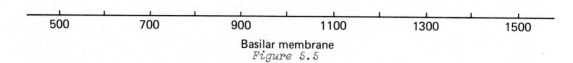

Basilar membrane
Figure 5.5

Suppose we play two tones at once to this monkey. If the operation of the
basilar membrane is the same as the human's except for what we have noted, what
determines whether both tones can be heard, in terms of what happens on the
30 basilar membrane? _____

_____

_____ For example, with one of the pairs of
tones in Figure 5.6, both tones will be heard, whereas with the other, only one
31 tone will be heard. Which pair will produce only one tone? _____
32 _____ For this pair, which tone will be heard? _____

_____

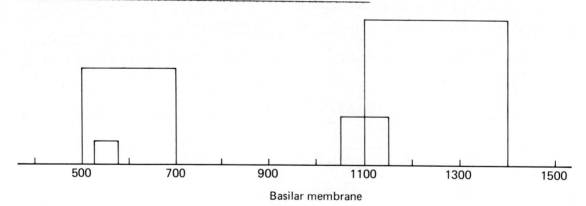

Basilar membrane
Figure 5.6

Now we are going to present the monkey with a series of pairs of tones, where one
tone of the pair is always the same. Call this constant tone the masking tone. Our
first masking tone will be 1000 Hz and 80 dB. Our varying tone will gradually
increase in frequency from 500 to 1500 Hz, and we would like to choose an intensity
for this tone such that it is barely audible to the monkey. You know the
threshold of hearing curve of this monkey and also what determines whether both
tones of a pair will be heard. What we need is a threshold of intensity curve,

given that there is a masking tone of 80 dB at 1000 Hz. You may want to experiment
by drawing in waves in the basilar membrane in Figure 5.7 until you are sure what
the threshold curve looks like. When you are sure draw it in the diagram below
the membrane.

33

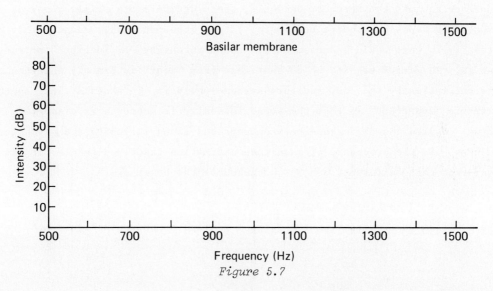

Figure 5.7

Now we will use other masking tones--both at 1000 Hz, but at intensities of 40 and
100 dB. For each masking tone the varying tone will again move from 500 to
1500 Hz at a barely audible level. Add these threshold curves to Figure 5.7, and
label the curves.

By now you are probably an expert at drawing threshold masking curves and it
is perhaps clearer to you what is meant by the phenomenon of masking. Comparing
this set of curves with the set of masking curves in Figure 5-7 in HIP, you can
see that one obvious difference is that our curves are square while those tend to
be rounded. This is because the waves on the monkey's basilar membrane are square
whereas the human's waves tend to be irregularly rounded. However, one could
compute the human's threshold masking curves by the same procedure that we used,
except that it would be more difficult to be precise because of the irregularities.

There is another difference between the sets of curves: Whereas the monkey's
are neatly symmetrical, the human's threshold curves come down much more slowly on

the right-hand side of the curves than on the left. Can you explain why this is so?

34 _____

_____

_____

DECIBELS VERSUS SONES

As we know from Chapter 4, true physical sound intensity can be measured in
dynes per square centimeter or decibels, where decibels are simply a way of
compressing dynes per square centimeter into a more manageable range. This physical
intensity is what would be measured by "sound intensity" or "decibel" meters,
that is, the meters are set up so that what they "hear" is exactly what the
physical intensity is. Our auditory system--which is, in a sense, just another
meter--is "imperfect" in that the sound intensity it measures is distorted. This is
one way to view the difference between physical sound intensity and psychological
loudness. By the procedure of magnitude estimation described in HIP, it has been
found that this difference can be described by the power law:

$$J = k \; I^{0.3}$$

This relation can be drawn in the form of a graph as shown in Figure 5.8.

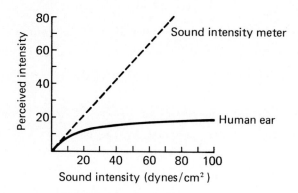

Figure 5.8

If the human ear were a perfect sound intensity meter, this graph would be a
straight line at a 45° angle, that is, for each unit of intensity that the sound
is increased, a unit of intensity would be measured on the meter. The fact that
this curve is not that steep indicates that, when the human ear measures sounds, it

tends to compress the range: High intensity sounds are not measured as loud as they
should be. Can you think of any advantage to making the ear "imperfect" like this?

_____

_____

_____

   Since the ear tends to distort the intensities of sound when it "measures"
them, it is useful to have a new set of units that express how it is measuring
intensity. Call these units *sones* and define sones as follows: 40 dB is 1 sone.
For each 10 dB more than 40, double the number of sones. For each 10 dB less than
40, halve the number of sones. Now we can use sones as the units on our perceived
loudness axis on our graph. Given the definition of "sone" and the way the units
are marked off on the scales below, draw on Figure 5.9 the line indicating the
relationship between perceived loudness and physical intensity. (Careful, it is
not exactly the same as in Chapter 5 of HIP.)

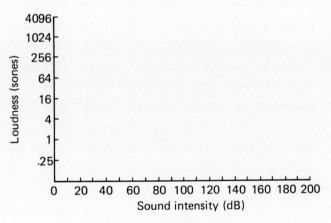

Figure 5.9

   Why is this graph not the same as Figure 5-10 in HIP? Those of you with a
strong math background should be able to answer this for yourself, but for our
purposes it is sufficient to say that one of the axes has been compressed in order
for the graph to fit in the book. Both graphs are perfectly correct, but the fact
that the graph here is a line less than 45° is a reminder that the ear perceives
more intense sounds as being less loud (intense) than they actually are.

Our definition of sone was only for tones of frequency 1000 Hz. What is the perceived loudness in sones of tones of other frequencies? Suppose we have a tone of 30 Hz and 90 dB and we want to know how many sones that is. All we need is Figure 5-2 of HIP: We find the tone of 30 Hz and 90 dB and find out what equiloudness curve it is on, then follow that curve to 1000 Hz. The point where the curve intersects 1000 Hz represents a tone that is equally loud to our tone. But we can find the sones of this 1000 Hz tone from the definition. In this case, the equally loud 1000 Hz tone is 60 dB and thus 4 sones. Therefore our tone of 30 Hz and 90 dB is also 4 sones. Using the same method, find the perceived loudness in sones of the following tones:

37   40 Hz, 70 dB   _____

38   6000 Hz, 50 dB   _____

39   50 Hz, 120 dB   _____

40   9000 Hz, 40 dB   _____

41   100 Hz, 30 dB   _____

You have a 3-year-old kid brother who has just discovered the family piano, and, being no Mozart, he has taken to pounding out single notes. Since this is the fifth time in a row he has chosen the G immediately below middle C, you are curious as to just how loud it really is. You have a meter which will measure sound intensity at a particular frequency, but a piano note unfortunately is not a single pure tone. However, since the perceived loudness of a complex sound is simply the sum of the sones of each of the pure tones (when they are in different critical bands, as in this case), we need only measure the sound intensity at each of the different frequencies that make up the note. For our purposes we will assume that this G note has a fundamental frequency of 200 Hz, and we will consider only the first two harmonics. Using the meter you find the following intensities: 200 Hz, 77 dB; 400 Hz, 56 dB; 600 Hz, 37 dB. What is the perceived loudness of

42   the sound as a whole? _____

Finally, we would like to alter Figure 5-2 of HIP such that it still shows equiloudness contours, but so that the vertical axis is measured in sones, as shown in Figure 5.10. Your task is to draw in the same equiloudness contours. (If you think about what the definition of sones is, this should be easy.)

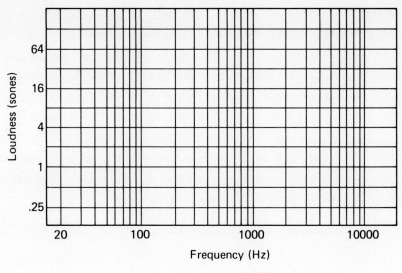

Draw in the 1, 4, 16, and 64 sone equiloudness contours

43

Figure 5.10

THE PERCEPTION OF FREQUENCY

Just as there are meters to measure sound intensity accurately, so there are ones to measure frequency. Again the ear, in perceiving frequency, can be considered one of these meters, and the ear makes much the same distortions as it does with intensity: Higher frequencies are not perceived to be as high as they should be. Thus, a new unit for perceived frequency or *pitch* is introduced, the *mel*, where a pitch of 1000 mels is what is heard when a 1000 Hz tone of 60 dB is played. We now have all the physical and psychological terms and units for two different dimensions, and you should be able to fill out Table 5.1.

Physical dimension	*Intensity*	*Frequency*
Physical units		
Psychological dimension		
Psychological units		

44
45
46

Table 5.1

In addition to the physical and psychological dimensions of frequency, there is a third way of measuring frequency--musically. One unit of measurement used here is the *octave*, which is related to hertz in the following manner: Given any two frequencies such that one frequency is twice the number of hertz of the other, then the first frequency is 1 octave higher than the second. The two frequencies are also said to *cover* one octave. For example, given a 300 Hz tone, a frequency

47 1 octave higher is _____ and one an octave lower is

48 _____ .

If you have to double a frequency twice in order to equal a second frequency, then the second frequency is 2 octaves higher than the first, three times for 3 octaves, etc. How many octaves do the following pairs cover?

49   30, 120 Hz   _____

50   1000, 8000 Hz   _____

51   35, 560 Hz   _____

52   100, 300 Hz   _____

You should not have been able to answer the last one exactly, that is, it is

53 _____ octave(s) from 100 to 200 Hz and _____ octave(s) from

54 100 to 400 Hz, so from 100 to 300 Hz is between 1 and 2 octaves. Which pair in each of the following groups of tones covers the largest number of octaves?

55   (A)   20, 80 Hz   (B) 3000, 6000 Hz   _____

56   (A) 120, 300 Hz   (B) 4000, 16000 Hz   _____

57   (A) 100, 200 Hz   (B) 1000, 2000 Hz   _____

Notice that, as in some of these examples, a larger range in hertz does not necessarily mean a larger range in octaves. If working with octaves seems like working with decibels, it is because they both are logarithmically related to other

58 scales, octaves to _____ and decibels to _____ .

59   As with sound intensity, one can ask where along the auditory pathway the ear distorts frequency in measuring it. Before examining this and exactly how the psychological dimension of pitch (measured in mels) differs from the physical dimension of frequency (using hertz), consider the following analogy to the place theory of frequency perception:

Suppose that you are in a soundproof room and the only way you can detect the frequency of sounds on the outside is through a friend who can hear the sounds on the outside and who communicates them to you by lightly poking you with a pencil

point at a particular spot on your back. For the lowest frequency sounds he will
poke you all the way over on your left and gradually move to your right as the
frequency increases, with the highest sounds signified by a poke to your far right.
You have to guess (in a certain number of mels) the frequency of the tone from
where he poked you on the back. Suppose your friend organizes his pokes fairly
evenly with respect to the actual frequency, but (unknown to you) tends to decrease
the distance between pokes as he gets toward the higher frequencies (say, he runs
out of room). Sketch a line in Figure 5.11 of how his pokes relate to the
frequency.

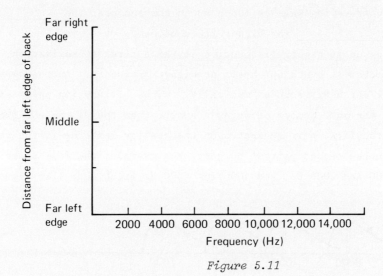

Figure 5.11

How are your guesses of the frequency (in mels) going to be related to the actual
frequency (in hertz)? _____
_____
_____
_____

    Relating this analogy to the ear, what part of the auditory system is analogous
to your back? _____ Your friend hears
a frequency and decides what location on your back to poke you. What operation
does this correspond to in the ear? _____
_____
_____
_____

You have tactile neurons that are sensitive to the pressure and location of pokes on your skin, and in this analogy, you have been converting this location to a pitch. In the auditory system, the hair cells below the basilar membrane play a very similar role to your tactile neurons, i.e., they are sensitive to bulges along the basilar membrane. In both cases, neurons are firing to indicate location of a disturbance. And here, as in the back analogy, your brain converts this location to a frequency.

The distortions of distance that your friend made in a similar fashion on the basilar membrane. The reason, of course, is not for lack of room but because of the irregular shape, stiffness, and mass of the membrane, which in turn cause
64   the peaks of the traveling wave to bunch up on the end near the _____
_____ for higher frequencies.

This bunching up at higher frequencies is, at a first approximation, quite similar to how octaves "bunch up" hertz at higher frequency. Another way of saying this is that the ear hears sounds "musically." Thus, if any two pairs of frequencies are the same number of octaves apart, then the distance between maximum bulges the first pair generates on the basilar membrane is the same as the distance between the second pair of bulges. For example, the four peaks generated by the pairs 1000 and 2000 Hz, and 4000 and 8000 Hz might look like Figure 5.12.

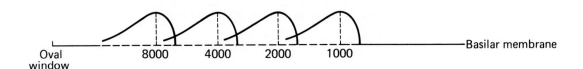

Figure 5.12

Notice that the distance between the 2000 and 4000 Hz peaks is the same as either of
65   the other two distances. Can you explain why? _____

_____

Remember, though, that this is only a first approximation. If this were truly how we heard, then the two lines in Figure 5-13 of HIP would coincide, and the right-hand graph in Figure 5-12 of HIP would be a straight slanted line. Alternatively, a musical piece could be played in any key and still have the same "character."
66   Explain this last point using distances along the basilar membrane. _____

_____

_____

Thus, distances between peaks of two tones along the basilar membrane are measured fairly accurately in terms of octaves. The reason why this is only a first approximation to how we hear is that these distances have to be "measured" in turn by the brain. Tactile distance is distorted by how dense the neurons are in that area of skin. You can test this for yourself: Let a friend poke you--lightly-- with two pencil points in the back of the neck, and try guessing how far apart they are. Compare this with two pencil points on the tip of your finger where you can't see them. You will probably find that a distance on your finger will seem somewhat larger than the same distance on the back of your neck. In fact, your friend may have to move the points an inch or more apart on your neck before you can even be sure that there are two points. The tips of your fingers are one of the most densely packed areas of neurons, while the back of your neck is one of the least.

67
68

A similar distortion occurs because of the distribution of hair cells along the basilar membrane. Because hair cells are more densely populated near the _____ (base or apex), a distance at that end is perceived to be larger than the same distance near the _____.   For instance, in our previous example, the octave from 4000 to 8000 Hz is perceived to be slightly larger, i.e., cover a greater number of mels, than the octave from 1000 to 2000 Hz (see Figure 5.13). Remember, though, that this is a small distortion compared to the "distortion" of frequency in terms of octaves instead of hertz. For each of the two pairs of tones in Table 5.2, state which pair covers the greater number of hertz, octaves, and mels. Write "same" if they are equal:

		Physical distance	Musical distance	Psychological distance
69	A. 100, 200 B. 500, 1000			
70	A. 120, 480 B. 3000, 12000			
71	A. 100, 300 B. 1000, 3000			
72	A. 100, 1600 B. 1000, 2000			
73	A. 1000, 2000 B. 2000, 3000			

Table 5.2

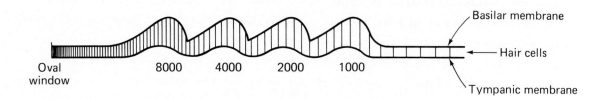

Figure 5.13

Note that the psychological distance in the last two cases in Table 5.2 are more difficult to judge. In the fourth case, A is clearly the much larger musical interval but B is in a denser area of the basilar membrane. Since the density of neurons is a much smaller distortion, A is larger psychologically. In the last case, the decision is much closer (A is one octave while B is some fraction of one), but the major distortion still wins out and A is psychologically larger. Try one last problem:

Your kid brother, the one who isn't Mozart, is now 7, and is being given piano lessons in order to try to redirect profitably his affinity for the piano. However, he now has an annoying habit of playing pieces he learns two octaves higher on the piano than where they should be played. Now the lowest note in a piece of music has a pitch of a certain number of mels, as does the highest note. Call the difference in number of mels between the highest and lowest notes the "range" of the piece. What happens to the range of pieces your brother plays two octaves higher as

74   compared to where they should be played? _____

75   _____ Why? _____

_____

_____

THE jnd

There is a second way to characterize psychological perception of frequency--

76   with the *jnd*, which is _____

_____ What would be a jnd in the back analogy above?

77   _____

_____

Explain why a jnd does not have to be equal to or smaller than the size of a

78   mel. (Think of the respective definitions and the analogy.) _____

_____
_____
_____

THE MISSING FUNDAMENTAL

In order to decipher the case of the missing fundamental, it is useful to know a little more about music, and the piano in particular. When a piano key is played, sounds of more than one frequency are generated. In fact, some lowest frequency is produced, called the _fundamental_, and all frequencies that are multiples of this fundamental are also produced, although they will have lower intensities than the fundamental. For example, given a fundamental of 100 Hz, other frequencies generated are 200 Hz, 300 Hz, 400 Hz, 500 Hz, etc. These are called the _first harmonic_, _second harmonic_, and so on. (These harmonics occur because of the physics of hitting a piano wire, which cause it to vibrate at all these frequencies.)

The pitch that one assigns psychologically to any complex tone is the pitch of the lowest audible tone, although one is aware that the other tones exist. In a piano note, the pitch is the pitch of the _____ if it is audible. If the fundamental is inaudible because it is played too softly, the pitch should be that of the _____, or the lowest harmonic which is audible. Try the following problem:

Suppose we have a 20 Hz fundamental plus the first two harmonics, which are at _____ and _____ Hz, respectively. As mentioned earlier, the fundamental will always have a higher sound intensity than the harmonics, no matter what level it is played at. Suppose the ratio of intensities is always 6 to 5 to 4. For example, if the tone is played at 120 dB, the two harmonics will be at 100 and 80 dB. From Figure 5-2 of HIP, which of the three tones will be perceived to be the loudest? _____ Now suppose that the same note plus the two harmonics is played at 60 dB, so that the first and second harmonics will be 50 and 40 dB in intensity, respectively. Which tone will be the loudest? _____ Which tone will you not even be able to hear? _____ _____ Why? _____

Thus, from what you know from above, the pitch of this complex sound should _____ as it is played softer. This does not make sense, and, in fact, the pitch does not change.

The reason why the pitch is unchanged has to do with the existence of _beats_. How are beats generated? Consider two tones that differ slightly in frequency, say 400 and 500 Hz (see Figure 5.14). Notice that at certain points the waves reach peaks

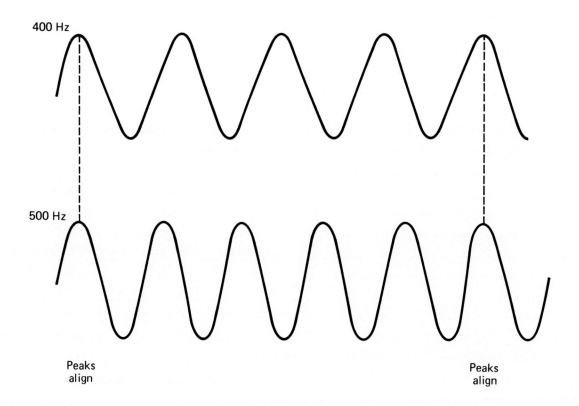

Figure 5.14

at about the same time, whereas at others one reaches a peak where the other reaches
a low point or trough. If these tones are played simultaneously, energies will
add when the peaks coincide, and the combined tone will sound louder. Beats occur
each time the energies add, and the frequency of these beats is the <u>difference</u> of
88 the frequencies of the two tones. In our example, beats will occur at _____ Hz.
The reason for the frequency being the difference has to do with the mathematics
of sine waves.

Now, in the periodicity theory of frequency perception, the hair cells can
basically be imagined to be firing at the peaks of a tone. When two tones are played
simultaneously and the peaks coincide, hair cells will be firing for each tone,
whereas at other times, the firings will not coincide. Clearly, this concentration
of firings will occur at the same frequency as the beats. Just as the brain uses
concentrations of firings of neurons to determine the frequency of a tone, so will

it notice the concentrations here, and think that there is a "tone" being played at
the beat frequency, where there is actually none at all. Since this beat frequency
is usually lower than the other frequencies in the complex tone, that frequency
is perceived to be the pitch of the tone. In our example, what is the pitch of the
89   combined tone? _____

90   Suppose the following tones were played simultaneously: 780 Hz, 940 Hz, 1100 Hz,
     1260 Hz, 1420 Hz. What tone would you hear in addition to these? _____
     Suppose masking noise were played on all frequencies from 500 to 900 Hz. Now
91   what tones would you hear? _____

     _____

     HIP never really expressly states why you do hear the missing fundamental,
     but you should now have all the pieces. Using these pieces and the preceding
92   paragraphs, explain why you do hear the fundamental at low intensity levels. _____

     _____

     _____

     _____

     _____

     _____

THE CRITICAL BAND
93   Give a brief definition of a critical band. _____

     _____

     _____ A 100 Hz and a 300 Hz
94   tone are played simultaneously. Are they in the same critical band? _____
     Each of these two tones is increased in frequency by a constant 5000 Hz to 5100 Hz
95   and 5300 Hz. Are they now in the same critical band? _____ What graph
96   did you use to determine this? _____ Can you
     explain why this makes sense in terms of distance between peaks along the basilar
     membrane? Assume that to be in the same critical band the peaks must be close
97   together. _____

     _____

     Now your kid brother is 8, and has quit piano lessons because he does not like
them, but he has learned that you can play more than one note at once. He has
gone to constantly pounding out more-or-less interesting chords. You begin to
notice that when he hits two notes that are very close together, i.e., a black key

and a white key right next to each other you can hear a pulsating beat in
addition to the two notes. However, if the notes he plays are further apart, say a
third or a fifth (see Figure 5.15), the pulsating beat seems not to be there.
(If you don't have a kid brother, you might want to try this on a piano yourself.)

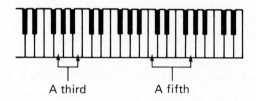

Figure 5.15

98   Why aren't the beats there? _____

_____

_____

As he continues to play his chords, you begin to notice that even with the thirds
and fifths there is a faint beat. What is causing these beats? (difficult question)

99   _____

_____

These faint beats are actually what piano tuners use when they are tuning. First
they set one note directly with a special pitch harmonica. Then since each chord has
its own special beat frequency, they play chords with the one note that they have
set and one other note, adjusting the tension on the piano wire until the "frequency"
of the beats sounds just right.

BINAURAL LISTENING

There are two ways or methods by which having two ears is useful in locating the
direction that a sound is coming from. Name these methods and describe their
characteristics in Table 5.3.

Method 1

100   Reason for being useful:

101   Frequency range for use in humans:
102   Reason for frequency range:

Method 2

103   Reason for being useful:

104   Frequency range for use in humans:
105   Reason for frequency range:

Table 5.3

Suppose it is found that elephants are much better at locating the direction of medium high frequency tones (2000–5000 Hz) than are humans. In terms of the
106 characteristics of the two methods, how would you explain such a result? _____

_____

_____

_____

How do you think elephants would compare with humans on lower frequency tones
107 (200–1000 Hz)? _____
108 Why? _____

_____

FREQUENCY PERCEPTION: PLACE THEORY OR PERIODICITY THEORY

During this chapter much evidence is given on both sides for the two major theories of how frequency is measured or perceived by the human ear. Although this battle ends up in a stalemate--both are partially correct--it is instructive to consider the evidence that was accumulated on both sides. In Table 5.4, briefly name three pieces of evidence that supported each theory.

	Place Theory
109	1.
110	2.
111	3.
	Periodicity Theory
112	1.
113	2.
114	3.

Table 5.4

6 Neural information processing

PRETEST

1. An axon of one cell generally synapses on a _____ of another cell.

2. The instrument which is used to record the firings of individual neurons is called a _____.

3. Neurons will fire even without stimulation. The pace of spontaneous firings is called the _____.

4. When a small spot of light is shone in the middle of the receptive field of an on-center, off-surround cell, it will fire temporarily at a high rate before settling at a lower rate. This initial activity is called a _____ _____.

5. A fiber which fires maximally for blue light will fire minimally for _____ light.

6. A couple of theories propose three channels to carry color information to the brain. These are called _____ theories.

7. Some processing of visual images is done by ganglia at the _____, but most of the complex processing and object recognition takes place in the _____.

8. _____ cells tend to detect features in a specific location.

9. Three types of ganglia have been found which conduct information to the visual cortex, the _____, _____, and _____ cells, with the _____ cells having the fastest conduction speed.

10. Cells which are sensitive to changes in the frequency of a sound are called _____.

1. dendrite; 2. microelectrode; 3. background rate; 4. transient response;
5. yellow; 6. opponent process color; 7. retina, visual cortex; 8. Simple; 9. W,
X, Y, Y; 10. frequency sweep detectors

INTRODUCTION

One theme which helps unify Chapter 6 is the concept of *separating* the various
types of information our nervous system is processing. For example, when a person
looks at a scene, there are several kinds of information to consider; an object
may have a particular color, texture, shading, location, and size as well as edges
at certain places. We know that people are capable of noticing each of these
features separately, so neural networks we devise must be able to extract one
particular type of feature while ignoring other features (e.g., edge detectors and
line detectors). In this study guide chapter we will consider what characteristics
of these networks allow them to separate features, and how they may interact to
affect our perception of the world.

THE NEURON

Without looking back at HIP, draw as much as you remember about what a typical
cell looks like in the space below. Label as many parts as you can:

1

Now look at Figure 6-2a of HIP and add any parts that you have left out. What is
the mechanism by which neural cells can receive inputs from more than one other cell?

2 _____

In general, a neural network consists of a set of cells at one end that
can react to patterns in the outside world and encode them in terms of neural
3
4   impulses. These cells are called _____ or _____ cells.
At the other end are a set of neurons in the brain that will receive the final
processed versions of the patterns. In addition to relaying the information, neurons
along the way must accomplish the processing: extracting the features and important

information in the patterns and perhaps discarding other information. Now suppose
each dendrite could be connected to one axon only, and each axon to only one
dendrite. Then each receptor cell must be hooked up to one final neuron, with a
string of neurons connecting them which is isolated from all other strings. (It
is useful to experiment with a few networks if you are not clear as to exactly why
this must be so.) Thus, using the symbols for receptors cells and neurons used in
HIP, a typical network will look like the one in Figure 6.1.

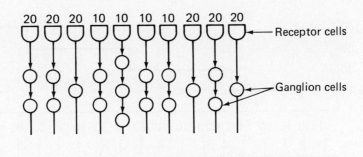

Figure 6.1

Take a typical light pattern like the one shown in Figure 6.1. Assuming gains of 1
5   for all connections, compute the output pattern in the blanks given.

       Given any light pattern in general, describe how this circuit would react to it.

6   _____

     _____

From all this, what would you say is the biggest advantage of allowing a dendrite
7   to receive inputs from more than one axon? _____

     _____

     _____

BUILDING NEURAL NETWORKS

       It can be shown that if neural networks are to extract features such as contours,
then simply allowing neurons to receive inputs from more than one axon is insuffi-
cient. One must require that some of these inputs be inhibitory. This mechanism by
which neurons at one level can inhibit the firing of neurons at the next level is
8   called _____ and is perhaps the most important principle
in neural information processing.

       In this section we will be working with increasingly complex neural networks.

Before beginning you should study Figures 6-12 to 6-14 of HIP and make sure you understand how the computations are done, and how the output patterns there were obtained.

The neural circuit of Figure 6-14 of HIP is reproduced as Figure 6.2, and is being presented with a light intensity pattern consisting of several Mach bands. Compute the output of each ganglion and sketch a graph below it indicating the shape of the response pattern. Assume that the light intensities at the ends of the light pattern extend forever.

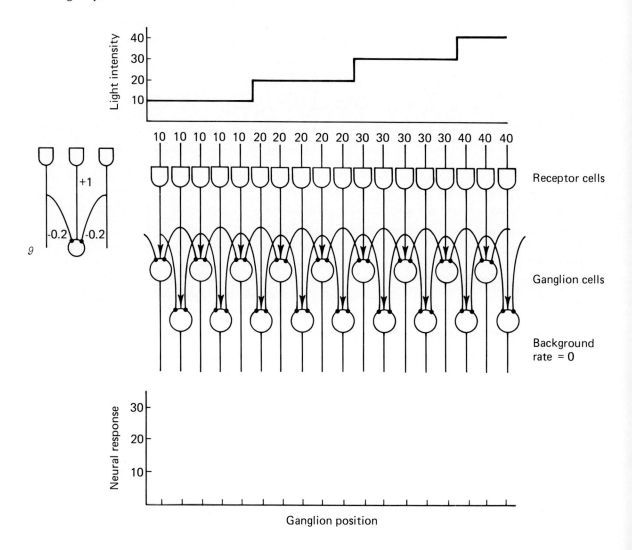

Figure 6.2

How does this differ from the idealized output pattern for Mach bands given in

10   Figure 6-16? _____

_____ Can you think

11   of any reasons why this might be true? _____

_____

_____

Now consider a slightly more complicated circuit but a somewhat simpler light pattern. Compute and graph the outputs of the ganglia in Figure 6.3. Again assume that the intensities remain the same beyond the edges of the light pattern.

12

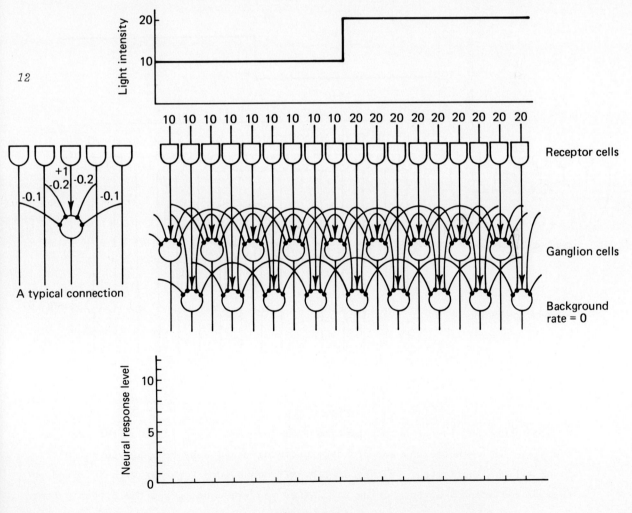

Figure 6.3

As you have probably noticed, this network is the same network as Figure 6-14 with inhibitory connections to cells both one and two cells away instead of just one away. Also, the input light patterns are the same. What is the difference in the output patterns? _____

13

_____

We are going to complicate the network even more, adding excitatory connections from adjacent cells, and inhibitory connections from cells up to four cells away (see Figure 6.4).

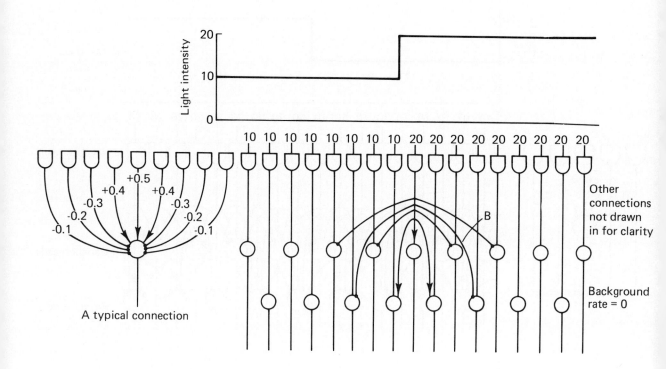

Figure 6.4

We are interested in the output pattern from the same light input as the previous example. The calculations are probably becoming tedious by now, if you haven't found all the shortcuts. If they are, by all means work together with a friend on them if you are not already doing so. After you are done, graph the output pattern in Figure 6.5.

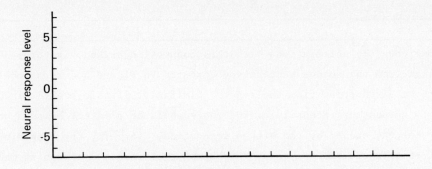

14

Figure 6.5

Comparing this to the output patterns of both previous networks, what trend do you

15 see? _____

_____ What in the structure of the

16 networks is causing this trend? _____

Figure 6-15b of HIP shows an output pattern typical of a ganglion cell when
exposed to an edge of light. Although you would probably agree that the output
pattern from our network here is closer than the one gotten in Figure 6-14 to the
experimental pattern, it certainly is not the same. Thus our network must be
altered further. Can you imagine how we would have to change it in order to

17 produce an output pattern closer still to the experimental one? _____

_____

Besides demonstrating the preceding point, the reason for doing all the calculations is to give you an idea of how messy they quickly become in even a moderately
complicated network. Although this last network will give you a flavor of working
with real networks, the real ones are in fact many times more complex. It is
understandable why detailed theorizing about networks can run into astronomical
computation problems.

IMPERFECTIONS

There is nothing in the body which makes sure that there are perfect
connections between each receptor cell and each ganglion in a neural network. What
happens when some connection dies, or becomes broken, or was never formed in the
first place? Let's consider what happens when such an event occurs in our last

network: Suppose the connection marked "B" in the above diagram has been broken.
In terms of the actual cells and cell terminology, what has happened in the network?

18   _____

_____

   If one does the calculations with this connection broken, it turns out that the
only change from the output pattern you computed in Figure 6.6 is a small bump in the
graph at the sixth point from the right.   Similarly, if this broken circuit were
exposed to a constant intensity of 10, there would be a little bump in an otherwise
constant output, caused by the broken connection.   (Briefly try computing the output
graph if this is unclear to you.)   This bump might induce a neuron to make a mistake.

19 What mistake do you think this would be?   _____

_____

However, as one increases the number of connections in the network, and concurrently
as the contribution of each connection decreases, the size of this bump becomes
smaller and smaller, virtually unnoticeable in relation to the rest of the output
pattern, and thus virtually undetectable by a ganglion monitoring it.

   The fact that the shape of the output pattern is not drastically affected by
the breaking down of a neural connection is one of the most important properties of
neural networks such as these, for the human brain is far from a perfect structure--
it must depend upon things being generally right and not exactly right.   This
property, sometimes called *graceful degradation* or *tolerance of error* is in some
ways analogous to the ability of a large organization of people to function despite
the illness or absence of some of its personnel.   With this in mind, what do you
expect would happen to the output of a simpler network such as the first one we

20 considered above, if a connection were broken?   _____

_____

21 Why?   _____

_____

CENTER-SURROUND CELLS

   The neural networks that are actually found in tests on mammals are, in general,
not as simple as the first circuits we considered; however, they are quite close to
a two-dimensional analogue of the last network in Figure 6.4.   Suppose we consider
a typical on-center, off-surround cell, and take a thin slice out of the middle,
as shown in Figure 6.6.

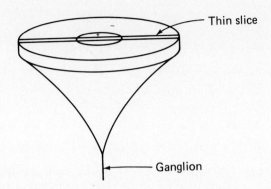

Figure 6.6

Sketch this thin slice as a neural network using the symbols we have been using
(showing a side view of the receptors, etc.):

22

If one imagines many of these on-center, off-surround cells with closely overlapping
fields, then cutting a thin slice straight through all of them, the network would
look much like the one in Figure 6.4. How would you change this network to represent
23 a thin slice from an off-center, on-surround cell instead? _____

_____

      Now let us return to the full two-dimensional version. What specific light
pattern would cause the greatest response from an on-center, off-surround cell?
24 (Ignore the complications of transient response for now.) _____

_____

What light pattern would cause the greatest response from an off-center, on-surround
25 cell? _____
Suppose we had a light pattern in the shape of a barbell, as in Figure 6.7.

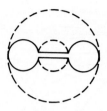

Figure 6.7

26   For which of these two types of cells would this cause the greater response? _____
27   _____ Why? _____

_____

     One can imagine ganglia that have center-surround fields like the ones just
considered, distributed all over the retina. One possible source of variation among
them is the size of the response field. It is argued in HIP that in order to make
the ganglion maximally sensitive to light, one should make the field as large as
28   possible. Why? _____

_____

However, this increase in size must be balanced against decreases in the amount of
detail that will be noticed in the light patterns. How does increased size make it
29   more difficult to notice detail? _____

_____

_____

_____

It is amazing how the human eye manages to get the best of both extremes. In every
place but the center (or fovea) of the eye, the response fields tend to be large,
allowing the eye to be sensitive to light and small changes in intensity. However,
when the eye needs to analyze a particular part of the visual scene in detail, it
can focus the fovea on that part, for there the response fields are extremely small,
often with each ganglion hooked up to just one receptor.

TRANSIENT RESPONSE

     Figure 6.8 shows a typical response of an off-center, on-surround cell
to the turning on and off of a spot of light focused on the middle of its receptive
field. Circle those portions of Figure 6.8 which are transient responses. Also
indicate where the light was turned on and off:

30

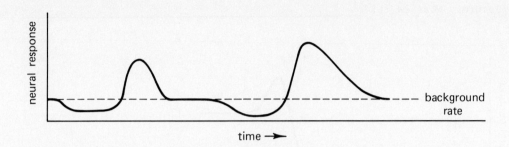

Figure 6.8

Again we are recording from a ganglion cell. Using a small spot of white light
we have figured out the response field. Now we focus a red light in the center of
the "on" area and observe the response, shown in Figure 6.9.

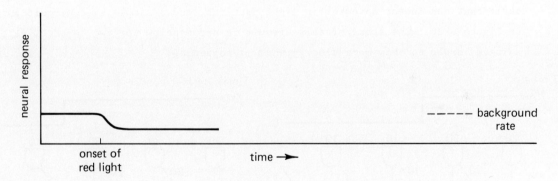

Figure 6.9

Without moving the dot we instantaneously change the color from red to a green light
of the same intensity and get the response shown in Figure 6.10.

31   Explain what is going on here. _____

32 _____ Continue the graph in Figure

6.10 to show what should happen when we change the green light back to red.

It was noted in the introduction that the purpose of many of these networks was
to extract one particular feature from the complex collection of information which
one sees in a visual scene. Most of the networks in the previous sections were
particularly good at extracting contours from a scene. Although transient responses

may at first seem only to cloud the working out of a neural theory, networks which
have these transient responses are in fact detecting another particular type of
33   feature.   What is it? _____

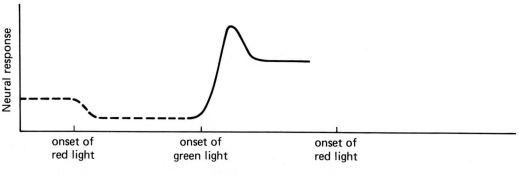

Figure 6.10

MOVEMENT DETECTORS

It is noted in HIP that if neural impulses can be delayed, then networks can be
built that can detect movement in light patterns, and a simple such circuit is drawn
in Figure 6-26. The state of this circuit is drawn below for two consecutive time
units in order to show more clearly what is happening:

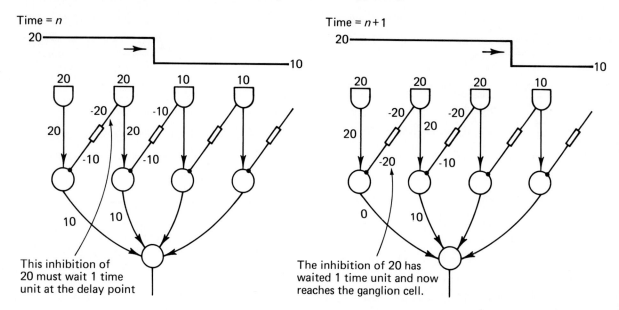

Figure 6.11

BRIGHTNESS CONTRAST

   Consider the network of Figure 6.12 and the light pattern shone on it. Compute
the response of each cell to the pattern and plot the output in the graph underneath
the network.

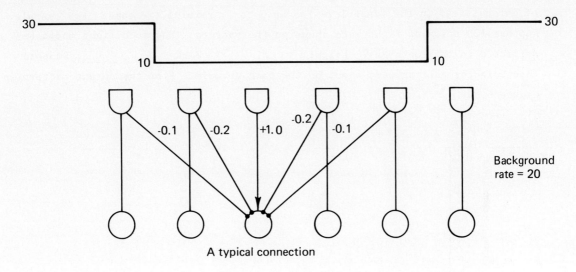

34

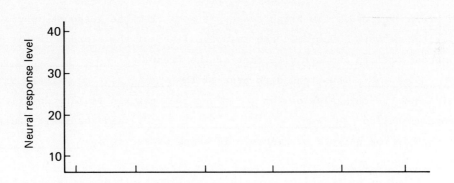

Figure 6.12

When we look at such a light pattern printed on paper (such as Figure 3-2 of HIP), what
we are actually seeing is the light that is shining on it and has been reflected to our
eyes. Bright areas appear bright because they reflect more light than dark areas. For
example, suppose that the bright areas of the pattern on the paper reflected all the
light shone on them, whereas the dark areas reflected only one third. If 30 units of

light were shone on this pattern, then we would get the input pattern shown in
Figure 6.12.

   What happens when we shine more light on this pattern printed on paper? The light
reflected from both the light and dark areas will increase in intensity, but the ratio
of intensities, in this case 1 to 1/3 or 3 to 1, remains the same. For example,
suppose 120 units of light were shone on the pattern. How much light would be
35 reflected in the two areas? bright _____ dark _____ Suppose
36 this brighter pattern were shone on the same network. Plot the output pattern in
Figure 6.13.

37

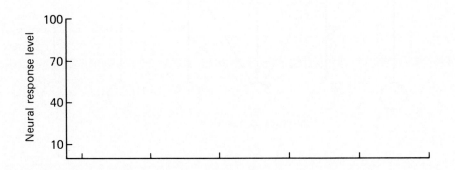

Figure 6.13

   The brain determines the brightnesses it sees from the response levels of each
neuron in the network. How does the response level of the neurons in the dark area
38 of the second pattern compare with that of the first? _____
39 _____ Thus, the dark area of the _____ pattern appears
40 brighter. Yet the dark area of the _____ pattern is more intense. This
41 phenomenon is called _____ and the basic neural
42 process used in the network of Figure 6.12 which causes it is _____

_____ .

   Plot the output of this same network to the input pattern in Figure 6.14. (The
only difference from the second pattern is that the dark area is wider.)

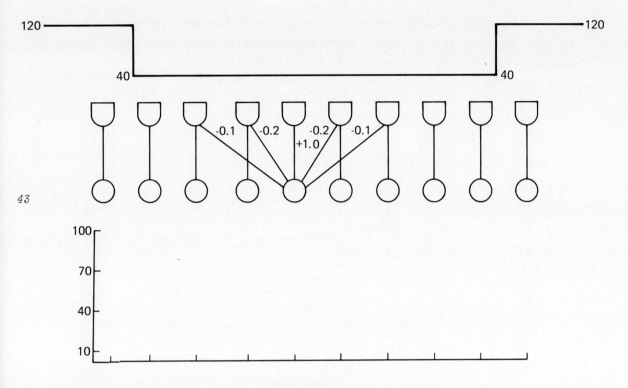

43

Figure 6.14

How does the output response of the middle of the dark area compare now to the first

44   pattern? _____

Thus, using this network, brightness contrast is actually limited only to the edges

45   of the dark part. Why didn't we notice this in the first two light patterns? _____

_____

_____

One may conclude that in general the dark patch must be sufficiently small, or else
the appearance that the whole patch is darker will go away. In real networks, the

46   dark patch can be wider than the four neurons here; can you explain why? _____

_____

     You may have noticed the similarity of the output pattern of Figure 6.13 to the
output of the same network to the Mach band input in Figure 6.2. It should be clear
now that what causes the Mach band effect is exactly what causes the brightness
contrast effect here.

INDUCED CONTRAST

We have poked a microelectrode into a neuron in the optic nerve of a monkey, and we vary the wavelength of a test light shone on that neuron's receptive field. Suppose we obtain the response graph shown in Figure 6.15.

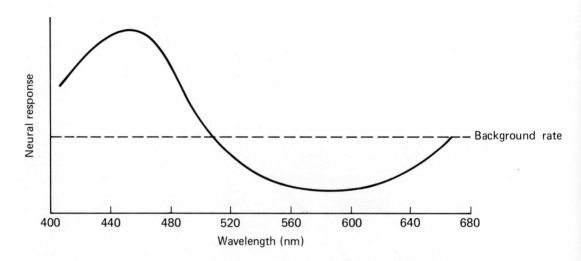

Figure 6.15

47 What wavelength is the neuron most responsive to? _____ Use Figure

48 3-19 of HIP to determine what color this is. _____ According to the

49 opponent process color theory, which channel should this be? _____

Now suppose the receptive field is exposed to intense blue light for 60 seconds.

50 At first the firing rate will be quite _____, but shortly thereafter it

51 will _____ because of fatigue. Immediately after the exposure another

52 graph is done of response versus wavelength. Sketch in Figure 6.15 what this new response curve might look like.

Consider the *opponent* neuron with the same receptive field. In Figure 6.16 draw approximately what its response curve looks like before exposure to blue light. (Let the intensity of the test light used be the same as before.)

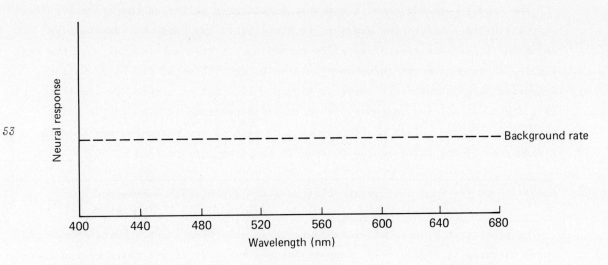

Figure 6.16

Explain why the response of this neuron will not be affected by blue light on its
receptive field. _____

_____

According to the first theory proposed in Figure 6-24 of HIP, both of these
neurons connect with a third neuron, one with an excitatory connection, one inhibitory, as shown in Figure 6.17.

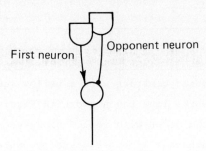

Figure 6.17

The brain can use this third neuron to decide on the blueness or yellowness of an
input, i.e., if it fires much faster than background rate, then it is a very
saturated _____, and if it is much slower than background rate, then
the input is a saturated _____. If it fires at background rate, where
along the blue-yellow dimension is the input? _____

Now suppose one had shone a somewhat desaturated yellow on the receptive field of these neurons before the exposure to blue light. By "somewhat desaturated" let us assume it is a mixture of a yellow of 600 nm, at the same intensity as the test light used to obtain the curve in Figure 6.16, and a blue of 510 nm of <u>half</u> the intensity used in the first curve in Figure 6.15. Let us assume for simplicity that if a light is half the intensity, then the response rate is also cut in half. Determine from the curves the firing rate of each of the channels, and thus the
58   firing rate of the third neuron (assume it has a background rate of 50). _____

59   According to the rule used, what color does the firing rate correspond to? _____
_____

Consider what happens after exposure to intense blue light: Using the second curve you drew in Figure 6.15, compute the new response of the third neuron to the
60   same desaturated yellow light. _____
61   What color does this correspond to, in comparison to the last color? _____
62   _____ This effect is called _____
_____.

A white light can be composed of equal amounts of blue and yellow light. Utilizing this fact and the same procedure you used above, what color will this
63   white light look like after exposure to blue light? _____
_____ Can you explain color afterimages using the same
64   theory? _____
_____
_____

Another form of induced contrast uses a yellow square inside of a blue background. Imagine having two networks like the network in Figure 6.12, one with blue-yellow channel receptors and the other with yellow-blue receptors, superimposed on each other. In addition, each pair of superimposed receptors is hooked up to a third neuron, just like in Figure 6.17 (see Figure 6.18). Suppose one now increases the intensity of the blue background without changing the yellow square. Using this network, can you explain briefly why the yellow square appears to be more saturated?
65   _____
_____
_____

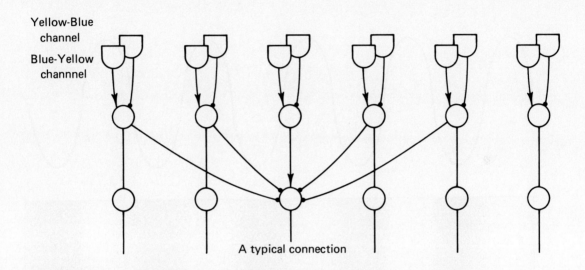

Figure 6.18

66 To what other effect is this form of induced contrast very closely related? _____
_____ And, as can be seen from the network of
Figure 6.18, these effects can be explained by much the same mechanism.

SPATIAL FREQUENCY ANALYSIS

    In HIP it states that letters stand out so well on a printed page because they
have "high frequency components." What does this mean exactly? A complex light
pattern can be broken up into a series of sine waves of light intensity varying at
different frequencies, just as a complex sound pattern can be broken down into a
set of sine waves of varying sound pressure at different frequencies. The major
conceptual difference is that, whereas sound waves involve variations in intensity
over time, light involves variation in intensity over space (you needn't worry if
this sounds fuzzy to you). Mathematically, the same set of operations apply.

    In general a light pattern will consist of both low- and high-frequency
components. Figure 6.19 shows a light pattern consisting of just a low-frequency sine

wave.   Underneath this is what the sine wave looks like that would produce this, i.e.,
when the sine wave reaches its peak the light pattern is at its brightest, and when
the sine wave is at a trough the pattern is darkest.   Notice that since the sine wave
moves gradually from peak to trough, the light pattern moves "fuzzily" from light to
dark.   If we add a higher frequency sine wave into this first wave, it begins to

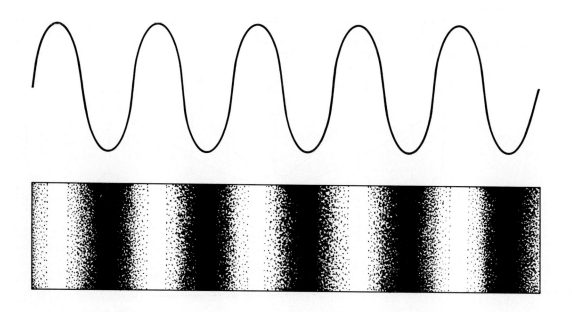

Figure 6.19

change in shape and character, as Figure 6.20 shows. Notice that the peaks and
troughs are somewhat flatter now, and that the wave moves more suddenly between these

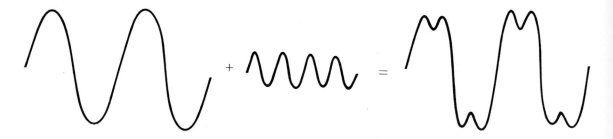

Figure 6.20

extremes. As one adds higher and higher frequencies, the peaks and troughs become even flatter, and the changes between them even sharper. The wave begins to approach a square wave, like that shown in Figure 6.21. As can be seen, a square wave looks like a normal stripe pattern or *grating* with peaks and troughs corresponding to light and dark stripes, respectively. Notice that the sharp changes in the waves correspond to the sharp boundaries between the stripes. Suppose one begins with a lower frequency sine wave before adding high-frequency components. How will the

67   resultant stripe pattern be different? _____

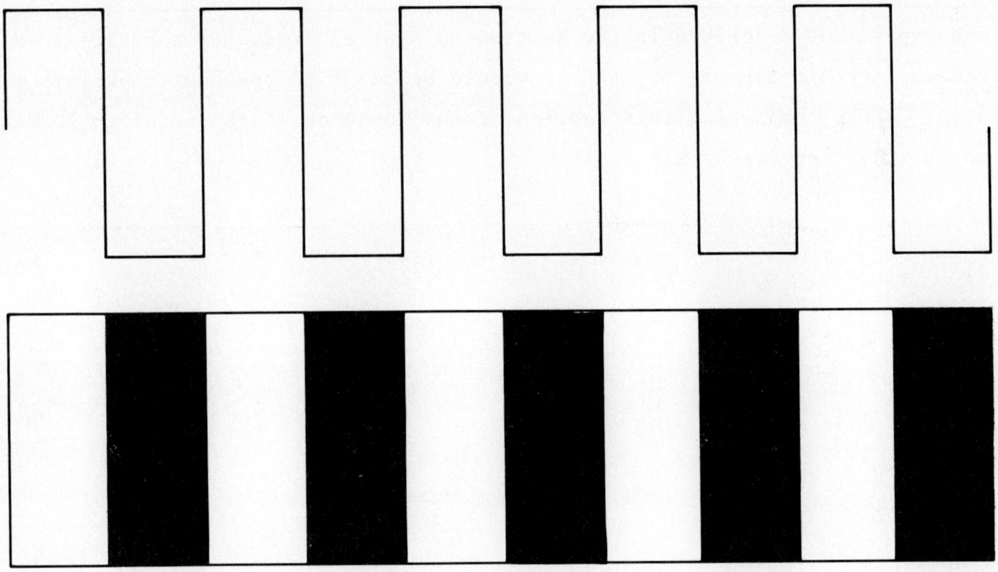

Figure 6.21

68   Can you explain why printed type contains high-frequency components? _____
_____
_____ How does the lowest frequency component compare

69   with the frequency used for our stripes? _____

_____

Suppose the visual cortex had neurons that were responsive to particular sine wave components, i.e., some neurons fire to coarse frequencies but not to medium or finer ones, others prefer medium frequencies, etc. The visual system could get an idea of a complex visual pattern by combining inputs from all these component neurons. Thus one perceives the fuzzy pattern in Figure 6.19 because only the low-frequency neurons fire, whereas one sees the stripe pattern in Figure 6.21 when both the low- and high-frequency components fire.

However, these component neurons are subject to the same fatigue after intense stimulation that the opponent process color neurons were in the previous section, and similar distortions can occur. Suppose one looked at a very bright pattern like the one in Figure 6.19. If you then looked at a striped pattern like

70   Figure 6.21, what frequency components could still respond? _____

_____ Therefore, what do you think would happen to your perception

71   of this striped pattern? _____

_____

The experiment described in the section on spatial frequency analysis in HIP is the reverse of this experiment, and it should be clear to you how to explain that result also. After completing this section of the workbook it is useful to go back and reread that section of HIP.

7 Pattern recognition and attention

PRETEST

1. A pattern recognition system that matches images as a whole against internal representations is called a _____ system.

2. A pattern recognition system that extracts features and matches them against internal lists of features is a _____ system.

3. The response of a _____ demon is determined by what proportion of features in the input match the set of features of the pattern it is responsible for.

4. A _____ matrix is a table showing the number of times each of a set of characters is misidentified as being another in that set of characters.

5. What do the words "sonorant," "round," "tensed," and "voiced" have in common?

_____

6. Give an example of two phrases with virtually identical speech waveforms but different meanings. _____

7. One can remember a list of words if they form a sentence better than if they do not because of the effects of _____.

8. _____ driven processing introduces expectations and hypotheses in the analysis of input information.

9. In the "specialist demon" model of pattern recognition, the message center of the demons is called the _____.

10. One demon changes a particular piece of information just as another demon is about to use it for another purpose. The mechanism which prevents this problem is the _____.

1. template; 2. pandemonium; 3. cognitive; 4. confusion; 5. features of opera-tions used to generate speech sounds; 6. "I scream" and "ice cream"; 7. context; 8. Conceptually; 9. blackboard; 10. supervisor demon

---

INTRODUCTION

The first chapter of HIP discusses the capabilities and limitations of human perception, the process by which people take in information from the outside world and recognize objects or familiar patterns. Chapter 7 of HIP considers this process--which is also called *pattern recognition*--in detail. This chapter describes how one can analyze complex objects by treating them as lists of features and simpler objects. Models for pattern recognition are designed to predict how perception should proceed. If the perceptual process does <u>not</u> operate as predicted, then at least part of the model is incorrect and must be discarded or modified.

Since human perception is limited in its processing capability, one is often faced with deciding what part of the world to attend to. Models of this process of *attention* are also built, and several of them are described in this chapter of the study guide. Because attending to some part of the world also involves perception of that part, a complete theory of perception also must agree with what we know about attention. The final theory in Chapter 7 of HIP tries to satisfy both requirements. This model for pattern recognition and attention uses *specialist demons* operating concurrently, communicating through a *blackboard,* and overseen by a *supervisor.*

The process of developing increasingly viable theories of attention and perception is a good example of the scientific method: gathering evidence, proposing a theory, predicting from that theory, and gathering more evidence based on the predictions. It is especially useful to participate by proposing models of your own and designing experiments to test them.

POSSIBLE THEORIES OF ATTENTION

Much of the progress of theoretical psychology can be summarized by a simple cycle: An abstract model is constructed to represent some psychological phenomenon. If the model is not too vague, it makes further predictions about other psychological phenomena. To test these predictions, one or a set of definitive experiments must be developed and run. If the results support the predictions, the model is also

supported. If not, the model must be either modified or completely rejected and a
new model proposed. No model will be completely right or supported--eventually
some evidence will be found that disputes parts of the model. Then it must be
modified or discarded and the cycle begins again.

An excellent example of this cycle occurs in the development of a theory of
attention, where a wide variety of models seem at least plausible. On the next few
pages, a series of possible attention models and experiments to test them are
presented. As you go through the models, it is useful to try to go through the
cycle process yourself, to propose experiments of your own that test the models
decisively, and to propose possible models of your own. Although the names used
in what follows are fictitious, the basic ideas follow approximately the history of
attention theory.

In a recent psychological journal, Dr. Ernest Forthright argues that the theories
of attention described in HIP are needlessly complicated, and introduces a very
simple *switch* theory of attention: If there are two separate streams of information
to attend to (for example, hearing two different conversations), and you are instructed to attend to just one, you simply "switch" your attention to that conversation without doing any analysis at all of the other one. The theory can be
diagrammed as shown in Figure 7.1.

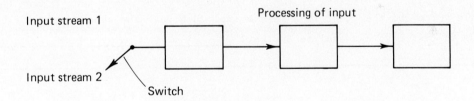

Figure 7.1

It is useful to describe here exactly what is meant by a "switch," since this
concept is utilized not only in attention theories but in many other psychological
models. Given two (or more) channels of information, a switch marks the point
where a clearcut decision must be made as to which channel will be processed further.
The fact that the switches in the diagrams point to one channel in particular does
not mean that that channel has been chosen; it simply indicates that a decision must
be made at this point.

Information from all other channels is lost forever beyond the switch. A

decision need not be final: If the information coming through each channel were
words, for example, one can make a new decision after each word as to which channel
to take the next word from. However, each decision must be made using only the
information known up to that point. For instance, in the case of Dr. Forthright's
model, each decision is assumed to be made before any analysis is done--before
anything is known about the tone, loudness, location, words, or meaning of either
channel.

    Do you think his theory has as good a chance of being true as any of the theories

1 presented in HIP? _____ If you think not, without doing any
experiments at all, how could you argue that his theory clearly must be incorrect?

2 _____

_____

_____

_____

_____

If you think his theory has a chance of being right, consider the following situation:
A female voice is talking slightly to the left of a subject, and a male voice is
carrying on a conversation, also to her left. She wants to listen to the female
voice, so she sets her switch as shown in Figure 7.2. Imagine the situation at any
particular time: There is one word entering the system from each channel, one in a
female voice and the other in a male voice. How does she choose which of the two

3 words to listen to and analyze further? _____

_____

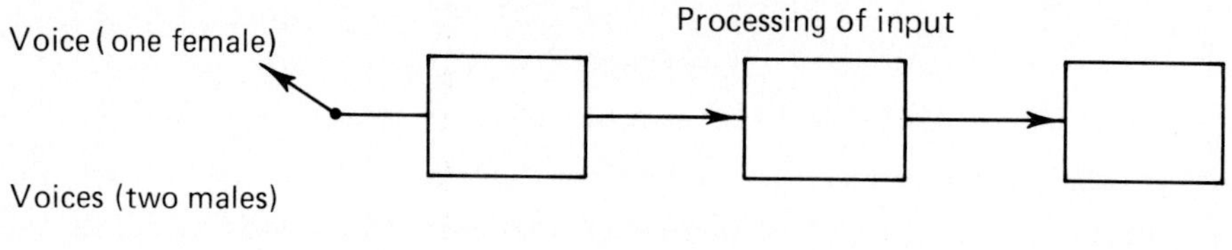

Figure 7.2

    Dr. Irene Arch proposes a second model which is slightly more complicated.
Before switching attention to one of two possible streams of information, basic
features are extracted from both, as depicted in Figure 7.3. For example, in the

case of two conversations, features such as the tone level and direction of the sound are noted before attending to one. How might this better explain the last

4 situation of the male and female conversations? _____

_____

_____

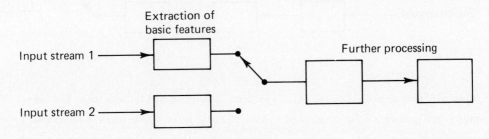

Figure 7.3

Suppose, however, the following experiment is run: The same person reads aloud a short passage in English and another short passage in Italian and records both of them on tape. A subject who understands only English listens to both tapes simultaneously coming out of the same speaker. The subject is asked to shadow the English passage only. It is shown that this can be done without difficulty. Why

5 might this second attention model have trouble explaining this result? _____

_____

Thus, if we are to salvage this model at all, we are going to have to move the "switch" further along in the analysis. Suppose we propose a third model, that analysis of input information proceeds until everything but the meanings of the messages are extracted before attention is switched to just one channel, as Figure 7.4 shows. In the case of two incoming conversations, both are analyzed until the identity of the incoming words is gotten, but attention is switched to one conversation before the meanings of the words are found. How would you explain the

6 results of the previous experiment using this model? _____

_____

_____

_____

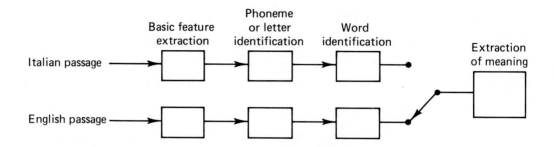

Figure 7.4

None of these proposed models say much about exactly how the features of the messages are going to be analyzed. One theory which has been suggested is called the *pandemonium system*. Since a simple version of this system fits nicely into our last proposed model of attention, we will now consider aspects of this theory further. Then we will go back to testing models of attention.

If the pandemonium system does fit into our last model, then the *feature, cognitive,* and *decision* demons must play roles in one of the stages of the model. In Figure 7.5 write the name of each of the types of demons under the stage you think describes its role.

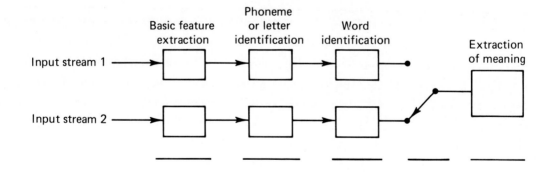

Figure 7.5

If you wrote the decision demon under the switch above, explain why you did so; if you did not, explain why not. _____

USING THE PANDEMONIUM SYSTEM

By about 1000 B.C. the people of Dalmatia, a civilization located along the coast of present day Yugoslavia, had developed a rather bizarre-looking alphabet, shown in Figure 7.6. (The Dalmatian civilization and its alphabet are from actual history.)

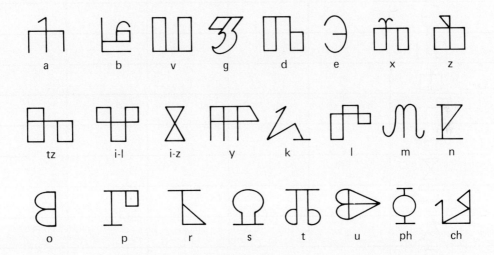

Figure 7.6

Suppose that a pandemonium-like system does in fact correctly describe how humans recognize letters. It is likely that the system has not changed much in the last few thousand years, so the Dalmatians would have been using much the same pandemonium system. Therefore, we should be able to infer a set of simple features (called a *feature set*) which uniquely describes each letter in the Dalmatian alphabet. Furthermore, one should be able to make several predictions (concerning the confusability of letters, etc.) from this feature system. Let's see where this leads us.

First, we need a feature set and a table specifying how many of each feature each letter has. Two candidate features are specified in the feature table (Table 7.1). You should go through the alphabet and count how many of each feature occur in each letter. Three other features are not specified, and you must infer what they must be from the few numbers in that column. (You may not agree with the set chosen, or feel that there is an equally reasonable set, but save your objections until later.)

Table 7.1
A FEATURE SET FOR THE DALMATIAN ALPHABET

	Horizontal lines		Right angles		
a					
b					
v			10		
g		0			
d		4			
e					
x					
z				1	
tz				0	
i-1				0	
i-2				2	
y					
k					
l					
m					
n					
o					
p		3			
r		1			
s		2			1
t					2
u					2
ph					1
ch					

In the pandemonium model the number of each feature in each letter is imagined
to be counted by a separate feature demon, which then responds accordingly to the
"cognitive" or "decision" demon. If this is so, for the Dalmatian alphabet, which

10 feature demon would have to have the most number of response levels? _____

_____

In Chapter 1 of HIP a template system is described in which the templates are
groups of receptors hooked up to have the same form as the patterns to be matched.
In this chapter it is mentioned that the pandemonium system can also be interpreted
as a type of template system. If this is so, what is the template for "g" in the

11 Dalmatian alphabet? _____
_____ In general, what is the template for any

12 letter? _____
_____

One of the advantages of the template system is that all the different templates
can be tested against a pattern simultaneously (or, *in parallel,* a common term in
models involving stages such as this). If this were so, which letter in the

13 Dalmatian alphabet would take the longest to recognize? _____

_____

However, it is quite possible that the whole system does not operate in parallel.
Although each of the feature demons may be counting the occurrences of its feature
simultaneously, they may not count them all at once (as you might do in estimating
the number of people in a crowd) but one after another (as you might count the
windows in a building). Another term for this second method is *in serial.* Suppose
the number of each feature is counted in serial, but the counting processes for all
the different features occur simultaneously. What will determine how long a letter

14 takes to be recognized? _____
_____ If this process is used in the pandemonium
system, which letter(s) of the Dalmatian alphabet would take the longest to be

15 recognized? _____

Errors and Confusion Matrices

According to this model, if two letters are very confusable, how do their

16 features compare? _____
If the feature sets of two letters are very dissimilar, in a recognition test for
one of the letters, what are the chances that a person will identify the letter as

17 being the other one of the pair? _____

You are flashing letters of the Dalmatian alphabet onto a screen for a short time (100 msec) and your subjects must identify each letter. Suppose the features one subject is able to extract from a particular letter are

3 horizontal lines
3 vertical lines
0 slanted lines
2 curves
10 right angles

Since this particular set of features does not match the feature set of any of the letters of the Dalmatian alphabet, he must guess from among the most likely alternatives. From the feature table you have constructed for this alphabet, find his most
18 likely alternative. ____________

Suppose in the preceding example that he did not extract either of the two curves. Name six other letters that also would then have been candidates, that is,
19 they might have been the letter that was flashed on the screen. ____________
____________ Of those six, which two do you
20 think would have been the <u>least</u> likely candidates? ____________

Let us assume that on a particular letter all that was extracted was one right
21 angle. Is "tz" a candidate? ____________ "k"? ____________ Why? ______
22
23 ____________
____

Suppose the letter-recognition experiment just described is run for a period of time using six letters from the Dalmatian alphabet: i-l, l, tz, b, z, and p. The response matrix shown in Table 7.2 is gotten.

Letter guessed

Letter presented	i-l	l	tz	b	z	p
i-l	A	B	C	D		E
l		F	G	H		I
tz		J	K	L	M	N
b			O	P	Q	R
z					S	T
p						U

Response matrix of letters from the Dalmation alphabet

(capital letters are only <u>labels</u> of particular boxes)

Table 7.2

Some of the boxes in the matrix have been marked with letters because particular questions will be asked about them. As an example, if "Q" were equal to 5, this would mean that the subjects guessed "Z" 5 times when the letter "b" was presented. Assume that we are testing the pandemonium system and that the feature table you constructed above is correct.

Consider the box marked "K" above. Describe which responses would be recorded
24 in this box. _____

_____

Now compare this response matrix to the confusion matrix in Figure 7-4 of HIP. How are the data recorded in this matrix different from the data recorded in that
25 confusion matrix? (Hint: Which matrix records only errors?) _____

_____

_____

Suppose that no confusion errors at all were gotten. Which six of the lettered
26 boxes in Table 7.2 would be greater than zero? _____
27 Why? _____

_____

Could then you conclude anything about the pandemonium model and the feature set
28 we are testing? _____ Why? _____
29

_____

_____

_____

For each of the following pairs of letters, the pandemonium model can predict one of three things: (i) the number of errors in the box corresponding to the first letter is _greater_ than the number of errors in the box corresponding to the second, (ii) the number of errors in the first box is _less_ than the second, or (iii) the pandemonium model with this feature set makes _no_ _prediction_ either way. Write "greater," "less," or "no prediction" after each of the following pairs:

30 C:D _____

31 L:M _____

32 Q:R _____

33 Q:T _____

34   G:H   _____

35   D:G   _____

36   G:J   _____

37   (Hint for 36: Must errors be symmetrical? _____) What rule did you use in

38   this pair to determine which box should have the larger number of responses? _____

_____

_____

_____

39   C:O   _____

If you answered "greater" on the last question, you have certainly chosen the
intuitively logical answer, for "i-1" is clearly more like "tz" than "b" is like
"tz." However, although this result is fairly likely, it is not a firm prediction
of the model, for whether this is actually true depends upon the other letters used
in the confusion matrix. In general, the model makes no prediction about two boxes
in the same column.

40   G:E   _____

41   G:I   _____

42   B:C   _____

43   F:G   _____

    As you have probably found out by now, there is one case in which the feature
set that we are using for this alphabet does not uniquely specify each letter
44   ("i-1" and "l"). Can you explain clearly why this is true? _____

_____ Because of this last point, the
pandemonium model predicts that the number of responses in several of the squares
in the matrix above should be very nearly the same. Can you find 4 of these 6
45   pairs? _____

    It is clear that people can distinguish between "i-1" and "l." Thus, something
must be wrong in our complete model, that is, either our feature set is wrong or the
pandemonium system itself is incorrect. Can you think of a feature in our current
set that one could modify, or a feature that one could add, so that each letter
46   would be uniquely identified? _____

_____

    This final question is just something to think about. One of the problems about our feature set and the feature set for the Roman alphabet in HIP is that if you rotate the letters 45°, then most of the letters are no longer recognizable by the system. Yet surely you can read tilted letters. How might you go about devising a feature set that is not disturbed by rotation, i.e., that can recognize the letters in any orientation?

A PANDEMONIUM SYSTEM FOR HEARING

Most examples given of pandemonium-type systems involve feature sets that utilize information obtained through vision. One major reason is that in this modality it is much easier to infer which features are important for pattern recognition and thus induce feature sets. Thus, in the case of vision, it is clear that lines, points, and angles are important features of visual objects. This is due in part to the fact that separate conceptual objects usually have definite visual boundaries and are separable in space.

In the case of other sense modalities, for example, hearing, it is not at all easy to decide what are features, and, more importantly, what features are utilized to distinguish patterns. This is partially because, in contrast to the visual domain, conceptual objects, e.g., words, often have no distinct boundaries and cannot be separated from other words around them. This problem is called the

47 _____ .

In general, given that one proposes a feature to be used in pattern recognition, how can you tell whether this feature is being utilized to distinguish between patterns? How might you devise an experiment to test if a feature is being used?

48 _____

_____

_____

Several feature sets have been proposed as a basis for pandemonium-type systems for hearing. One possible feature set using *phonemes* is given in Table 7-2 of HIP.

49 What is the procedure by which one phoneme can be distinguished from another? _____

_____

Why is it unlikely that this phoneme feature set could provide a basis for a

50 pandemonium system? _____

_____

_____

A second feature set is proposed which is based on how speech sounds are produced by the mouth. This is given in Table 7-3 of HIP. Notice that whereas the features used for the Dalmatian alphabet could be counted, here each feature can only be either present or absent. In terms of counting, this might be interpreted as 1 and 0, respectively. Suppose for a moment that this feature set is the one used by humans for the recognition of speech. Let us see what such a model would predict experimentally, much as we did with the visual feature model above. Using just the phonemes "f," "v," "b," and "s," consider the confusion matrix in Table 7.3.

Phoneme guessed

	b	f	v	s
b		A	B	C
f			D	E
v		F		
s		G	H	

Phoneme presented

Confusion matrix of phonemes

(capital letters are labels for boxes)

Table 7.3

As in the earlier response matrix, some of the boxes have been lettered. Much as you did with the previous table, write "greater," "less," "same," or "no prediction" in the blanks below depending upon what relation the number of errors in the first box has to the second:

51   A:B   _____

52   A:D   _____

53   B:C   _____

54   G:H   _____

55   D:F   _____

(Hint: On the last one: What rule did you use for symmetricality before?)

A parallel can be drawn between the stages used for the visual pandemonium system and the stages in this last model for hearing. In Table 7.4, write the corresponding stage in the auditory pandemonium system for each visual stage.

	Printed language	Spoken language
56	features: lines, angles, curves	
57	letters	
58	words	

Table 7.4

However, the two systems are quite different in one facet: Whereas in printed language, each feature, letter, and word is clearly separable, in spoken language, none of the corresponding levels have been found to be separable.

MORE POSSIBLE THEORIES OF ATTENTION

In our last theory of attention it was proposed that analysis of several input streams of information proceeded until everything was analyzed but the meaning of the information, before attention was switched to one particular stream. Furthermore, pandemonium systems like the ones we have just considered might be a reasonably detailed model of the first stages of analysis before the "switch." Is this model satisfactory, or is there another experiment that would contradict even this model?

Suppose a single person read aloud two different prose passages, both in English, and again recorded both on tape. Again they are played simultaneously through the same speaker to a subject. The subject is told to follow just one of the prose passages. Although this task is quite difficult, the subject can still follow that passage. Yet our present model would predict that the two passages could not be separable since they differ only at the meaning level.

Therefore, even meaning must be analyzed in all the input streams before attention can be switched to a particular message. Our model of attention must now look like the one shown in Figure 7.7. But this last model is no theory of attention at all: We are saying that each channel must be completely analyzed before attention can be switched to any one, but then why do you need to concentrate attention at all, since all the messages have now been completely analyzed? Furthermore, this last situation is clearly not possible--have you tried to listen closely to three conversations at once, or read a difficult book and listen to a lecture simultaneously?

It is becoming evident that all "switch-type" models of attention are unworkable.

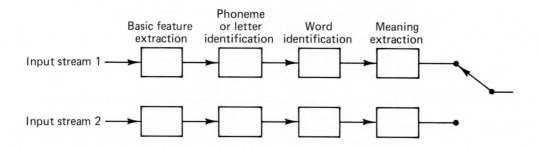

Figure 7.7

But why not throw the switch out of the model completely? In other words,
attention is never switched to one channel to the total stopping of analysis of
other messages; instead the majority of analysis effort is spent on the attended
message, while the other messages receive what is left over. Moreover, analysis
is assumed to proceed at all levels on all channels; that is, not only are a few
basic features extracted from the unattended channels, but a little of the meaning
of those messages which are not attended to is analyzed. Another way of looking at
this new model is that attention does not need to be given in one lump sum to one
channel but can be parceled out in continuously varying amounts to each of the
channels.

However, this does not completely solve the problem, for how does one know on
which channel to concentrate the attention in the first place? Take the last experiment where two English prose passages are being read simultaneously. Our subject
must pick out from the overlapping stream of words those words which belong to the
one passage she is following. Suppose she has followed the passage up to a particular
point. How does she know what part of the next overlapping pair of words is perti-
nent to her passage unless she analyzes that overlapping pair completely? The key
to solving this problem is that, if she has been following the message up to some
point, she must be obtaining the meaning up to that point and therefore has *expectations* about how that passage should continue, i.e., what comes next should make
sense in relation to what has come before. For example, suppose the passage she
was following has gone:

*Juan had just finished studying and he knew that he had to get something to
eat before he went to bed. The ice cream parlor was a couple of blocks
away and he got there just a minute before it closed. As usual he chose*

his favorite _____

Then the system would probably expect the next word to be "flavor."

Let us stop for a moment and link this process with the terminology used in HIP. The information around any particular word being analyzed is called that word's

59   _____. If that surrounding information provides expectations about the word being analyzed, then the information is said to be repetitive, or

60   _____. The demons that are in charge of introducing

61   these expectations are called _____. What

62   would happen to this last process if humans had no memory? _____

_____

_____

_____

Using these expectations (for example, that the next word is "flavor"), the system can allocate most of its attention to finding features that are in line with this theme (in our example, one could look first for the features of the letter

63   "f," etc.). This process is one of the duties of the _____ as

64   described in HIP. What are its other two duties? (i) _____

_____

65   (ii) _____

_____

Thus, there are two types of processes that work on the analysis of an input message. One is a process activated by the input data--a *data-driven* process (like the pandemonium system). Parts of this process can be allocated more or less attention. The second type operates on the first by monitoring the context of the message and keeping a set of expectations as to what should come next, and also by using these expectations to control the allocation of attention--both these roles are *conceptually driven* processes.

An example of the interaction between conceptually driven and data-driven processes in pattern recognition is given below. Note that the whole process probably took less than a couple of seconds to complete, and much of it, especially the data-driven parts, was not conscious. Your job is to identify the marked sentences as to whether they refer mostly to data-driven (D) or conceptually driven (C) processes. Although you need write no more than that, it should be clear in your mind why you chose the particular process in each case.

After arriving at your 3:00 physics class you open the door and take a seat very close to the entrance.

66 _____ *You are somewhat worried that you are late.*

67 _____ *Thus you look up near the upper left-hand corner of the front wall.*

68 _____ *You find an object there of which all you notice is that it is round.*

69 _____ *Since you know this room quite well, you postulate that this object is a clock.*

70 _____ *More features of the clock become clear--that there are two thick dark lines forming an oblique angle at the center of the object.*

71 _____ *Since you have assumed that you have found the clock, you can convert this hand position to time.*

Just as you suspected. You are 10 minutes late. This also explains the frown on the person in front of the room who must be your professor. (You have just sampled a few features--color of hair, shoulder width, frown-- data-driven processing). Since you expect a person, one which is specifi- cally your professor (conceptually driven), you jump to that conclusion on such a small amount of information. And you are probably right, although your initial conclusion would be wrong if the person just looked like the professor, or perhaps even if it were a well-made manikin.

72 _____ *Moving your eyes down from the professor's face, you find an object which looks black and has a few straight-line features.*

73 _____ *You hypothesize it must be the lecture counter, the same one that's been there for at least a year.*

74 _____ *Meanwhile, a shiny silvery flash slightly higher up catches your eye.*

75 _____ *This must be the faucet to the sink on top of the counter. This also helps confirm that the dark object with the straight lines is the counter.*

76 _____ *Next to the shiny flash is a long, gray tube attached to other dark shapes. There is a glint of white light at one end of the tube.*

77 _____ *This must be the slide projector. The glint must have been the glass lens.*

78 _____ *You wait for the confirming sound of the projector fan and look*

for slide trays.

79 _____ *Features for neither object nor sound are noticed.*

80 _____ *More features for the long tubular object are being iden-*
tified. There are several long, thick, curved lines grouped around and
below the tube, and you notice a small flash of magenta near the middle of
the object. Neither of these new features fits in with the initial hypo-
thesis that the object is a slide projector, and the flash of magenta in
particular is surprising enough for you to stop sensory processing on other
objects and concentrate on this now-unknown object (the initial hypothesis
has been discarded).

81 _____ *You hypothesize that the long curved lines must be wires.*

82 _____ *You suddenly remember that the professor has mentioned*
bringing a ruby laser to class sometime. This must be it!

83 _____ *The glint of magenta must have been the ruby crystal.*

A Few Conclusions

1. Processing in this system is viewed to be a constant interaction between
   (a) data-driven processes introducing new sensory information to be fit
       in, and
   (b) conceptually driven processes proposing identifications of the current
       incomplete input information, and continually directing the effort of
       further data-driven processing to important or surprising results.
The second activity of the conceptually driven processing is what attention is in
this model.

2. The conceptually driven process will often make a hypothesis based on a few
features or bits of information and move on to something else without processing
additional features of the object. For instance, in recognizing the clock in the
situation above, one left the clock without noticing that it has a brown metal rim,
that the hands are pointed, and that the glass covering the clockface is actually
missing.

3. Initial snap conclusions are usually right--the world is fairly regular and
predictable--but there are times when the system may be fooled by hypothesizing too
quickly (the laser).

4. A particularly surprising or important piece of data may interrupt this
interactive data-driven and conceptually driven processing and the conceptually driven
process may direct further processing to that feature.

8 The memory systems

PRETEST

1. Which memory system provides brief storage for encoded, categorized stimuli? _STM_

2. Which memory system contains information which was once in consciousness but has now passed into a large, interconnected store? _LTM_ _____

_____

3. Which memory system is bound up with perceptual processes and pattern recognition? _sensory information storage_

4. What is the approximate duration of information in the sensory information store? _~~msec~~ 150-500 msec_

5. Which type of rehearsal only refreshes material in short-term memory but does not help material get into long-term memory? _maintenance_

6. What is the name of the experimental device which has three fields for the presentation of visual displays, and which is capable of fine degrees of control of exposure time and brightness contrast? _tachistoscope_

7. 2000 msec = _2_ seconds; 40 msec = _.04_ seconds.

8. The _reconstruction_ process of memory is responsible for a subject's ability to recall or identify an item when only a portion of that item's attributes remain in memory.

9. In one theory of short-term memory, items in memory are thought to lose strength when new items arrive. This is the _item decay (interference)_ * theory.

10. In another theory of short-term memory, items in memory are thought to lose strength with the passage of time. This is the _time decay_ theory.

1. short-term memory; 2. long-term memory; 3. sensory information store; 4.
150 - 500 msec; 5. maintenance rehearsal; 6. three-field tachistoscope; 7. 2,
0.04; 8. reconstruction (or reconstructive); 9. interference; 10. time-decay

---

AN OVERVIEW OF THE MEMORY SYSTEMS

In Figure 8.1, the boxes represent the memory systems, whereas the arrows between
the boxes represent the processes that must apply in order for information to be
transferred from one information system to another. Using the blank spaces provided,
label the boxes and arrows in Figure 8.1.

1

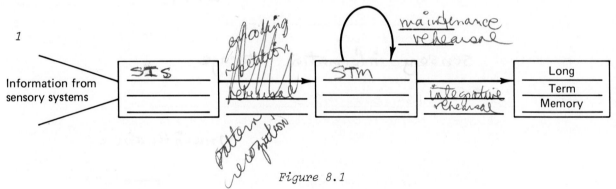

Information from
sensory systems

Figure 8.1

Whether all memories of longer duration can properly be thought of as part of
long-term memory is problematic. Suppose someone is able to say over and over again
a list of seven words for 3 solid days. (Perhaps this is an attempt to
get into The Guinness Book of World Records.) Sixty seconds after stopping this
silent repetition, this person can no longer remember most of the words on the list.
During the 3 days was this person practicing maintenance rehearsal or integrative

2   processing? _maintenance rehearsal_____ Was the list of words in

3   short-term memory or in long-term memory during this time? ___STM___
_____.

SENSORY INFORMATION STORE (SIS)

Several different types of devices are available for the controlled presentation
of visual stimuli in experiments on the nature, size, and duration of the SIS.
Computer-controlled displays are one such device. What experimental device has the

4   following advantages over computer-controlled displays? ___*tachistoscope*___

    a. More accurate control of presentation duration

    b. Possibility of much better color

    c. Higher contrast potential

The next group of questions will all deal with tachistoscopic experiments on the nature of the SIS. Subjects are shown displays that consist of rows of letters. The displays are flashed for very brief durations, say, for 90 msec. The experimenter wants to discover how much information is available in the SIS at various times after the presentation of the display. You will be asked to consider the results of this experiment in three different conditions: A Report-All condition, a Probe condition, and a Detection condition. You should try to evaluate the effectiveness of each condition as a means of learning about the information content of SIS.

A. *The Report-All Condition*

In this condition, subjects are shown the 90-msec displays and are supposed to try to report all the letters they saw in the display. If the display has nine letters (three rows of three letters each), then about how many letters will be

5   correctly reported, on the average? ___4-5___ If the display is shown for 180 msec rather than 90 msec, will the information be available in the SIS for

6   twice as long? ___no___ Explain. ___amt of time in SIS important, not duration of event. (presentation time)___

_____

_____

Since the experimenter in the Report-All condition wants to find out whether the amount of information in SIS changes with time, subjects are asked not to begin reporting all the letters from the display until they hear a tone. The experimenter arranges the experimental trials so that sometimes the tone sounds immediately after the display goes off, sometimes 100 msec after the display goes off, sometimes 200 msec later, and so on, up to 1000 msec after the offset of the display. Use the graph provided in Figure 8.2 to sketch the results which you would expect the experimenter to find.

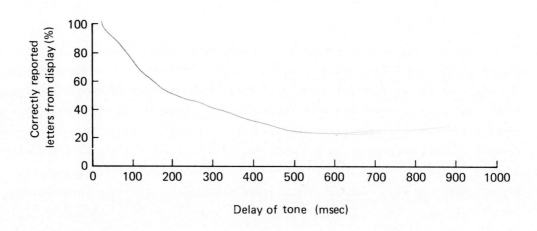

Figure 8.2

7

The experimenter may be tempted to draw some naive conclusions about SIS on the basis
of the experiment. On the basis of the results you have graphed in Figure 8.2,
what does the capacity of the SIS appear to be? (How many items can it hold?)

8 _____4-5_____The duration of information in the SIS appears to be at

9 least how long in this experiment? _150_ msec ̶/̶ several seconds.

10 What is wrong with the naive conclusion drawn on the basis of Figure 8.2? _____

_____

Let us assume that the experimenter publishes his results in the Report-All
experiment, and claims that his conclusions are correct. A critic responds to these
claims by saying that the number of words recalled is not really a function of the
limits of SIS in this experiment at all. Rather, the critic claims, the number
recalled is a function of either the size of short-term memory, or of the time
required to transfer information from the SIS to the STM (that is, SIS may decay
before pattern recognition processes have transferred all of it to STM). Do you

11 tend to agree more with the experimenter or with the critic? _Critic_____

Why?_____

_____   _____

Suppose that the Report-All experiment was carried out with a display of 16
letters (arranged in four rows of four letters each) rather than a display of 9

12 letters. What differences in results would you expect? Why? _worse — too_____

many!

_____

_____

_____

B. The Probe Condition

The critic just mentioned decides to conduct an experiment to find out more about what the real limits of SIS are. This experimenter (whom we'll call Experimenter 2) shows subjects 90-msec displays, which are followed by a bar marker that singles out one of the nine letters of the display as the target. If the bar marker appears under the target's location immediately after the display of nine letters goes off, then what percentage of the time will subjects be able to correctly report the

13   target letter? _____ *100%* _____   Because Experimenter 2 wants to find out how the information in SIS changes with time, the time of onset of the bar marker is varied. Sometimes the target is marked with the bar at the time of the offset of the display, sometimes 100 msec later, sometimes 200 msec later, and so on. Use the graph provided in Figure 8.3 to sketch the results you would expect the experimenter to find.

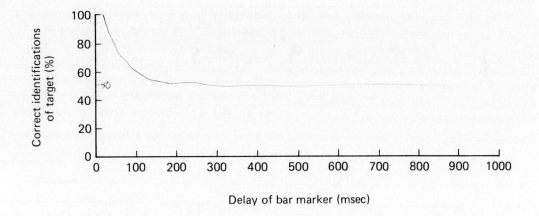

14

Figure 8.3

One way of estimating the capacity (number of items it can hold) of the SIS in the Probe experiment is to multiply the percentage of correct identifications times the number of possible targets in the display. On the basis of the results you have

15   graphed in Figure 8.3, what is the estimated capacity of the SIS? _____
_____ Does the capacity decrease

16 with time following the offset of the display? _____ The duration of

17 information in the SIS appears to be about how long in this experiment? _____

_____

    Notice that the percentage correct value does not decay all the way to 0%. Why

18 should this be the case? (Keep in mind the comments of the critic above.) _____

_____

_____

    Reconsider the answer you gave to question *5* (How many letters are correctly

reported in the Report-All condition with a nine-letter display?) Compare your

answer with the answer you gave to question *15*. Which condition (Report-All or

19 Probe) does <u>not</u> seem to be really testing the capacity of SIS? _____

20 What do you think this condition <u>is</u> testing? _____

_____

C. *Detection Condition*

    Subjects in the Detection condition are told that each briefly presented visual

display will have either an <u>S</u> or a <u>T</u> (but not both) in it. They are required to

say whether an <u>S</u> or a <u>T</u> was present. The location of the target (<u>S</u> or <u>T</u>) is randomly

varied among the nine possible positions of the nine-letter display. As a means of

studying the capacity of SIS, does this condition seem more like the Report-All

21 condition or the Probe condition? ~~Report All~~ *Probe* Why? *Need to*

what's in all 9 positions.

_____

    Subjects ordinarily do very well in the Detection condition. The percentage

of correct identifications is close to 100 in the nine-letter display condition.

What does this result imply about the relative durations of the pattern recognition

22 process and the preservation of information in SIS? _____

_____

_____

    One difference between the Detection condition and the Report-All condition is

that subjects have a much better chance of scoring a "correct identification" in

the Detection condition even when they did not see the target letter. A subject

in the Report-All condition who has not seen the target or who fails to remember

what it was must guess by randomly choosing one of the 26 letters of the alphabet.

A subject in the Detection condition who has not seen either of the two targets

need only randomly choose between them. If a subject in the Detection condition always had his eyes closed during the 90-msec display, what percentage of his

23 responses would be correct, on the average? ___*50%*___

Assume for the moment that the graph you drew in Figure 8.3 is an accurate representation of the amount of information from the display that is present in SIS. (That is, ignore the fact that approximately 4% of the time that subjects do not remember the target letter they will still guess it correctly.) If you were to graph the results of the Detection experiment on Figure 8.3, would the curve be higher than, about equal to, or lower than the actual amount of information in SIS,

24 as depicted in Figure 8.3? _____

Now consider a possible modification of the Detection experiment. Subjects are shown displays of letters and required to say either "S" or "T," depending on which letter they believe is present. For 45% of the trials, a $\underline{T}$ is actually present; for 45% of the trials, an $\underline{S}$ is present, and for the remaining 10% of the trials, neither an $\underline{S}$ nor a $\underline{T}$ is present. Displays A and B show two of the displays used for the trials in which neither target is present.

I	K	L		C	B	J
X	M	F		Q	D	P
N	W	H		R	G	O
Display A				Display B		

Subjects are shown these displays under conditions that make full analysis of the material in SIS very difficult. The displays are shown for only 30 msec, and then a bright light is flashed to "clear" the SIS, thus, it is very hard for subjects to be sure that they did not see all or part of one of the two target letters.

One of the findings of this experiment is that subjects are much more likely to say they saw a "T" when they have seen Display A. They are also more likely to say

25 "S" than "T" when they have seen Display B. Why? ___*Physical characteristics*___
___*more similar to item looked for.*___

Does this result suggest that subjects make use of partial information in visual

26 processing? ___*yes*___ How might they use such information in this task? ___
___*look for shared ~~that~~ phys characteristics +*___
___*eliminate*___ In the section entitled "Attri-
butes of Memory" in Chapter 8 of HIP, an example is presented in which the retention of some of the attributes or features of a stimulus enables a subject to reconstruct the original stimulus. Presumably there is some difference in the visual attributes of Displays A and B which causes subjects to think that they see an "S" in Display B

27 and a "T" in Display A. What attributes of Display A suggest "T"? _Vertical |_

_____ What attributes of Display B suggest "S"?

Horizontal + more rounded.

Mention was made above of the use of a bright flash to "clear" or erase SIS
after the presentation of a display, so as to further limit the duration of processing.
What measures can an experimenter take to clear or erase from the SIS only one

28 character of the display, rather than the entire display? _O._

_____

_____

If a display of one letter is presented for 10 msec, with no erasure, then about

29 how long is the memory of that display in the SIS? _at least 10 msec — much more 150 - 500 msec_

If a display of one letter is presented for 10 msec, and is then subjected to the

measures you outlined in answer to 28, then for how long is the memory of the

30 display in SIS? _same — the item_

SHORT-TERM MEMORY (STM)

Imagine that you have just looked up a telephone number in the book and are
walking to the other side of the room to use the phone. Before you get to the phone,
however, a friend, who is an experimental psychologist, stops you and asks you to
spell your first and last names backward as fast as you can. Suppose you comply
immediately. Do you think you'll remember the phone number after doing this? _No_
Recall the short-term memory task of Peterson and Peterson, in which subjects were
required to recall three letters only seconds after presentation, but had to spend
those seconds performing a difficult interference task. Draw an analogy between
the task of spelling your names backward and some aspect of the Petersons' experi-

31 ment. _Interference knocked out material which had been rehearsed._

Suppose that instead of being asked to spell your first and last names backward, you
are asked to spell "cat" backward. Would you expect to remember more or less of the

32 phone number in this condition? _More_   Why do you suppose the results

are different in the two cases? _Takes less involvement to do_

Cat - shorter - can keep rehearsing.

Is short-term memory concurrent with pattern recognition, or does it precede

33 or follow the pattern recognition process? _follows._

Human beings are able to relate items of information they read as written
language to items of information they hear as spoken language. In other words, if
you read something about tachistoscopes and if you hear something about tachistoscopes

you are able to put the information from the two sources together. This is very
useful, since it may enable you to draw conclusions you might not have been able to
reach on the basis of the information from either source by itself. These facts
imply that information from all language sources may be stored in some common format
in long-term memory. Which use of language do you suppose evolved first: reading

34 and writing, or speaking and hearing? _____ *Speaking + hearing* _____
Which type of language-encoding, one based on acoustic/articulatory factors or one

35 based on visual/spelling factors, is most likely to have developed first? _____
_____ *acoustic / articulatory.* _____

Below there are two groups of possible errors which subjects might be found to
produce when trying to recall the letter T (as part of a string of letters to be
memorized):

    Error Group 1:   C, G, V
    Error Group 2:   I, L, J

(In each error group, the most common error is listed first.) Consider the visual
and acoustic attributes of these error groups. What, if any, acoustic attribute(s)

36 do the members of Group 1 share with T? *end in ē sound* _____
What (if any) visual attributes do the members of Group 1 have in common with T?

37 _____ ~~Vertical lines~~ *None* _____ What (if any) acoustic attributes

38 do the members of Group 2 have in common with T? *None* _____
_____ What (if any) visual attributes do the members of

39 Group 2 have in common with T? *Vertical lines /* _____
_____ Which of the two error groups would we expect to find in

40 the experiment if a memory system is based on an auditory or articulatory base? *2*
Which of these error groups would you think a group of subjects would be more likely
to display as "misrecallings" of the letter T in a list of nine letters which they

41 read once and then rehearsed for 60 seconds? *1* _____
In a list of nine letters which they heard once and then rehearsed for 60 seconds?
_____ *2* _____ If your answers to 41 were the same, explain why.

42 If they were different, explain why. *Hard to do 2 visuals or
2 auditories at once*

The section in HIP Chapter 7 on Attributes of Memory introduces the idea that
items may not always be stored in memory as unitary concepts. Rather, concepts
in memory may consist of groups of attributes or features. In HIP, some of the STM
results with acoustic errors are explained in terms of lost acoustic attributes.

Problems 11-13 of this problem set deal with errors in SIS due to missing visual attributes. An essential aspect of explaining either sort of error with a theory of attributes is the function of the attributes of a concept which are not lost or forgotten. These remaining attributes of the concept serve to define a *candidate set*. A candidate set is the group of items which is consistent with the remaining attributes. In the example given in HIP Chapter 7, the attributes of the word "hose" are the sounds h, o, and z. If the attribute h is lost, then the remaining attributes o and z define a candidate set with these members: doze, goes, hose, Joe's, nose, pose, those, chose, shows, foes, lows, bows, mows, rose, sews, and toes. These are all English words which begin with some sound and end with the sounds o and z. What are the chances that "hose" will be correctly recalled, given

43   that a choice of responses is made randomly from this candidate set? _____

_____ 1/16 _____ Suppose now that the word "receipt" is given and that the attributes of "receipt" are the sounds, r, ee, s, ee, and t. If the attribute r is lost from memory, then the remaining attributes define a candidate set with these members: deceit and receipt. What are the chances that "receipt" will be correctly recalled, given that a response choice is made randomly from the

44   candidate set?_____ 1/4 _____

These examples reveal two aspects of partial information which are important to the reconstruction process in remembering partially forgotten information. What is the relationship between number of features (or perhaps proportion of features)

45   remembered and probability of correct reconstruction?_____

_____

What is the relationship between number of alternatives possible based on the

46   remembered attributes and probability of correct reconstruction? _____

_____

Below are two lists of words. Read list 1 once, then look away and silently rehearse the list for 60 seconds. How many of the words were you able to recall at the end of the 60 seconds?_____ 3 _____ Now read list 2 once, look away, and silently rehearse for 60 seconds. How many of the words were you able to recall at the end of the 60 seconds?_____ 4 _____

	List 1		List 2
	box		container
	scared		timorous
	glue		adhesive
	bright		luminous
	insult		criticize
	tool		implement

47   Why is one list remembered better than the other? *more familiar*

_____

48   Which list takes longer to say? _____*2*_____ One possible conclusion that can
be drawn from this experiment is that one can maintain by rehearsal in STM only as
much as one can say aloud in a certain short period of time. Give another

49   explanation for the results of this experiment. *familiar words take*
                    less time to remember or rehearse

How might one try to determine which of these two explanations is more nearly

50   correct? _____

_____

There are two widely held theories about how information is lost (forgotten)
from STM. The *interference theory* holds that we forget because new information
enters our low-capacity short-term memories, and thereby degrades or "crowds out"
the older information. The *time-decay theory* holds that it is merely the passage of
time that causes information to be lost from STM. In this view, a piece of information is strongest just as it enters STM, but as time passes it rapidly decays,
unless it is refreshed through rehearsal. Suppose a psychologist announces that a
way has been discovered to prevent rehearsal that does not require interfering with
items in STM. If subjects are run in a short-term memory experiment under this

51   condition, what results will the interference theory predict? *perfect.*

_____

52   What results will the time-decay theory predict? *problems*

_____

53   Does such an experimental condition exist? ~~Yes~~ *No*   If so,
what is it? _____

_____

We have already seen that there is some evidence that linguistic material may
have an acoustic/articulatory code in STM, whether the material was presented

auditorily or visually. Take care to realize that this does not mean that everything
in STM must necessarily be in acoustic/articulatory form. Most people agree that
they can have brief visual memories (longer in duration than those of the SIS) which
intuitively do not seem to be verbal in nature. The experiments by Brooks, discussed
in Chapter 8 of HIP, can be taken as further evidence that there may be different
types of codes in STM. The basic structure of Brooks' evidence is to show that
response modes which are similar to the modes in which stimuli are presented make
the task considerably more difficult than response modes which are different from
stimulus-presentation modes.

     Give an example of a task in which the stimulus material is verbal and the

54   response is verbal. *sentence - yes to nouns*
                                    no to others

Give an example of a response task for the above stimulus material which is visual/

55   spatial. *Y N - point*

56   Which type of response task is easier with this type of stimulus material?
               Y N - point - visual

     Think about the overall structure of the memory systems which you labeled in
Figure 8.1. In this chapter we have dealt with the sensory information store,
short-term memory, and some aspects of maintenance rehearsal. Chapter 7 treated
pattern recognition, the link between the SIS and STM. The next chapter will deal
largely with the nature of the integrative processes responsible for the transfer of
information from short-term memory to long-term memory. In addition, Chapter 9 will
discuss how information in LTM is accessed, and, in particular, how information can
be stored so as to improve the chances for its successful retrieval. A discussion
of the actual form of the information in LTM is postponed until Chapter 10.

9 Using memory

1-3. The three major components of long-term memory are _recognition_, _comparing to other items_ and _decision making_.

4. A strategy for remembering an item or group of items which depends upon mentally associating the item or group with some previously learned material in an unnatural way is called a _mnemonic_.

5. "_Depth_ of processing" refers to the degree of meaningful thought and elaboration which an item receives.

6. The general term used to describe the manner by which material in short-term memory is transferred to long-term memory is _elaborated rehearsal_.

7. Another term for the allocation of processing resources is _____

8. In a _recognition_ test of memory, subjects are asked which items have been presented before in the experiment.

9. Another way to test what is remembered from a list is to require the subject to either say out loud or write down all the items from the list that are remembered. This is a _free Recall_ task.

10. In some list-learning experiments, subjects are required to recall many lists of words immediately after each presentation. The results (in terms of percentage correct recalls) are plotted against the position of the recalled words in the originally presented lists. The resultant graph is called a _serial position_ curve.

*1-3. the monitor, the interpreter, the data base; 4. mnemonic; 5. Depth; 6. inte-
grative processing; 7. attention; 8. recognition; 9. recall; 10. serial position*

INTRODUCTION

In order for information to be available for recall some time after its original
presentation, after it has disappeared from short-term memory, it must be integrated
with old information in long-term memory in such a way that it can be retrieved when
needed. One of the most common cues for retrieval seems to be the <u>meaning</u> or
significance of the item to be remembered. One effective integrative process is to
think about the meaningful relationships between new and old information in memory.

The transfer of words on a list from short- to long-term memory is necessarily
quite a personal experience. List learning experiments must miss much of what is
most interesting about the integration of new information, precisely because such
experiments ignore the personal, idiosyncratic nature of the transfer. Nonetheless,
experimental designs such as the *serial position curve* experiments described in
Chapter 9 of HIP can give us some ideas about the gross relationships between STM
and LTM.

FROM STM TO LTM

Consider a serial position curve experiment in which lists of 20 words are
read to subjects at the rate of one word per second. At the end of each list,
subjects are told to recall the list. Graph the results of such an experiment in
Figure 9.1. You should be more concerned with the shape of the curve than with the
precise values on it.

1

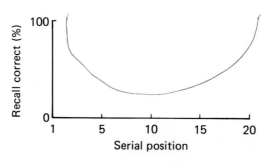

Figure 9.1

For which positions on the curve is recall determined primarily by long-term

2   memory? _____*begining —primacy*_____

3   For which positions is recall determined by both STM and LTM? _*middle*_

_____

    Suppose that a new set of subjects is given the same lists of words that were used to obtain the serial position curve you gave for the last problem. However, at the end of the presentation of each list, subjects are now required to do rapid mental multiplication problems (37 x 9 = ?, 48 x 7 = ?, etc.). The subjects solve as many of these problems as they can in 30 seconds without making use of pencil and paper. Then they try to recall the list they were just given. Sketch the shape of the serial position curve for these subjects in Figure 9.2.

4

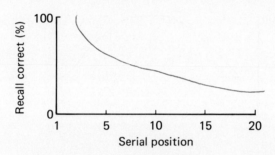

Figure 9.2

What accounts for the difference between this curve and the one you sketched in

5   Figure 9.1? _____*interfered w/ short term memory.*_____

    Now consider the probable effects of changing the nature of the lists you present to the subjects. The list to the right is an example of a list in which the seventh through the fifteenth items can be combined to form a sentence, with a few adjustments. In this case, a possible sentence formed from these items is "The secretary of state didn't want to testify before the senate committee." If Items 7 to 15 of each of your lists can easily combine to make sentences, you might expect different results for the serial position curve.

List
clove
thus
play
coo
stuff
cling
the
secretary
state
didn't

  want

                                                    testify

                                                    before

                                                    senate

                                                    committee

                                                    elk

                                                    howl

                                                    shop

                                                    pen

                                                    rock

Sketch in Figure 9.3 the type of serial position curve you would expect with
these kinds of lists.

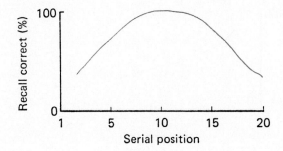

Figure 9.3

7   How does this curve differ from the one you drew in Figure 9.1? _____ *opposite* _____

_____

Do you think the structure of Items 7-15 facilitates their storage in and retrieval
8   from SIS, STM, or LTM? _____ *LTM → put in* _____ How? _____

_____ *+ chunk - go back + remember* _____

TESTING MEMORY

     Many psychological approaches to the testing of memory seem dull and artificial
because they use unnatural stimuli, such as lists of apparently unrelated words.
Why not ask subject to remember things of importance to them? Wouldn't this be a
fairer test of human memory as it was meant to be used? Here is an example of the
problems that can arise with such an approach:

In the course of a project on long-term memory, an investigator asked
a personal acquaintance to try to remember what he had been doing just before he heard that John F. Kennedy had been assassinated. The acquaintance
struggled hard to remember for several minutes, while giving the investigator a running commentary on his thought processes. Suddenly he remembered,
"Why, I was playing tennis with you!" The investigator was greatly surprised, and later tried to check this out, only to discover that she had
been attending a conference in another city at the time. Her acquaintance's
memory had been completely false.

Technical terms for this sort of erroneous report are *fabrication* or *confabulation*.

When the use of attributes as partial information for the recall of items in
memory is discussed in HIP Chapter 8, Lindsay and Norman do not refer to the
process as one of "guessing from a candidate set." Instead they use a term that
designates a more intelligent, guided process for building up the missing item.

9   What is that term? _____ Could this term be applied

10 to the process of "remembering" the tennis game just discussed? _____

If so, what might the "attributes" be which form the basis for this process? _____

_____

_____

Because of these kinds of problems, psychologists will often present lists to
subjects and then either instruct them to recall items or ask them whether they
recognize items as being on the list. In terms of percentage correct, will
subjects in general score higher on a recall test of memory, or on a recognition

11 test? _____recognition — less retrieval_____

MEMORY AND ATTENTION

In HIP Chapter 7, the concept of *attention* is tentatively equated with the
allocation of processing resources, which are assumed to be limited. Limits on
attention (such as our inability to follow all of three conversations at one time)
are thus explained. But consider the problem of listening to a nearby conversation
at a noisy cocktail party. People are often very good at doing this, even though
they may be tuning in on only a very small fraction of the total sound available to
them in the room. How do you explain this ability to follow the conversation in

12 these circumstances (in terms of the theory just discussed)? _shadowing_

recall one

recognize the other

Now if all the conversations suddenly were to cease, would you be able to say
whether the person who was speaking directly behind you (who was not part of the
conversation you were listening to) was a man or a woman (assuming their voices

13   would have a different pitch)? _____ *Yes* _____

What if, in the midst of all the hubbub, the person directly behind you had
uttered your name as part of a conversation you were <u>not</u> listening to. Would you

14   be likely to notice this? _____ *Yes* _____

What modifications or additions to your answer to *12* are called for because of

15   the phenomena brought up in *13* and *14*? _____ *selectively attentive* _____

_____

_____

Integrating information into long-term memory undoubtedly requires the allocation
of processing resources. To learn material one must <u>attend</u> to the material--think
about it. When subjects are required to shadow words presented over earphones to
one ear while a list of common English words are presented to the other ear (with
many repetitions), what percentage of the words in the unattended ear were they

16   able to recall later? _____ Explain this result. _____

_____

_____

ORGANIZATION AND INTEGRATION

You will recall that Bransford and Johnson found that using a different title
for the same prose passage (either "Watching a peace march from the 40th floor" or
"A space trip to an inhabited planet") made an important difference in the way in
which the prose passage was remembered. This suggests that many of the phenomena
we try to understand as facts about memory may really be better thought of as facts
about understanding. An essential aspect of understanding any body of material is
imposing some organization (usually meaningful) on the material. Read the following
paragraph.[1]

> The procedure is actually quite simple. First you arrange things into
> different groups. Of course, one pile may be sufficient depending on how
> much there is to do. If you have to go somewhere else due to lack of
> facilities that is the next step, otherwise you are pretty well set. It
> is important not to overdo things. That is, it is better to do too few
> things at once than too many. In the short run this may not seem important

1. Adapted from Bransford, J.D. & Johnson M.K., Considerations of some problems of comprehension.
In W.G. Chase (Ed.), *Visual information processing*, New York: Academic Press, 1973.

but complications can easily arise. A mistake can be expensive as well.
At first the whole procedure will seem complicated. Soon, however, it
will become just another facet of life. It is difficult to foresee any
end to the necessity for this task in the immediate future.

17 How well would you say you understand this paragraph? _*well*_

If you were now required to turn the page and try to write out the paragraph from

18 memory, how well do you think you would do? _*Bleh!*_

Now read the paragraph again, being aware that the title is "Washing clothes."

19 How well do you understand the paragraph now? _____ Do you

20 think you would do better on a recall task because you know the title? _*No*_

21 To what do you attribute the difference?_____

_____

In the construction of any information storage and retrieval system, decisions
must be made about how much effort should be put into storing items and how much
effort into the retrieval of the items. Storage can be accomplished very quickly
indeed if there is no requirement for indexing, cataloging, or in some other way
way providing an address for the stored item. In a system with this sort of

22 storage principle, is retrieval likely to be fast or slow? _*slow*_

What implications for studying academic subject matter does the principle of a

23 tradeoff between storage time and retrieval time have? _*slow storage - fast*_
*retrieval*

In the section on Integrative Processes, the authors of HIP point out that we
often bring a very great deal of structure to bear on the problem of learning new
things. (They show that we may use many associations to remember the names "rods"
and "cones.") What implications does this have for the practical problem of learning

24 academic material that one may have a need for quite some time in the future? _____
*associations help to bring thing back.*

_____ Items of information that are
not naturally integrated into our memories can sometimes be integrated through the
use of special techniques that set up artificial associations between these items and
material already in long-term memory. These techniques are called mnemonics, and
their use and function are discussed below.

DEPTH OF PROCESSING AND INTEGRATION

What is the least effective commonly used technique for remembering new infor-

25 mation (such as a new list of familiar items)? _*rehearsal*_

Subjects are presented with a list of words and asked to perform one of the following tasks. (Different subjects are asked to perform different tasks with the list.)

1. Think of a synonym for each word.

2. Notice how many consonants each word has.

3. Imagine a scene in which all the objects the words stand for play sensible parts.

4. Notice whether the word is singular or plural. (This requires more than just looking for an "s" on the end of the word, since some plurals, such as "women," do not end in "s.")

Order these tasks along a depth-of-processing dimension.

26   Greatest depth of processing   _____2 3_____

                                          _____3 1_____

                                          _____4_____

        Most shallow processing   _____2_____

Subjects assigned to which task are likely to perform best on a later memory test?

27   _____3_____

MNEMONICS

Adults are aware of some of the properties of their own memories. They have strategies to help them learn material and strategies to help them retrieve information they think they ought to know. What is the technical term for this knowledge about

28   our own knowledge? ____metamemory____ Give an example of a

29   simple, everyday strategy to help learn something, say a telephone number._____

                        Chunking

Give an unsophisticated strategy to aid in retrieval of something, say the name of

30   Hubert Humphrey's running mate in the 1968 presidential election. _____

        _____image for association_____

There are a number of more esoteric approaches to learning and retrieval strategies, which can be grouped together under the rubric of *mnemonics*. All these approaches try to teach fairly complicated storage strategies that are compatible with fairly simple (usually) retrieval strategies.

In ancient Rome, politicians found that effective speech making in the forum was an essential aspect of their careers. Since notes were not considered cricket, a

umbrella
bottle
photograph
desk
carpet
envelope
restaurant
coat *barbell*
broom

good memory was essential. The speaker would memorize all the dimensions and interior spaces of some large building with many distinct areas. In preparing a speech, the speaker added mental images representing the topic he wished to cover to these mental areas. The first room might have a broken sword on the floor if the first topic to be covered is the inadequacy of the Roman army, and so on. What is the

31 name for this mnemonic method? __Loci (places)__

Recall the list of words that rhyme with the numbers 1-10 presented in Chapter 9 of HIP. (One is a bun, two is a shoe, three is a tree, four is a door, five is a hive, six are sticks, seven is heaven, eight is a gate, nine is a line, ten is a hen.) Read the list of ten unrelated items below slowly to yourself. As you read each item fix in your mind some meaningful or bizarre picture that relates the item to the appropriate rhyme word above. The word *umbrella*, for example, you would associate with *bun*, perhaps by thinking of a bun with an umbrella sticking out of it.

1. umbrella
2. bottle
3. photograph
4. desk
5. carpet

6. envelope
7. restaurant
8. overcoat
9. barbell
10. broom

Now close your eyes and recall the list in order. If you have problems with any item, try to think of a more unusual or interesting image. Now close your eyes and say the whole list backward. Were you able to do it? _____ Do you think you could have done as well if you had used the amount of time that you spent establishing the images to simply repeat the list above over and over again to

32 yourself? __No__ Why or why not? __would have gone out of STM__

What is the eighth item on the list? __overcoat__ Do you think the rote repetition method would allow you to retrieve items associated with arbitrary

33 numbers as easily as this method? __No__ Why or why not? _____

34 What is the name for this mnemonic method? __Peg words (images of association)__
Name two principles that seem to underlie most mnemonic methods, and that have validity

35 for the process of academic study as well. __association + chunking__

ANSWERING QUESTIONS

Take a look at Figure 9-10 of HIP, which shows the three major components of a long-term memory system. The interpreter is a translator. It takes inputs (which have, of course, already been processed and partially analyzed by the sensory systems) and converts them into a format compatible with the rest of information in memory. It also takes information in memory and converts it into some output form. The data base contains all the information in LTM in some standard or universal form. Information from all sources is translated into this form. In the theory presented in Chapter 10 of HIP, a possible standard form is presented, *a semantic network*. The monitor governs the functions of the interpreter, using some of the information in the data base. It decides higher-level issues in input and output. For example, it examines incoming assertions and checks them for possible internal contradictions and for contradictions with what is already stored in the data base. In cases of information conflict, the monitor may direct a search for a possible resolution elsewhere in the data base or may even decide to reject the assertion and not allow it to be encoded in the data base. The monitor also checks what the interpreter outputs. For example, if the interpreter is about to output an answer to a question, the monitor tries to ensure that the answer is both comprehensible and informative for the questioner.

Imagine that as you pass a conversation at a cocktail party, you hear someone say "They are cooking apples." You understand the speaker to mean that the apples in a bowl on the other side of the room are not eating apples, but are rather cooking apples. In fact, however, the speaker was answering a question about the current activities of Elmer and Hortense, who are in the kitchen preparing cooked apples. Which of the three major components of LTM in Figure 9-10 is responsible

36   for your error? _____ *interpreter* _____

If someone asks you "What is John Quincy Adams' telephone number?" you don't even seem to try to find it in memory. Which of the three major components of LTM

37   is responsible for this? ____ *monitor* _____

Xaviera erroneously believes that France has landed men on the moon on two occasions. Now someone correctly tells her, "France just landed a team of astronauts on the moon." As a result, she now believes that France has landed three parties

38   on the moon. Which of the LTM components is responsible for her error? _____
_____ *monitor* _____

The following example[2] should give you a better idea of how the monitor might function to ensure that the answers to questions are relevant. Imagine that the network shown in Figure 9.4 is a portion of the network that represents some person's knowledge about geographical relationships. This person (hereafter referred to by his initials T.P.) is the one whose monitor we are going to model. T.P. can answer questions about the geography shown in Figure 9.4.

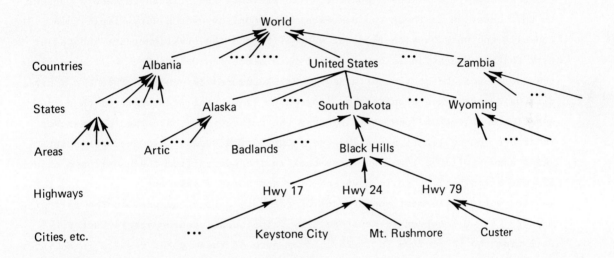

Figure 9.4

The arrows in Figure 9.4 are all meant to represent the relation *is located in (or on)*. Naturally, T.P. is aware that *is located in* is a transitive relation; that is, if Hwy 79 is in Black Hills, then it is also in South Dakota and in the United States.

Consider now some of the many possible contexts in which T.P. could be asked this question: "Where is Mt. Rushmore?"

Context 1: T.P. is in an Albanian bar talking about his travels of the previous summer, and mentions a hike up Mt. Rushmore. An Albanian who has been listening at a neighboring table asks in heavily accented English, "Where is Mt. Rushmore?"

Context 2: T.P. is working as an attendant in a gas station on Hwy 17 in the

---

[2]*This example of how where-questions are answered was developed by David Rumelhart and Jim Levin.*

Black Hills. Some tourists in a car with Alaska license plates pull in to the station and ask him, "Where is Mt. Rushmore?"

One of the true answers to the "Where is Mt. Rushmore?" question is "In South

39 Dakota." How appropriate would this answer be in Context 1? _____
_____ In Context 2?_____

40 What is the problem with this answer? _____

_____

Fortunately, T.P. has a monitor which prevents the "In South Dakota" answer to this question in these two contexts. The monitor uses a very simple rule. It consults the data base to find out where T.P. and the questioner are located at the time that the question is asked. Call this place the Q-location. It also finds the questioned object (in our example, Mt. Rushmore) in memory. Then the monitor directs two searches along the *is located in* links—one starting from the questioned object and one starting from the Q-location. When the two searches intersect in one location (called the *intersection node*), then the appropriate level answer will be found one step back in the search from the questioned object. If, for example, T.P. is in Keystone City and someone asks where Custer is, T.P.'s monitor selects the most appropriate of the many correct answers in the following manner. The Q-location is Keystone City. The questioned object is Custer. Following the *is located in* links up from each of these nodes results in an inter- section at "Black Hills." Going one step down on the *is located in* chain from this intersection point toward Custer brings the monitor to Hwy 79. This, therefore, is the appropriate level answer.

If T.P.'s monitor uses the appropriateness rule just outlined, what answer will

41 T.P. give to "Where is Mt. Rushmore?" when it is asked in Context 1? _____
_____ (You may assume that T.P.'s data base includes full knowledge about where this bar in Albania is, even though this is not represented

42 in Figure 9.4.) What is the intersection node in this example? _____
_____ If the question is asked in Context 2, what is

43 the Q-location? _____ Again, in Context

44 2, what is the intersection node? _____ And

45 what is the appropriate answer according to the monitor in this context? _____

_____

Let's try applying this procedure to another context.

Context 3: T.P. is somewhere in the Arctic portion of Alaska, and mentions

that it was this cold on Mt. Rushmore when he hiked there last year. Someone
hears this and asks, "Where is Mt. Rushmore?"

46   What is the intersection node? _____ What

47 answer does the monitor deem appropriate? _____
Do you think this is an appropriate answer? _____

So far, this simple rule has done fairly well. Now let's see if there are
circumstances in which a monitor with this simple a rule (and with access to this
simple a data base) will run into problems.

Context 4: T.P. is working at a gas station on Hwy 24 in Keystone City. A
tourist asks, "Where is Mt. Rushmore?"

What will T.P.'s monitor choose as the appropriate answer to this question in

48 this context? _____ Can you think of
a simple rule that could be added to the rule the monitor already uses to get a
better answer to this sort of question and context? (You can assume a more detailed

49 data base is available.) _____
_____
_____

Here is another context.

Context 5: T.P. mentions a hike he took on Mt. Rushmore to his friends in an
Albanian bar. An Albanian at a neighboring table says, "I spent three years
in the Midwest of your country, but I seem to have forgotten my geography.
Where is Mt. Rushmore?"

50   What will T.P.'s monitor select as the appropriate answer? _____
_____ Why isn't this completely appropriate?

51 _____
_____ What is a more appropriate answer from

52 T.P.'s data base?_____ What does this

53 suggest about the nature of this simple monitor and the rules it uses?_____
_____
_____

54 How would a more sophisticated monitor solve these problems? _____
_____
_____
_____

Answering questions that require one to recall information from the distant past often involves hard mental work, with many problem-solving characteristics. Recall the work of Williams, discussed in HIP Chapter 9, in which subjects must spend hours trying to recall the names of their entire high school senior class. One of the properties of subjects' protocols is *overshoot*--they continue to recall lots of information about a person even <u>after</u> the person's name is recalled. Overshoot seems to have two functions: verification and further search. Explain

55 the verification function. (What is being verified?) _____

_____

56 Explain the search function. (What is being sought?) _____

_____

In this chapter we have studied how information is incorporated into long-term memory from short-term memory. We have also seen some aspects of the organization of long-term memory, particularly with respect to the importance of organization in storage and retrieval. In the next chapter the internal organization or structure of the information in long-term memory will be considered.

10 The representation of knowledge

PRETEST

1. Does *semantic* memory (as opposed to episodic) consist mainly of *primary* or *secondary* nodes? _____

2. Statements that characterize properties or relationships are expressed in the semantic network by _____.

3. The semantic representation is so designed that the properties of <u>particular</u> concepts can be inferred from the properties of _____ concepts.

4. True or false: Images must be a very different kind of stored information from other types of memories. _____

5. Will the *definition* of a term be directly associated with a primary concept or a secondary concept? _____

6. The relations in memory between a verbal concept and the concepts of the individuals who participated in the action represented by that verbal concept are called _____ relations.

7. The relation that goes from an instance to its primary node is labeled _____.

8. The representations in memory for detailed sensory memories are called *sensory images*. What are the representations for the control processes for muscle movements called?_____

9. The representation in memory for the generic concept COW includes the relation between COW and ANIMAL. How is this relation labeled in a semantic memory diagram? _____

10. In the semantic representation of the sentence "The cat scratched the dog," a propositional node labeled SCRATCH represents the basic action. What is the name of the relation that points from this node to the node that stands for the cat?_____

1. primary; 2. propositions; 3. generic (or primary); 4. False (or We don't know yet); 5. primary concept; 6. case; 7. isa; 8. motor control images; 9. class; 10. agent

---

INTRODUCTION

We have seen that long-term memory consists of a monitor, an interpreter, and a data base. Consider the wealth of information in memory--tens of thousands of words and their meanings, many times that many individual incidents or experiences are all stored. Obviously the form in which this information is stored in the data base is a very important topic in psychology. Chapter 10 of HIP presents a model for the representation of information. This chapter of the study guide has been prepared with two goals in mind. First, we hope it will help you to become familiar with the representational format and able to use it yourself to represent concepts. Second, you should become aware of general issues associated with the representation of ideas about objects and events, issues which any psychological model of memory must try to solve.

REPRESENTING THE MEANINGS OF WORDS

The basic unit of memory is a *record*, a piece of information in the data base. Records are represented in semantic memory diagrams by *nodes*. Figure 10.1a represents the record for the name "person." Figure 10.1b shows how the concept PERSON is related to the name "person."

Figure 10.1a   Figure 10.1b

1   What is the number of the record that represents the name "person"? _____

What is the number of the record that represents the generic concept PERSON _____

_____?

A generic concept is one that represents not just one particular thing but rather a class of things. Generic nodes in the semantic network are represented by black dots. Mental concepts for specific individuals, such as Ross Bott, an author of this book, are represented not by generic nodes, but by *specific* nodes. A specific node is represented by angle brackets. (See Figure 10-4 in HIP.) Particular things are represented by specific concepts; classes of things are represented by generic concepts. Is node *501 in Figure 10.1b a specific or a

2   generic node? _____

Figure 10.1b is an incomplete representation of PERSON. A complete representation should include the *meaning* of the concept, not merely its name. Suppose that we can define the meaning of PERSON in some simple manner, say, "A PERSON is a thinking

3   animal." According to this definition, what *class* does PERSON belong to? _____

What other information *applies to* the concept of PERSON? _____

Use the space provided below to draw a representation for PERSON using the above definition. Continue to use the numbers *501 and *500 for the concept PERSON and the name "person." Note that you will have to add new nodes for the generic concept ANIMAL and the name "animal." Use *499 for the former and *498 for the latter.

4

If you are uncertain how to draw this representation, consult the "Nodes and Relations" subsection of Chapter 10 of HIP and HIP Figure 10-4.

5   The relation *class* points from node _____ to node _____
6   (use the node numbers). What relation points from node *499 to node *498?_____
     _____ What proposition *applies to* the concept
7   PERSON? _____

        Dictionary definitions tend to be circular, in that they make reference to each
     other. The representation of the meanings of words in semantic memory is partially
     circular, since definitions do include pointers to other records in the data base.
     The representation of meaning in the mind is not completely circular, however,
     because certain types of concepts do not refer to the meanings of other concepts.
8   The two types of concepts are _____ images and _____
     images. Because the two types of concepts are often intimately related to each
9   other, they are sometimes referred to as _____ schemas.

REPRESENTING INDIVIDUALS

        An important type of specific concept in the data base is one that is an
     instance of some generic concept. Instances of concepts are related to their
     generic nodes by the *isa* relation.   Use the space below to represent these ideas:

                  Helen *is a person*.

                  Jacques *is a person*.

     Include in your representation all the information about the meaning of PERSON that
     you used in your answer *4*.

Assign new node numbers to the appropriate nodes in your representation. Which nodes

11 are instances of the concept PERSON? _____

Which node represents the name "Helen?" _____Is the represen-

tation you drew in *10* different from the one you would draw to represent the idea

12 that *Helen and Jacques are persons?* _____ Explain._____

_____

Semantic memory representations are more abstract than language representations such
as words, sentences, or paragraphs. Essentially the same information in memory
(the same semantic memory structure) can be phrased differently depending on the
context in which an utterance is made. Semantic memory represents the *meaning*
rather than the *form* of sentences.

Using the knowledge about typical persons contained in the definition of PERSON,

13 what default values can be assigned to Helen and Jacques? _____

_____

One property of the *isa* relation is that it tells us where to go to look for
default values about specific concepts.

Which type of node, generic or specific, corresponds to *primary* concepts?

14 _____ Which type corresponds to *secondary* concepts?

_____

Figure 10.2 is a simple representation which includes both primary and secondary

15 nodes. What does this figure represent? _____

16 Add to the representation the fact that two of the individual entities are homeless.
Use the space below to represent the idea that *elephants are large.*

17

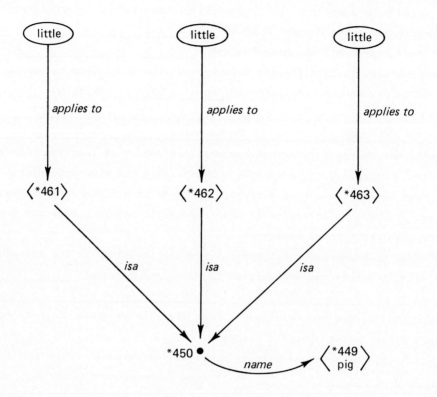

Figure 10.2

Use the space below to represent the concept of *a large elephant*.

18

19 Explain the difference between your answers to *17* and *18*._____
_____
_____

REPRESENTING RELATIONSHIPS

Propositional nodes (which appear as ovals in our representation) can be used to represent many different types of information. One important type of propositional information in memory is *relational* information. A relational node is a proposition that has pointers to two nodes in the data base. Give an example of a relational

20 proposition from Figure 10-4 in HIP. _____

_____

Use the space below to represent the idea that *Helen is bigger than Jacques.* You need not include the information that Helen and Jacques are PERSONs, and so on.

21

Another type of relationship is that of *owning*. The proposition *own* has two pointers, point a to the concept of the owner and point b to the concept of the thing owned. In the space below represent the following information:

Mary has a car.
John has a car.
John's car is larger than Mary's.

22

How many specific cars (that is, representations of individual cars) does your
23   representation have? _____. How many abstract, generic cars
(that is, representations of the general concept, CAR)? _____.

     Henceforth in this chapter we will use the shortcuts for drawing semantic
memory diagrams described in the section "Primary and Secondary Concepts" in HIP
Chapter 10. The word "applies-to" will be omitted from the relations between
propositions (ovals) and the nodes to which they apply. In addition, the "name"
relation will not be explicitly shown. Instead the name of each node will be
written directly on the node. Redraw your answer to *10* in the space below,
using the shortcuts.

REPRESENTING EVENTS

Of course, a memory system that can store all the complicated events that people remember must have a way of storing more than ideas about objects and the simple relationships between them. There must be some way of representing memories about events. Figure 10.3 represents the meaning of the sentence *Ethelbert washed a dog*. (Time information is excluded for simplicity.)

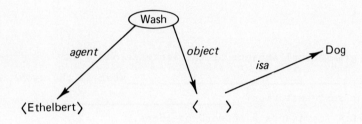

Figure 10.3

Use the space below to draw the representation for the sentence *Martha washed her car*.

25

Can you think of another way to express in English the meaning of the representation

26 you just drew? _____

Use the space below to represent the sentence *Sam's car was fixed by Joan*.

27

28 What is the grammatical subject of the sentence *Sam's car was fixed by Joan?*_____
_____What is the *agent* of the washing
29 event in your representation? _____
    Figure 10.4 represents a network of ideas.

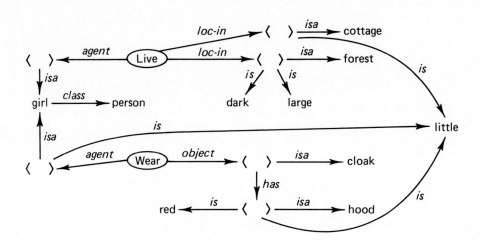

Figure 10.4

30 How many people are represented in this network? _____ From the
31 network representation can you tell whether the cottage is in the forest? _____
Whether the forest is in the cottage? _____ Do you think a model of
human understanding should be able to make one or another of these inferences?
32 _____ On what basis might such inferences be made? _____
_____
_____

33 Who is little, according to Figure 10.4? _____

34 Can you tell from the network whether the hood is little? _____ Whether the

cloak is red? _____

35   Write a few sentences that express all the ideas in the representation. _____

_____

_____

_____

_____

EPISODIC AND SEMANTIC MEMORY

   Spend a few minutes trying to solve the following memory problems, then record

your answers. As you try to remember what the question calls for, be aware of the

steps you take in arriving at the answer. How many windows were there in the place

36 that you lived in two places ago? _____ Did the answer to this

question come to you really quickly? _____ If not, use the space below

to list some of the things you had to remember before coming to the answer.

   Try to remember whether each of the following is an English word and <u>circle</u>

those which are:

       acrobat   *frablous*   *halve*   *symmetry*   *marvish*

37   _____   _____   _____   _____   _____

Use the blanks under the words to fill in your estimate of how long it took you to

come to a decision in each case. Were you aware of any steps that you took in

arriving at your answers? That is, did you have to remember other things (other

38 words or whatever) to decide? _____

_____Would you characterize your answer to Question

39 *36* as coming more from semantic memory, or more from episodic memory? _____

40 How about your answers to Question *37*? _____ In general, what is the

nature of the difference in retrieval time for episodic as opposed to semantic

41   memory? _____
_____

In which of the two memory problems just posed above does the task require that

42   primary concepts be retrieved? _____

Which secondary concepts? _____

VIEWING THE DATA BASE

     In Chapter 10 of HIP, the authors suggest that the interpreter may be able to
"view" only a limited number of nodes in the data base at one time. What other
human memory system is characterized by a limitation on the number of items it can

43   hold at one time? _____

     Remember Kosslyn's experiment in which different size boxes were used to tell
subjects what size images to create? When subjects created larger images, they
were faster at answering questions about details of the imaged object.

     Postulate some relationship between different size images, as cued by the boxes,
and different size spotlights on the data base from the interpreter (as in Figure

44   10-21). Explain. _____
_____

_____

One problem with this "explanation" for images of different degrees of completeness
is that we drew an analogy between the beam from the interpreter and short-term
memory. What does this analogy imply about the amount of information in short-term

45   memory when different size images are created? _____
_____

VISUAL IMAGES

     Some students feel that the representation of concepts that is presented in
Chapter 10 of HIP is too abstract. They protest that memory is more closely
related to experience than this sort of representation would suggest. One of the
arguments that they most commonly bring to bear on this issue is that of mental
imagery. Images, they say, are extremely detailed and are so similar to real
objects as they are perceived that it would be awkward indeed to try to represent
them with any semantic network representation. Let us try to demonstrate just
how detailed and accurate images are.

     First, remember what a telephone looks like. After thousands of experiences
with phones, you must have a very good image of their appearance. Think of a dial

phone, rather than one with push-buttons. Figure 10.5 is a sketch of a telephone
dial with the numbers and letters missing.

46

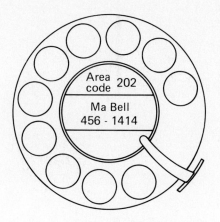

Figure 10.5

Consult your image of the phone and put the letters and numbers in their appropriate
places in Figure 10.5.

Now compare the answers from your image with a real phone dial. Any errors?

47 _____ How confident were you as you completed the sketch? _____
_____ Do you think you lack sufficient
experience with telephone dials to have built up an adequate image? _____
What conclusions about the nature of mental images does this demonstration

48 experiment suggest? _____
_____
_____

11 The neural basis of memory

PRETEST

1. The four pairs of lobes which constitute the cerebral hemisphere are
(i)_____, (ii)_____, (iii)_____,
and (iv)_____.

2. The point of contact between two neural cells is called a _____.

3. A contact between two neurons that decreases the chance of the second cell
firing is called _____, whereas one that increases the
chances of firing is _____.

4. Three possible ways of encoding the memory of an object are as a _____
_____, _____, or _____
_____.

5. Transfer of information from a temporary to a long-term memory is called
_____.

6. What is the basic purpose of the "rat on the pedestal" experiment? _____
_____

7. In _____ amnesia, the last 10 minutes (approximately) of
memory is never recovered.

8. _____ processing seems to be located in specific areas of the
cortex, but little is known about the locations of higher cognitive functions and
memories.

9. In a right-handed person, language production tends to be located in the
_____ hemisphere. This can be distinguished from language
_____, which can be done by both hemispheres.

10. A phenomenon based upon language (verbal or reading) processing conflicting
with nonlanguage processing is the _____.

1. frontal, parietal, temporal, occipital; 2. synapse; 3. inhibitory, excitatory;
4. unique cell, unique pattern of cells, unique firing pattern (or code); 5.
consolidation; 6. to show that memory is initially encoded in some electrical form;
7. retrograde; 8. Sensory; 9. left, recognition or understanding; 10. Stroop
effect

INTRODUCTION

Chapter 11 of HIP discusses brain function while focusing on the neural basis of
memory. As a result of studying sections of the brain, we believe that memory must
begin in some electrical form and then change to a chemical or structural form;
that sensory processing appears to have quite specific locations in the brain while
higher functions are much less localized; and that, at least in humans, the two
hemispheres appear to have specialized functions. These general principles are
introduced in this chapter and extensive experimental evidence is given to support
them.

The brain is so complex that a single experimental result can have several
reasonable interpretations. Electric shock or brain injuries often affect large
areas of the brain, so that if a certain behavior is noticed, it is impossible to say
exactly which area or function was the cause. Thus, for example, we must sometimes be
satisfied with saying that memory of something decreases proportionally with the amount
of the brain that is removed, without being able to pinpoint where that memory is locate
or what specific network holds it. And we can suggest that one hemisphere of the brain
concentrates on spoken language without knowing specifically how or why this happens.

This chapter of the study guide proposes possible experimental results, so that
you can think through how each experiment is constructed and decide how such
results support the theoretical principles of brain functioning that are being
investigated.

PINPOINTING THE LOCATION OF A MEMORY

In an animal that you are experimenting with you find that the memory for a
particular behavior is stored somewhere within a network of a few neurons.
This behavior is associated with, but not the same as, a set of stimuli and a
response. By testing with the stimuli and observing the response, and by using
direct anatomical experiments to follow the pathways of the neurons, suppose you

are able to diagram at least part of the neural network that holds the memory for
the behavior. A common variation of this network is shown in Figure 11.1.

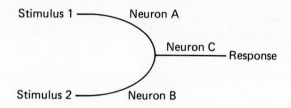

Figure 11.1

Remember that the <u>behavior</u> held in memory by this circuit is different from both
stimuli and response, and might be something like "execute this response only once
a day, or at exactly midnight each night." (The relationship between this
behavior and the response will become clearer in our first example.) The problem
you will now have is that, although you have an idea of the neural connections,
you have no real idea of what neurons in the network hold the memory--does the
effect come from neurons A and B with C serving some other purpose, or from C and
not A and B?

Situations like this involving alternative structures or functions occur
extensively in neuropsychology. One has not begun by building up from single neurons;
instead there is some information at some higher level from which one must work back
down to the structure and connections among neurons. Usually, as we do here, we
need more information in order to decide among the alternative structures. The
experiments that provide this evidence are often quite clever and perhaps will require
some thought to understand at first. However, with practice, it is possible to get a
knack for devising such experiments. As they are a quite powerful and often-used
tool, we will go over a couple of these experiments, and then you will be able to try
composing a couple of your own.

Our first example concerns *habituation* in the Aplysia, as described in Chapter
11 of HIP. It is useful to reread that section now and then continue. Before

1   we start, define habituation in your own words. _____

_____

_____

_____

_____

What is the pair of stimuli in this example? (Ignore dishabituation for now.)

2 (i)_____

3 (ii)_____

4 What is the response elicited by either of these stimuli? _____
_____ In a diagram similar to the last
one, label the parts appropriately for this example, using A, B, and C as before:

5

Up to this point there has been no memory for a behavior. Now we poke the

6 Aplysia's siphon repeatedly. Exactly what is the behavior that develops? _____
_____
Thus in this case the relationship between behavior and response is that the behavior
is the <u>absence</u> of the response. In the diagram you drew, darken that path through
the network which was affected by our experiment. Which two neurons are possible

7 candidates for the memory of the behavior? _____ The

8 behavior in this case is called _____. With the
information we have so far, can you think of a way to determine which of these two

9 neurons holds the actual memory for the behavior? _____
_____
We now run a second experiment on a different Aplysia, poking the purple gland
with water repeatedly. Which two neurons are implicated in the memory for the

10 behavior that develops this time? _____
Again it is not possible, with the information we have so far, to determine which
of these two neurons holds this second memory. However, if we combine these two
experiments on one Aplysia, we can find information on both memories: We habituate
an Aplysia on the gill response to the siphon, then test the animal on its response
to poking the purple gland. Suppose we find the same response as on a fresh
Aplysia, i.e. the memory for the second behavior does not exist. Which of the two
candidate neurons for storing the first behavior must actually hold the memory?

11 _____ Why? _____
12 _____

_____

Have we also located the memory for the second behavior? (Think about this before
13 answering.) _____ If not, what experiment must be conducted to isolate
14 the memory? _____

_____

_____

   Suppose that in the first experiment in the paragraph above, habituation of the
siphon caused complete habituation of the purple gland. Which neuron is likely to
15 hold the memory for both behaviors? _____ As stated in HIP, actual results
indicate that this memory is located in A and B. Assume this is true in what follows.
   In a second experiment we find that touching the neck of the Aplysia makes the
snail sensitive to both earlier stimuli again, even if they have both been
habituated. Thus there must be a neural connection from this new stimulus (squirting
the neck) to our present network. There are four possibilities as to where in the
network it could connect, and you should be able to use this experiment to reject
all but one of them.
   First, the neuron telling our network about the jet of water to the neck could
hook up with either the A or B neuron as shown in Figure 11.2.

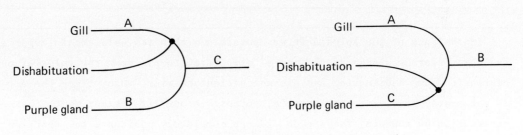

Figure 11.2

16 Is this a possibility? _____ Why or why not? _____
17

_____

   The neuron could hook up to both A and B, as Figure 11.3 shows. Is this a
18 possibility? _____ If not, why not? _____
19

_____

_____

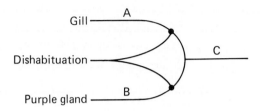

Figure 11.3

Finally, the neuron could connect with C as in Figure 11.4.

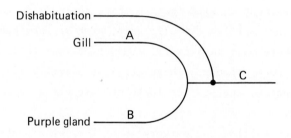

Figure 11.4

20   Is this possible? _____ Why or why not? _____
21   _____

_____

In the case of the Aplysia it was possible with a few well-chosen experiments
and some prior knowledge of the neural structure, to pin down the roles of particular
neurons in some habituation and dishabituation behavior. Many times the situation
is not nearly as clear. For example, suppose in our first experiment, that
habituation by touching the siphon did not completely habituate the reaction to
poking the purple gland, but caused partial habituation instead. Here it is not
22   possible to point at any neuron in particular. Can you explain why? _____

_____

_____

_____

_____

_____

Although one might argue that the habituation response is divided among neurons in this case, there would be a great suspicion that the situation is more complicated, that we do not know about all the relevant neural connections. As often happens in these experiments, one hopes for a particular result from which to draw a clear conclusion; in our case, the hoped-for result is that habituation of one stimuli has no effect on habituation of the other. Fortunately, in this case, nature has provided this result.

It is known that if one observes a pattern moving in one direction for several minutes (for example, a waterfall or the moving spiral shown in Figure 1-48 of HIP) that when one looks at a finely textured pattern (like a bedspread) later, there will appear to be motion in the opposite direction for a while. In Chapter 1 this motion aftereffect is attributed to antagonistic systems of neurons, each responding to motion in one direction: When there is no motion in a pattern the response rates of the two systems will balance each other. However, when one system is used heavily (as with a pattern moving in one direction), it becomes fatigued, and when the movement stops the two systems will no longer balance, with the opposite system temporarily responding more heavily. Therefore, motion is "perceived" in the

23 other direction. The stimuli in this case are _____

24 _____ What is the response? (careful) _____

_____ And finally, the behavior

25 which is being stored by the network is _____

_____ .

Let us treat each set of opposing systems as the equivalent of one neuron in the previous example. The antagonistic sets of neurons that actually store the memory could be located anywhere along the paths from each retina to the brain. At some point these paths from the two eyes join into one path going into the visual cortex. In terms of the rough diagrams that we have been using, how would you draw these pathways? Label the stimuli and response appropriately.

26

Our task is to discover whether the motion aftereffect behavior is stored
somewhere along the pathways before the junction, or somewhere afterward. (Although
each of the paths is not just one neuron as before, and may consist of several
connecting bundles of neurons, it is still very useful to attempt to narrow down
the location.) Can you think of an experiment to decide where the memory for
this behavior is located? (<u>Hint</u>: Consider the form of the experiment used with the
27   Aplysia.) _____

_____

_____

_____

_____

Suppose that you found in your experiment that the aftermotion effect transferred
28   to the other eye. What could you the conclude? _____
29   _____ Why? _____

_____

_____

_____

_____

MEMORY INITIALLY IS ENCODED ELECTRICALLY

A rat is placed in a two-room box with a door between the rooms that it can push
open. The walls to the box are opaque. In the other room from the one the rat is
placed in, a small dish of food is placed in one corner. The setup is shown in
Figure 11.5.

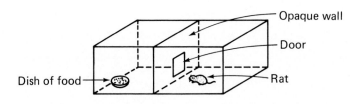

Figure 11.5

The rat's natural exploratory behavior will eventually lead it to push open the door and find the food in the other compartment, and it will quickly learn that it should do this right away upon being placed in the box. However, suppose that immediately after it opens the door and finds the food the first time and each subsequent time, you take the rat out and give it an electroconvulsive shock (ECS). Describe what

30   the rat's behavior will be like. _____

_____

Can you conclude from this that the rat's memory of the food in the other compartment is stored initially in some electrical form and thus is being wiped out by the ECS?

31   _____ Why or why not? _____
32
_____

_____

33   Can you explain the general problem with experiments like this? _____

_____

_____

In another experiment a rat is placed in the same two-room box. However, this time the room it is placed in is intensely lit, while the other room is dark, but the floor of that room is electrified. The bright lighting will make the rat quite uncomfortable, and once it finds the door to the dark room it will jump in to escape the light, only to be shocked when it hits the electrified floor. Eventually it will learn to stay in the first room despite the intense light, since the alternative is worse.

Now each time the rat jumps into the dark room and is shocked, you take it out

34   of the box and give it an ECS. What will the rat's subsequent behavior be? _____

_____

_____ Can you conclude anything about whether memory

35   is encoded electrically initially? _____ Why or why not? _____
36
_____

_____

What are the necessary characteristics of an experiment like this in order that

37   one can really conclude that ECS has erased memory? _____

_____

_____

RETROGRADE AMNESIA

38   Describe what typically happens in a case of retrograde amnesia. _____

_____

_____

One could argue that there is another reason why those last 10 minutes before the
accident are never remembered. The shock of the accident could act as an aversive
stimulus against remembering, much as the ECS might have been associated with
entering the second room and eating in the first experiment with the rat. How could
39 you argue from the second experiment that this is unlikely? _____

_____

_____

_____

       Since it is the older memories that are least affected by retrograde amnesia,
one could argue that old memories are stronger. Since this seems somewhat unreason-
40 able, can you provide an alternate explanation? _____

_____

_____

       What is the difficulty in objectively testing the degree of loss in cases
41 of retrograde amnesia? _____

_____

In such amnesia cases the people who are afflicted often believe their memory loss
is greater than outside observers think. In a sense they certainly are closer
than anybody to what information was in their mind before and after the amnesia.
42 Why not measure memory loss by asking the patient? _____

_____

_____

       This self-knowledge of one's own memory is sometimes called *metamemory*, and the
problem with using it is similar to the general problem of using *introspective*
evidence, that obtained by examining one's own thoughts and actions: The direction
many mental processes take can be biased by what one hopes or fears is true or by
the very act of observing one's own thoughts. Other processes may be totally
hidden to one's own consciousness, and thus completely left out as evidence. This is
not to say that introspective evidence is useless; it may provide a crucial idea or
indication that can then be confirmed by more objective tests.

MEMORY IS EVENTUALLY ENCODED CHEMICALLY OR STRUCTURALLY

Describe a simple experiment using a rat (you can even use a modification of one of the previous experiments) to show that memory does not stay in a permanently

43 electrical form. _____

_____

_____

_____

_____

Thus a memory that is initially encoded electrically must eventually be encoded in some chemical or structural form if it is to be unaffected by ECS. This process

44 of recoding is called _____.

Ribonuclease is a chemical which, when injected into the brain of an animal, will inhibit the production of protein in neural cells. Although chemicals with such effects do exist, the results and conclusions from their use in psychological experiments are hotly debated. In the hypothetical experiment that follows, pay attention not so much to the particular results as to the logic of the experiment and conclusions.

We rerun the second experiment with the rat (involving the lighted room) except that, instead of applying an ECS after taking the rat out of the second room, *ribonuclease* is injected after some period of time. Assume that this chemical is an effective inhibitor of protein synthesis in neural cells of the rat for several hours. If memories are gradually encoded in terms of proteins, at what time after the rat is taken out of the second room would the injection of the chemical have

45 the most effect on memory? _____ Why? _____
46
_____

_____

_____

One way of measuring how well the rat has remembered the task is to count the number of trials the rat takes to *relearn* the task, i.e., that it shouldn't leave the first room. This task usually takes only one trial to learn, so the rat knows the task before you give it the injection. If you waited several hours before injecting, we are assuming it will have encoded the task in protein, and 0 trials will be needed for relearning. If you inject it immediately after it is taken out of the

47 second room, no protein synthesis will occur, and the task will take about _____ trial(s) to relearn. Suppose you vary the time of injection from immediately to

several hours. The task cannot take a fraction of a trial to relearn, but in an
intermediate case, the rat might learn the task sometimes and not learn other times,
which would average out to a fraction of a trial. In Figure 11.6, sketch what you
would expect to be the general shape of the curve if you plotted time of injection
versus trials of relearning.

48

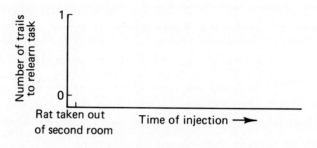

Figure 11.6

Convert the graph in Figure 11.7 to a graph of memory strength versus time given for
encoding.

49

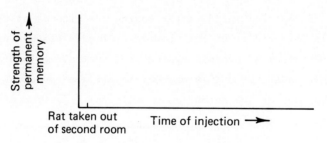

Figure 11.7

Chapter 11 mentions a subject, N.A., who has a very interesting memory deficit.

50 What was his memory difficulty? _____

_____

51 How was this condition caused? _____

_____

We have been considering the possibility that memory is encoded in terms of
proteins in neural cells. Yet, assuming that this is the basis for long-term
memory, it seems inconceivable that a small cut in the brain, as N.A. received,
could destroy the ability of all neurons in the brain to encode in terms of
proteins. Therefore, suppose that they still have this ability, and that N.A. is

still permanently encoding memories. Can you give an alternate explanation for

52   his condition? _____

_____

_____

   A distinction is made in this chapter between N.A.'s ability to recall new
material, where he has much trouble, and his ability to recognize, where he is
virtually normal. In recall, you are given a clue, such as "Who was the Secretary
of State in 1976?" from which you must retrieve both a name and then verify that
it is the piece of information you are looking for. In recognition, you are already
given the information, such as "Is Olympia the capital of Washington?" and you need
only to go through the verification step. Considering N.A.'s ability on these two

53   measures of memory, can you give another explanation for his condition? _____

_____

_____ Does this agree with your

54   previous explanation of N.A.'s condition from the protein-encoding hypothesis? _____
If not, can you see how this second explanation would not conflict with the protein-
encoding hypothesis?

TWO SEPARATE BRAINS

   The communication link between the two hemispheres of the brains of mammals is

55   called the _____. What is it composed of? _____
56

57   What is the role of the optic chiasma in mammals? _____

_____

_____

58   What is it made of? _____

   The following experiment is run on a cat: First its corpus callosum is severed.
Then its right eye is covered and it learns to go through a maze to some food at the
end, using only its left eye. The eye patch is now transferred to the left eye and

59   the cat tested on the maze. What will the results be? _____

60   _____ Can you conclude anything from this experiment? _____

_____

61   Why or why not? _____

_____

_____

In a second experiment, the optic chiasma is cut instead of the corpus callosum. The same procedure is used, except that, right before testing, the corpus callosum is also cut. If the result was that during the test the cat acted as though it knew nothing of the previous learning, what could you conclude about
62 the learning processes in the different hemispheres? _____

_____

_____ What result actually occurs in this
63 experiment? _____

_____ What do you
64 conclude? _____

_____

_____ Assume this result
in predicting the outcomes of the experiments below.

   Potassium chloride is a chemical that, if injected into a brain will put all or part of the brain in a state called *spreading depression,* depending upon the amount and location of the injection. In this state, that part of the brain is essentially nonfunctional and will not accept inputs from anywhere. However, this state is temporary, and, when the drug wears off, the brain is completely normal again.

   We run an experiment using a cat again; however, this time we cut only the optic chiasma. Right before training we inject the left hemisphere of the cat's brain with potassium chloride, enough to put the whole hemisphere to sleep. The left eye of the cat is covered during the time it learns the maze. Then the cat's corpus callosum is cut and it is retested on the maze with only its right eye covered. (In this case, as in those which follow, assume that we wait until the effects of the drug have worn off before testing.) What will the cat's behavior be like? _____

_____
66 Why? _____

_____

_____

_____

Suppose both eyes are uncovered during learning, but the right eye is still
67 covered during retest. Will this experiment work as it should? _____ Why or
68 why not? _____

_____

_____

Suppose just the right eye is covered during learning. What would happen then?

69 _____ Why? _____
70 _____
    _____

Even assuming that the knowledge of the task is transferred across the corpus callosum during learning, it is not clear whether it is transferred over all at once, or gradually during the learning process. How could you utilize this chemical to obtain a curve of amount of learning transferred with time? (reasonably

71 difficult) _____
    _____
    _____
    _____
    _____
    _____

Suppose you obtained a curve like that shown in Figure 11.8.

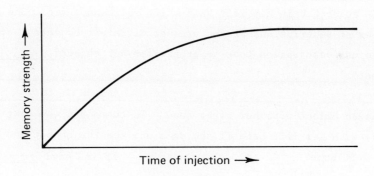

Figure 11.8

72 What would this say about how learning is transferred? _____
    _____

There is an alternative explanation for what's going on, though. Can you give another reason why such a curve might be obtained? (<u>Hint</u>: Consider some of the

73 earlier experiments with rats.) _____
    _____
    _____
    _____

DIFFERENT ROLES FOR THE HEMISPHERES

The following questions concern a right-handed patient who has had her corpus callosum cut. After you have read the book and understand the principles, it is useful to answer these questions by thinking them out and referring to the book only after you are done.

You put a book in one of her hands where she can't see it. In which hand would

74 she be able to describe it verbally? _____ Why? _____

75 _____

_____

You show the word "hammer" to her right visual field and the word "rock" to her left visual field. Given a bag of objects of which she can feel the shape, what

76 will she pull out with her left hand? _____

In question *76*, without seeing what she has pulled out, she is asked to draw the object with the same hand. Then, without looking at what she drew, she is

77 asked to verbally identify the object in her picture. Can she do it? _____

78 Why or why not? _____

_____

_____

She holds an object in her left hand which she cannot see. She is verbally given a series of descriptions of the uses of different objects. Will she be able

79 to choose the use description that is proper for her object?_____

80 Why or why not? _____

_____

She holds an object with her right hand. Is there any way that she can draw a picture of it with her left hand if she does not see the object and does not touch

81 it with her left hand? _____ If so, how? _____

82 _____

_____

The following experiment is run on a strongly right-handed person. Throughout the experiment the subject will be wearing earphones through which different messages will be presented to each ear. All four of the following conditions will be run:

(i) A series of words are presented in the right ear and simultaneously random clicks are presented to the left ear.

(ii) The same as (i) except that words are presented to the left ear and clicks to the right.

(iii) A series of three tones is presented to the right ear and simultaneously random clicks are presented to the left ear.

(iv) The same as (iii) except that tones are presented to the left ear and clicks to the right.

In conditions (i) and (ii) the subject must remember the words so that they can be recognized among a larger group where some of the words will be ones which have not been presented. In conditions (iii) and (iv) the subject must remember the trios of tones again so that they can be recognized in a larger group of trios of tones.

The random clicks during any one presentation will usually be separated from each other; however, occasionally, two clicks will occur as a closely spaced pair. When this occurs, the subject must press a button immediately.

After each condition has been run (which will include 100 words or groups of tones), the recognition test is given and an error rate is computed from words the subject did not recognize and words falsely recognized, and similarly for tones. Suppose the results were as shown in Table 11.1.

	Words	Tones
Right ear	5	35
Left ear	8	18

Error rate (%)

Table 11.1

83 In which condition, tones or words, was the right ear better? _____

84 In which condition was the left ear better? _____ From what you have read

85 about specialization of hemispheres in HIP, how would you explain this result? _____

_____

_____

_____

_____

    The random clicks are not tested for later. Why then is it necessary to include

86 them in the experiment above? _____

_____

_____

_____

_____

_____

12 Language

PRETEST

    1. Both speaker and hearer make assumptions during conversations which depend upon their tacit agreements about the rules that govern conversation. These assumptions are called _____.

    2. An unambiguous sentence can be represented by how many meaning structures in the data base of long-term memory? _____

    3. In English, the grammatical roles that the words of a sentence bear are communicated to a hearer through _____.

    4. In phrase structure grammar, what do these abbreviations stand for:

        S _____

        NP _____

        VP _____

    5. _____ rules allow parts of sentences to be shuffled about or transformed.

    6. Suppose someone tells you, _Some foreigners_ threw a party for _the prime minister_. Which underlined noun phrase contains a _definite_ article? _____

    7. The parts of words which are the smallest units of meaning are called _____.

    8. People understand many implications that are part of the meanings of the words they hear. The analysis of a word into its underlying structure is called _____.

    9. Because of the limitations of short-term memory, the analysis of a spoken sentence must procede _____.

    10. Language processing which starts at the highest level--meaning structures-- and works down to the lowest level--the arriving sounds--is called _top-down_ or _____ _driven_ processing.

1. conversational postulates;   2. one;   3. word order;   4. S: sentence, NP: noun phrase, VP: verb phrase;   5. Transformational;   6. the prime minister;   7. morphemes; 8. lexical decomposition;   9. from left to right (in the order in which the words are heard);   10. conceptually

---

INTRODUCTION

Human language understanding and production is one of the least well-understood areas of human information processing. There are a large number of competing theories in this field, and none of them is able to account for the facts about language that are already known, not to speak of what we have yet to learn. These conditions conspire to make the study of language and language processing a chaotic, exciting, and very enjoyable endeavor.

In Chapter 10, some facts and theories about the meaning structure of language were introduced. This chapter is concerned with the function of language and with what is known about how a person's various cognitive capabilities cooperate in the processing of language.

The first topic deals with what kinds of knowledge must be brought to bear in the activities of language understanding and production. The multiplicity of knowledge sources that are used in processing language is illustrated first by the specialized processing of linguistic forms that is required by *translating* from one language to another. In order to understand some of the processes which must go into translating, we examine a series of progressively more sophisticated translating machines. The point of these exercises (Problems 1-13) is not that you should learn how to build a good automatic translator, but rather that you understand that even ordinary uses of language often call for as much complicated processing as do these translation exercises. Problems 14 and 15 take a different approach to the question of what must be known to use language by asking what is involved in telling a lie. The next two exercises deal with a special type of knowledge about the goals of conversation, called conversational postulates. The last problems that are specifically concerned with using a variety of knowledge sources in language processing are 18-19. This material relates to the speaker's need for knowledge about his hearer's knowledge. We find that sometimes a conversation can be doubly or triply sidetracked as the participants in a conversation each tries to find out what the other knows, so as to make his own contribution more relevant.

The second topic we deal with is that of making reference. One of the essential aspects of communication is being able to direct one's hearer to access particular concepts in long-term memory. Some grammatical devices for accomplishing this are dealt with in Problems 20-26.

The third topic, which is only briefly treated in this problem set, is the relationships possible between meaning structures (in the data base) and sentences. In particular, Problems 27-30 deal with the notions of ambiguity and synonymity.

The fourth and largest topic is English grammar. The exercises and text have two purposes. The first is simply to acquaint you with some of the facts of English sentential structure and the possible manners of describing it. The second is to help you get some idea of how a psychological theory of grammatical processing might work. Two grammatical theories are discussed: phrase structure grammar and transformational grammar.

AUTOMATIC TRANSLATION AND LANGUAGE UNDERSTANDING

For a number of years, people have been trying to build automatic translating machines to translate from one natural language (like Chinese) to another (like English). Every few months one can find in the back pages of the newspaper, a press release from one company or another claiming that within 6 months of a year they will put on the market a computer-controlled translator. For one reason or another, these systems never seem to appear. Let us use some of the facts about language that were presented in HIP Chapter 12 to see why we might expect language translation to be a complicated endeavor. As we shall soon see, automatic translation would require a very complete model of how it is that people ordinarily process language for understanding. By thinking about what is needed for translation, we come to understand the wealth of different types of knowledge which must be brought to bear in even the most ordinary or language-understanding situations.

To begin with, we will consider five hypothetical translating machines. When we find that such a translator is unable to translate correctly a sentence that a human translator who knew both languages could translate, then we will have learned something about the human ability to use language. What are some of the similarities between the task of understanding a sentence in your native language and the task of

1 translating a sentence from your language to another you know equally well? _____

_____

_____

_____

Translating Device (TD)1

     Most of this machine is simply a huge dictionary. In this dictionary, the most
common meaning of each word or morpheme in the foreign language is stored in English
next to its entry. To translate a sentence into English, TD1 examines each word or
morpheme in the foreign language in the order in which it encounters it, going from
left to right. It finds the item in the dictionary and prints out the English
"translation" it has stored for the word. Here is a simple sentence in Mojave
(a Native American language spoken in parts of Arizona) together with the English
translation provided by TD1.

    Mojave: *posh-ny-ch*   *hatchoq-ny*   *taver-k*
    English: cat the   dog the   chased

2   Is this "translation" a grammatical English sentence? _____ What do you think
it means? _____

Actually, the sentence should be translated 'The cat chased the dog'. (The Mojave
-ny is a definite determiner, hence its translation as English 'the'. The *-ch* of the
first Mojave word marks that word as subject; it is not translated, since there is no
corresponding English morpheme. The *-k* of the last word is a marker of past <u>or</u>
present tense; because sentences are more often about past events, TD1 translates
<u>all</u> instances of *-k* as the English past tense morpheme, 'ed'.)

    What is the major problem with the preceding "translation," as a sentence of

3   English? _____

_____

What response would you make to the claim that language understanding is nothing
more than the successive looking-up of word meanings in a mental "dictionary"?

4   _____

_____

Translating Device 2

    Translating Device 2 is smarter than TD1. It has grammars of both Mojave and
English in addition to the dictionary. As a result, it gives English sentences of
normal word order, and it moves determiners into their correct positions in English,

5   in front of their nouns. How would TD2 translate the example Mojave sentence?_____

_____

Here is a sentence which raises some problems for TD2.

> Mojave: *hatchoq-ny-ch*   *'-intay-ny   taver-k*
>   dog the   my mother the   chased
>
> English   'The dog chased the my mother.'

(To make the sentence clearer, we have shown the intermediate stage, before correct English word order is imposed on the translation. The '- of the second word means roughly 'my' in English, but unlike the English, it is not necessarily definite.)

6 What is wrong with the above English "translation"? _____

_____

7 Give a simple rule to avoid this sort of ungrammaticality. _____

_____

Do you think that language understanding might consist simply of a "dictionary look-up" process plus a few rules about the significance of certain word-order

8 relationships in sentences? _____ Explain. _____

_____

_____

Translating Device 3

Translating Device 3 incorporates a fix that prevents English strings like *the his father* or *the their uncle*, which TD2 might produce. There are still problems, however. For example, the Mojave word *inyaq* has both a noun meaning-- 'younger sister'--and a verb or adjective meaning--'funny'. If <u>funny</u> is the more common use of *inyaq*, only that translation will be stored in this TD's dictionary.

> Mojave: *'-inyaq-ny-ch   inyaq-k*
> English: my funny   funnyed

9 What do you suppose a better translation would be? _____

_____

Translating Device 4

Translating Device 4 has a more sophisticated dictionary. Its entries are marked as to whether they are verbs, nouns, or some other part of speech. If a word has one noun meaning and one verb meaning, then that word will have two entries in the dictionary, marked appropriately. When TD4 is translating a sentence, it makes use of its grammatical knowledge (the same knowledge that TD2 needed to put the words in the correct order) to decide whether a word is probably a noun or a verb.

Of course you're not surprised to learn that there are still problems. For example, the Mojave word *inyaq* discussed on the previous page has not just one noun meaning, but two. It can mean either 'younger sister' or 'great grandmother'. This sort of ambiguity can make for problems even for very good human translators. How is one to decide whether *'-inyaq-ny-ch inyaq-k* means 'My younger sister is funny' or 'My great grandmother is funny'? Suppose that the translator knows the speaker of the Mojave sentence and is aware that the speaker does not have any younger sisters.

10   How would the sentence be translated? _____

_____

Consider what is required to build a translating device that is capable of making this kind of judgment. Not only would the device have to understand the meanings and uses of all the words of both languages as well as their grammars, it would also have to store knowledge about the speakers of sentences. Rather than a simple dictionary, its main memory would have to be a full complex data base with semantic knowledge <u>and</u> knowledge about particular events. *Translating Device 5* has these features. Its knowledge base, which includes the meanings of words and much detailed knowledge about the world, is a semantic network like that developed in HIP Chapter 10. Do you think that people ordinarily use essentially nonlinguistic knowledge, knowledge about the past history of the speaker, the physical setting for the conversation, and other information in understanding everyday discourse? Or is a combination of semantic (word meaning) and syntactic (grammatical) analysis enough?

11
_____

Even with this much cognitive processing power, some of the English sentences TD5 produces are a bit strange. For example, the English sentence below is a translation of an offer made in a language that has special "pejorative markers."

Do you want some more of this yecch-cake?

(*Yecch* is used here as the closest translation of the pejorative.)
This translation is not really adequate, because the speaker (who is probably the baker of the cake) does not really mean to imply that the cake is objectionable. Rather, the speaker is simply being polite. It is not considered polite to put the hearer in one's debt by offering something of value to him or her. Therefore, speakers of this language conventionally deny the worth of their offers by using a word that means 'yecch'. A better translation into English would be something like

this:

You must have some more of this cake.

12 How does this translation differ from the earlier one? _____

_____

13 Does it convey the same politeness? _____ If so, how?; If not, why doesn't

it? _____

_____

_____

These exercises have demonstrated that the understanding of even relatively
simple sentences may require quite complex cognitive processing. Language understanding requires the use of many sources of knowledge. To understand sentences
one must make use of knowledge of the meanings of words, knowledge about the grammar
of the language the sentence is spoken in, knowledge about the rules of conversation,
knowledge about the speaker, shared cultural knowledge, and much else. One usually
has to know the context in which the utterance is made, a context defined either by
previous utterances or by some aspect of the physical situation.

The most advanced translating device we have discussed still lacks many of the
most basic skills every native speaker of a language brings to bear in understanding
sentences. In particular, the examples we have discussed don't even begin to
scratch the surface of the needed semantic and grammatical knowledge. (A problem
we did not deal with is that of the translation of idioms. Do you think that a
native speaker of a foreign language could make sense out of a literal translation
of the English sentence *Henry Abelson kicked the bucket last night?*)

SOCIAL CONTRACTS IN LANGUAGE USE

A little thought about some common speech situations will reveal many types of
knowledge which must be available for the formulation or understanding of utterances.
Consider the act of *lying*. Imagine that you want to tell someone a lie. What sorts

14 of knowledge do you have to make use of in order to tell a successful lie? _____

_____

_____ Which of these knowledge sources would you

15 use in making an ordinary assertion? _____

_____

Conversational postulates are rules that express some of the knowledge speakers
have about what they can expect utterances to mean in given situations. In parti-

cular, they are concerned with what a speaker *intends* when he makes an utterance. Here is a list of conditions that must hold when a speaker asks a question as a request for information (we call such questions "real" questions):

Conditions on real questions

1. The speaker does not know the "answer."
2. It is not obvious to the speaker that the hearer would provide the information without being asked.
3. The speaker wants the information.
4. The speaker intends that as a result of his utterance, the hearer will tell him the "answer."

Now think about a different type of question, namely "test" questions, such as a teacher might ask a student. Using the space below, list some conditions which must hold for this type of utterance.

16   *Conditions on test questions*

     Were any of the conditions the same for both types of questions? _____
17   If so, which? _____

Searching for Common Knowledge

     Most uses of language can be viewed as an attempt to transfer knowledge structures from a speaker to a hearer. But in order to transfer such a structure, the participants in a conversation must first discover what knowledge they have in common. The search for common knowledge is important for two reasons. First, it can prevent the assertion of facts already known, thus saving time; second, it can enable the person who is acquiring the new information to tie in the new knowledge structures to closely related ones, thus making the new knowledge more accessible and better understood.

Consider the following sample conversation:

1. A: *Can you tell me where the student health center is?*

2. B: *Do you know where the main library is?*

3. A: *Is that the weird building on the other side of the eucalyptus grove?*

4. B: *Do you mean the eucalyptus grove east of Third College?*

5. A: *Yes.*

6. B: *Yes, it is.*

7. A: *OK, I know it.*

8. B: *Well, the health center is about 150 feet south of the library.*

9. A: *OK, thanks.*

18 Why didn't B answer A's first question immediately? _____
_____

19 Utterances 5-8 in this conversation are all answers to questions, but only one of them is immediately preceded by a question. Why did this occur? _____
_____
_____

REFERENCE

     A very important aspect of the process of making common contact in communication is being able to direct a hearer to find the appropriate *referent* in memory. A *referent* in this use is a concept for some individual, whether it be a particular person, object of event. *Reference* is a linguistic process by which a speaker directs a hearer to the appropriate referent in memory. There are two types of reference, definite and indefinite. In indefinite reference, the speaker tells the hearer that he does not expect the hearer to find a preexisting referent in memory on the basis of the utterance. If a friend tells you that a mutual acquaintance has married "a musician," then you do not know which particular musician is meant. This is an example of indefinite reference. In this case you should create some new referent in memory. If, however, your friend points out a streetcorner guitarist, saying that *Sally married that musician,* then you can presumably find the unique intended referent in your data base. This is an example of definite reference. In the case of definite reference, the speaker expects the hearer to find a specific

referent in his memory to which to attach the new information. The hearer will
know which referent is intended for one of a number of reasons: There may be only
one such concept in memory (a *unique* memory); the referent may have been introduced
earlier in the conversation; some aspect of the setting for the utterance may
specify the referent; the utterance itself may contain a specifying description of
the referent.

Consider these two sentences:

20   *I saw* <u>*an elephant*</u> *at a shopping center today.* _____

        Carter wants to shoot <u>*the elephant with the*</u> _____

        <u>*ingrown toenails.*</u>

Imagine a likely context for each sentence. In the space provided, write by each
underlined noun phrase whether that noun phrase is definite or indefinite.

        We have just described four ways in which a hearer might be able to find a
definite referent in memory are described. Choose the most likely of these ways for
each of the underlined noun phrases in the following four sentences (you should
imagine that each sentence is uttered in some appropriate setting).

21   a. *Don't sit on* <u>*that bench!*</u> _____

        b. *He has orbited* <u>*the moon.*</u> _____

        c. *So I laughed at* <u>*the woman.*</u> _____

        d. <u>*The elephant*</u> *was white.* _____

        Sometimes none of the strategies for finding the concept defined by a definite
referent described above seem applicable. This sentence is a case in point:

                    The whale is an aquatic mammal.

How would you phrase a rule to enable a hearer to find the appropriate concept in

22   memory given this type of definite reference? _____

_____

_____

PERSONAL PRONOUNS

        In English, the use of personal pronouns involves acts of definite reference.
Consider the following brief conversation.

        A: *Do you know* <u>*Judy,*</u> <u>*who*</u> *is trying to raise* <u>*15 prize rabbits*</u> *and*
                          1   2   3
            <u>*100 prize cabbages*</u> *for* <u>*the county fair?*</u>
                4   5

B: *Yes.*

A: *Well, <u>they</u> got out of <u>their cages</u> and ate <u>them</u> all.*
         6   7   8

Which of the above numbered nouns or noun phrases represent acts of definite

23 reference? _____ Which indefinite

reference? _____ Do any of the underlined

24 nouns or noun phrases have the same referents? _____ If so,

which ones? (If 3,4, and 5 all have the same referents, write 3=4=5.) _____

_____

There is something strange about some of the acts of reference in the following
conversation. Use the space provided to explain what.

A: *Do you know Henry and William, the James brothers?*

B: *Yes.*

A: *Well, he got mad and hit him yesterday.*

25 _____

_____

Do *proper nouns* (such as names like Judy or Henry) usually direct the hearer to

26 find a preexisting referent in memory, or to create a new one? _____

_____ Are proper nouns usually definite or

indefinite? _____

LANGUAGE STRUCTURE AND MEANING STRUCTURE

The relationships between grammatical structures and meaning structures are
varied and complex. The next few problems are designed to help you to understand
some of them.

Do linguists use the term *surface structure* to refer to meaning structures such

27 as those discussed in HIP Chapter 10? _____

Here is a pair of synonymous sentences:

        a. *John gave Harry a minsoc.*

        b. *John transferred possession of a minsoc to Harry.*

Comment on the relationship of the surface structures of these two sentences, and

28 on the relationship of their meaning structures. _____

_____

Here is an ambiguous sentence:

c. *Visiting professors can be boring.*

29   Explain why this sentence is ambiguous. _____

_____

_____

In terms of meaning structures, what does it mean for a sentence to be ambiguous?

30   _____

_____

ENGLISH GRAMMAR

In the "English Grammar" section of HIP Chapter 12, a *phrase structure grammar* of English is presented. A phrase structure grammar is a formal device for describing the syntactic structure of grammatical sentences. Another way to view a phrase structure grammar is as a device to <u>produce</u> the grammatical, but not the ungrammatical, sentences of a language. Here, in condensed form, is the phrase structure grammar from HIP:

1.   S $\longrightarrow$ NP + VP

2.   VP $\longrightarrow$ $\begin{cases} V + NP \\ V + PP \end{cases}$ (The symbol $\{$ means that to apply the rule you should choose just <u>one</u> of the lines to the right of the symbol.)

3.   NP $\longrightarrow$ Art + N

4.   N $\longrightarrow$ Ad + N   (<u>Ad</u> has the special property of being able to apply more than once when this rule is used)

5.   PP $\longrightarrow$ Prep + NP

The dictionary

V $\longrightarrow$ *lives, eats, sings, . . .*

N $\longrightarrow$ *man, tree, house, limerick, oyster, . . .*

Art $\longrightarrow$ *the, a, an*

Ad $\longrightarrow$ *old, many, few, very, tree, . . .*

Prep $\longrightarrow$ *in, on, at, by, to, . . .*

Given this grammar, we should be able to determine the structure of any grammatical sentence by discovering what sequence of rules must apply to produce the sentence. For example, the sentence *The old man lives in the tree house* can be produced by first applying Rule 1, then Rules 3 and 4 to get the first noun phrase *The old man*, then Rules 2, 5, 3, and 4 (in that order) to get the verb phrase *lives in the tree house.*

In the next series of problems you will be asked to judge for each of a group of sentences first, whether the sentence could be produced by the above grammar, and second, whether in your opinion the sentence is grammatical in English. The first of these problems has already been answered, as an example.

	Sentence	*Produced by above rules?*	*Grammatical English?*
	The old man sings	NO	YES
31	The very old oyster eats the tree.	_____	_____
32	The old man sings the limerick.	_____	_____
33	The old man sings the house.	_____	_____
34	The old very oyster eats the tree.	_____	_____
35	An old oyster lives in a tree.	_____	_____
36	An old oyster lives in a limerick.	_____	_____
37	Man eats oyster.	_____	_____
38	Man sings.	_____	_____
39	A man sings by the few very tree.	_____	_____

You probably found that your grammatical intuitions did not always agree with the product of the phrase structure rules. Did the rules produce sentences you consider ungrammatical, or did it fail to produce some sentences which you feel are

40   part of English? _____

The manner in which a phrase structure grammar produces a sentence can be thought of like this: First, the grammar decides to produce a sentence; then it realizes that it needs a noun phrase, so it follows Rule 3; now it must choose an article, so it picks one of the entries after <u>Art</u> in the dictionary; when it finds it needs a noun, it picks one of the entries under <u>N</u> in the dictionary; and so on. Does this seem

41   to you like a good model of how <u>people</u> produce sentences?_____
Give some defense or some criticism (make it clear which) of phrase structure grammars as psychological models of sentence production. _____

_____

_____

TRANSFORMATIONAL RULES

There are a variety of reasons why one might want to use transformational rules as part of the grammar of a language. They were invented in order to reduce the number of phrase structure rules needed in that type of grammar, and to relate

sentences which would not otherwise be formally related to each other (like passive
sentences and their active counterparts). It is possible to find more psychologically
interesting motivations for transformational rules, however. For example, transformations can be thought of as the psychological mechanisms that translate concepts,
which exist in some nonlinguistic format in the data base, into sentences, which can
be spoken. Let us look at an example.

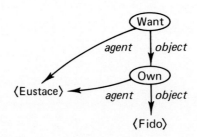

Figure 12.1

Figure 12.1 represents a small portion of the data base of a potential speaker.
In fact, Figure 12.1 represents just those concepts that the speaker plans to try to
communicate in his next utterance. Some series of rules must apply that can
translate the semantic relations like "agent" and "object" into sentential positions
(i.e., agents are usually subjects of sentences, and thus the first word in a simple
English sentence). Similarly, there must be a rule that inserts a "to" before the
verb "own" in the sentence. When these rules have applied, a string something like
this is the result:

(a) *Eustace wants Eustace to own Fido.*

At this point, a transformational rule called *EQUI NP deletion* (*EQUI* for short)
applies. A transformational rule applies only when its *structural conditions* are
met (hold true for the meaning structure which is being made into a sentence). Here
are the structure conditions for EQUI:

1. The meaning structure must consist of two sentential ideas, one of which is
   the <u>object</u> of the other, higher, sentential idea. (In the example we are
   discussing, the concept that *Eustace wants something* is the higher sentential
   idea; the concept *Eustace own Fido* is the <u>object</u> of this idea.)
2. The verbal concept of the higher sentential idea must belong to a restricted
   class which includes WANT, LIKE, HATE, and TRY.

3. The <u>agent</u> of the higher sentential idea must be the same referent as the <u>agent</u> of the lower sentential idea (*Eustace = Eustace*).

If all the structural conditions for EQUI are met, then EQUI causes the second mention of the referent to be deleted from the string. Thus, in our example, (a) becomes (a') by EQUI.

(a') *Eustace wants to own Fido.*

The next set of problems consists of a number of grammatical English sentences about which you are to make a number of judgments. For each example, you should indicate whether EQUI has applied, and, if it has not, which of EQUI's structural conditions were not met by the meaning structure.

Sentence	*EQUI applied?*	*Condition(s) not met?*
Eustace wants to own Fido.	YES	--
42 *Penelope hates to arrive early.*	_____	_____
43 *Ingeborg wants Horst to come home early.*	_____	_____
44 *Eloise wants a soft drink.*	_____	_____
45 *Penelope hates Max.*	_____	_____
46 *Alexander liked to laugh at his own jokes.*	_____	_____
47 *Alphonse liked Marie to laugh at his jokes.*	_____	_____
48 *Theodore believes he is infallible.*	_____	_____

Naturally, EQUI is only one of a number of transformations in English. Earlier we mentioned rules which look at meaning structures and decide what the word order should be in a simple sentence to communicate those meaning structures. The easiest kinds of transformations to explain, however, are those which we can study by looking at *sentences* which are related to each other. Consider this pair of sentences:

(c) *Prudence called Andrew up.*
(d) *Prudence called up Andrew.*

What is the relationship between the meaning structures for these two sentences?

49 _____

The same sort of relationship seems to hold between (e) and (f).

(e) *The realtor pointed the house out.*
(f) *The realtor pointed out the house.*

It might be nice to relate pairs of sentences like this to each other by means of transformation, which we could call *Particle Movement*. In the pairs of sentences above, which type of sentence seems more basic (closer to the form of its meaning structure) to you, the (c)-(e) type of the (d)-(f) type? _____

50

51   What structural conditions must apply for Particle Movement to occur? _____

_____

_____

_____

What is the effect of the Particle Movement transformation if all the structural conditions apply? (Notice that Particle Movement is an *optional* transformation-- it can either apply or not, and the result is still a grammatical sentence, as

52   examples (c)-(f) show.) _____

_____

_____

GARDEN PATH SENTENCES

     In garden path sentences, one or more than one word in the sentence is at first interpreted as belonging to some other syntactic class than the one to which it actually belongs in the sentence. The person trying to understand the sentence assigns some perfectly normal syntactic function to the troublesome word or words, only to discover later in the sentence that none of it makes any sense, given that earlier wrong turning. The only way to understand the sentence then is to go back, to try to find what word was assigned the wrong syntactic role in this particular sentence.

     One place this backtracking behavior shows up quite clearly in is in reading. When people read a garden path sentence, they usually find that they have to go back and reread earlier parts of the sentence, often several times. Here is an example of such a troublesome sentence:

The old man the boats.

Some of you may read this correctly the first time; others may have to think about it for some time before coming to the correct, grammatical interpretation. How many

53   times did you have to read the sentence to understand it? _____ What does the sentence mean? Paraphrase it. _____

_____

     Those of you who felt there was no challenge to understanding that sentence are welcome to try your luck on this one:

The plastic red boxes are made of is flammable.

(Those of you who are still having trouble with *The old man the boats* might find enlightenment by thinking about the use of *man* in *They want to man the stations with Americans,* and the use of *old* in *The old often survive on Social Security.*)

At this point you have encountered several approaches to the grammatical structure of language, although all the examples in this problem set are much simplified versions of the theories that really attempt to account for the form of utterances or the process of understanding utterances. You should be aware that the study of language is in a period of great uncertainty, and that at present there seem to be no serious contenders for the title of "comprehensive theory of linguistic structure." This makes the study of language one of the most exciting and potentially productive areas of psychological research today.

13 Learning and cognitive development

PRETEST

1. What is the name of the following "law of learning": The outcome of an event serves as information about that event? _____

2. Animals who fail to try to escape electric shocks because their earlier attempts to escape did not succeed are exhibiting _____

3. Human beings exhibit goal-directed behavior, including the use of intermediate steps to achieve goals. Do they share this characteristic with any other species?

_____

4. A six-month-old baby might be observed to pick up and drop a bean bag repeatedly, varying its hand and arm positions, apparently observing the result of each action very carefully. Such a child could be said to be learning by _____

_____.

5. What are the labels which Piaget applies to the stages of cognitive development in the child? (The age ranges given are only approximate.)

birth-18 months _____

2-7 years _____

7-11 years _____

11- _____

6. A young child who has recently learned the word "doggie" applies the term only to large brown dogs, not to smaller dogs or dogs of different colors. This child is exhibiting _____.

7. As a general rule, would you expect people first to learn a word, or the concept for which the word stands? _____

8. How important is imitation in children's language learning? _____

9. Language spoken by mothers and fathers to children who are just acquiring simple sentences is usually marked by simplified structure and by reduced length. This type of language is called _____

10. One phase of the learning of complex materials is the adjustment of the memory schemas for adequacy and efficiency. This phase is called _____

_____.

1. The law of information feedback; 2. learned helplessness; 3. yes, with a few primate species; 4. experimentation; 5. sensorimotor development, preoperational thought, concrete operations, formal operations; 6. overdiscrimination; 7. concept first; 8. not very; 9. parentese; 10. tuning

---

INTRODUCTION

As a result of a quirk in the development of psychological theory and research over the last 80 years, the terms *learning research* and *memory research* have applied to very different, and often antagonistic theoretical approaches. *Learning* theorists usually studied subjects from animal species, most often not very clever species such as pigeons or rats. *Memory* theorists studied people. The former group tried to work with very simple motor responses or autonomic responses. The latter group often dealt with very complicated language behavior. The first sections of Chapter 13 of HIP show that these approaches can be dealt with in one theoretical system. The first section of this problem set is also concerned with relating the two approaches to what should be a single problem--learning and memory.

CONTIGENCY LEARNING

Figure 13.1 represents that portion of a pigeon's conceptual structure which can be attributed to the experiences it has had in an experimental chamber. The concepts are labeled for your convenience, although the pigeon certainly cannot associate these concepts with any abstract symbols. In a few sentences, express what the pigeon

1   learned in this experiment._____

_____

What innate predisposition in pigeons does the design of this experiment take ad-

2   vantage of? _____

Cognitive psychologists believe that for an animal to learn the relationship between a specific action and an outcome, the animal must believe there is a causal relation between them. How does the pigeon's conceptual structure, as represented in Figure

3   13.1 express this belief about a causal relation?_____

_____

_____

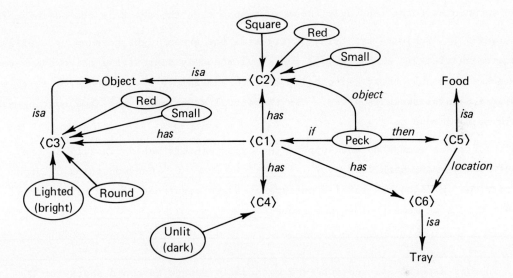

Figure 13.1

One of the principles of the cognitive approach to learning is that most learning involves awareness. For example, in operant learning experiments, the subject discovers that some outcome is contingent on the performance of some action. In order for learning to take place, the subject must become aware of the contingency.

Naturally, we do not want to accept the awareness hypothesis on faith, so we should think about the results of some experiments that might bear on the issues. The first problem is deciding which subjects are aware of the contingency in an experiment.

Propose some way of dividing a group of subjects into an *aware* and an *unaware*

4   subgroup._____

_____

_____

_____

_____

Consider the following *avoidance* experiment. Human subjects are seated at a panel with eight switches, and shock electrodes are connected to their left legs. The panel has an unlit green light.

Group 1: Subjects are told, "Under certain conditions, you may receive an electric shock. Here is an example of the shock." At this point a painful shock is given. In the actual experiment, the green light flashes on for 3 seconds before the shock is administered. If the subject should happen to depress simultaneously the third and seventh switches (and only those switches) then the shock is not administered.

Group 2: Subjects are told, "Every time the green light goes on, you will receive an electric shock, unless you simultaneously depress the third and seventh switches (and only those switches). Here is an example of the shock." At this point a painful shock is given. In the actual experiment, the same contingencies hold as for Group 1.

Which of these groups do you suppose the experimenters would classify as the

5 *contingency-aware* group?_____ Can you think of any conditions in which the label "contingency-aware" might not really be properly applied to some member of such a group?_____

_____

_____

In this experiment, subjects who eventually manage to avoid shock for 20 consecutive trials are said to be conditioned. In a group of 50 trials, is it likely

6 that some Group 1 subjects will fail to become conditioned?_____ Why or why not?_____

_____

In a group of 50 trials, is it likely that some Group 2 subjects will fail to become

7 conditioned?_____ Why or why not?_____

_____ Which group would you expect to "condition"

8 faster?_____ Why?_____

_____

Some of the conditioned subjects in this experiment can be observed to practice a strange ritual whenever the green light comes on in this experiment. One such subject always holds his breath, taps his feet three times quickly, and only uses his little fingers to depress the switches. What is the term for such behavior?

9 _____ Which group is this subject

10   more likely to come from? _____ Why? _____
11   _____

     _____
     Can you think of some reason why the two groups might not condition at the same rate
12   that involves more than "contingency awareness"? _____

     _____

     _____
     A number of subjects fumble with the switches for the first 20 or 30 trials, but
     are never able to avoid being shocked. Then they simply sit still through the rest
     of the session, looking painfully resigned whenever the light comes on. What is the
13   name for their condition? _____ Which group
     of subjects is underline{un}likely to have such subjects? _____ How could the
     experiment be designed so that a much larger number of subjects would act like this?

14   _____

     _____
     Here is quite a different experiment designed to discover whether awareness is
     essential to conditioning. The experimenter instructs the subject to say individual
     words, at the rate of about one every 2 seconds. Whenever the subject says a
     plural noun, however, the experimenter mutters "umhumm" (this, the experimenter
     believes, reinforces the subjects' tendencies to produce plural nouns in this
     situation). If subjects are producing plural nouns for more than 80% of their
     utterances by the end of the session, then they are said to have been conditioned
     to produce plural nouns.

     The first time the experimenter does this experiment, 60% of the subjects become
     conditioned, according to the criterion just mentioned. At the end of the experiment,
     the experimenter asks each of the subjects, "Did you realize that I said 'Umhumm'
     every time you said a plural noun?" and records their "Yes" or "No" answers. The
     experimenter finds that none of the subjects who failed to condition say "Yes," but
     that only 1/6 of the subjects who did condition say "Yes." The experimenter therefore
     concludes that 5/6 of the subjects who conditioned did so without awareness of the
15   contingency. Do you agree with the experimenter's conclusions? _____ Why
     or why not? _____

     _____
     One of the experimenter's students (who will hereafter be referred to as
     Experimenter 2) worries that the procedure for assessing awareness may not have been
     complete enough. Experimenter 2 repeats the experiment, but at the end of each

experimental session the subject of that session is required to fill out a
questionnaire about the experiment. One of the questions asked by the questionnaire
is: "Experimenter 2 sometimes said 'Umhmm' during the experiment. When was
Experimenter 2 most likely to do this?" Here are the different types of answers
Experimenter 2 got for this question:

a. The "Umhmms" were randomly distributed.

b. When I mentioned something I could see in the experimental room.

c. When I mentioned animals, like "giraffes," "lions," and "dogs."

d. When I mentioned jewels, like "rubies," "pearls," and "diamonds."

e. When I cleared my throat.

f. When I mentioned plural nouns.

g. When I mentioned groups of things, like "people," and "books."

h. When I mentioned types of people, like "teachers," and "liars."

i. When I mentioned actions, like "running," and "selling."

j. When I mentioned psychological terms, like "stimuli," "subjects," and
"reinforcements."

The responses were evenly divided among these 10 answers to this question.
Experimenter 2 replicated the earlier experiment in certain respects. For example,
60% of the subjects "conditioned" by the rule mentioned earlier. By the measure of
awareness used by E, what percentage of E2's subjects were aware of the reinforcement

16 contingency? _____Do you think that 60% of the subjects who gave each
type of answer above (a-j) would condition and 40% not condition, or would you
expect that those who gave certain answers would be more likely to condition (to

17 produce at least 80% plural nouns toward the end of the session?) _____

_____

If you suspect that those who gave certain answers were more likely than those who
gave other answers to condition, then which answers were given by those who

18 conditioned? Letters:_____

In this experiment, could a subject develop an incorrect hypothesis about the

19 reinforcement contingency and yet appear conditioned?_____ Explain_____
20
_____

_____

Is it fair to say that the conclusions that one draws from these experiments depend

21 very much on how one defines "awareness of contingency" in this context?_____

22 Explain. _____

Reinforcement is treated as information feedback in HIP Chapter 13. What sort of feedback do subjects such as those mentioned in Problem 19 get, if they

23 consistently act on the basis of their hypothesis? _____

Recall the taste aversion experiments described in Chapter 13 of HIP. Animals who become ill will later shun any novel food that was consumed several hours before the onset of the illness. They will avoid this new food even if the food itself had nothing to do with the illness, as in the case in which the illness is brought on by

24 exposure to radiation. Give a cognitive learning explanation for this result._____

_____

_____

COGNITIVE DEVELOPMENT

The Swiss psychologist Jean Piaget has proposed that there are four fairly distinct stages of cognitive development in children. Four conceptual tasks that represent the abilities of children at different stages of development are listed below:

a. A child is shown a round lump of clay. The clay is then placed on one tray of a balance scale. A number of small lead weights are placed on the other tray of the scale, until the two trays balance each other. The experimenter then removes the lump of clay from its tray, shapes it into an elongated oblong, and prepares to return it to its tray. (This is all done in full view of the child.) Before replacing the clay on the balance, the experimenter asks the child whether more or fewer lead weights will be required to balance the clay. The child says that exactly the same number are needed.

b. A child is shown a globular lump of clay, which is then immersed in a glass beaker full of water. The clay sinks completely, and the water level in the beaker rises to a level which is then marked on the outside of the beaker with a blue crayon. The lump is then removed from the water and shaped into an elongated oblong. Before replacing the lump in the beaker (it will obviously be completely immersed again), the experimenter asks the child to mark with a red crayon exactly where he thinks the water will rise to when the clay is put back in the water. The child marks a point right next to (at just the same level as) the blue line.

c. The child is lying on its back, looking at the ceiling. The experimenter enters the room without the child noticing. But when the experimenter speaks to the child, it turns its head toward the sound of the voice.

d. The child is able to name many of the objects and simple events that are part of its **environment**.

At which of Piaget's stages in cognitive development is each of the abilities represented in the tasks a-d <u>first</u> present in the child.

25   Task <u>a</u> _____

26   Task <u>b</u> _____

27   Task <u>c</u> _____

28   Task <u>d</u> _____

For each of the characteristics listed below, list the stage of cognitive development which it is most characteristic of:

29   Use of propositional logic _____

30   Egocentrism _____

31   Mental hypothesis testing _____

32   Learning to control gross body musculature _____

Piaget believes that there has been too much emphasis on the notion of four distinct stages in the development of the child's thought on the part of his American followers. He also feels that too much emphasis has been placed on the exact age ranges for the stages of cognitive development. What does Piaget see as a more crucial contribution of his theory toward the description of children's cognitive development? That is, in what way does his theory claim that cognitive development

33   is restricted?_____

_____

_____

LANGUAGE LEARNING

A child learning to speak and understand language has a great deal to learn. Learning how to use language includes problems like these:

(1)   The social rules of conversation must be learned. One must know about taking turns in conversations, about preserving one's turn, about interruptions, about polite ways of saying things.

(2)   Facts about the world must be learned. Linguistic symbols have no inherent meaning--they merely stand for concepts about objects and events in the world. Children must acquire some of those concepts before being able to talk about them.

(3)   Something about the grammar of their language must be learned. They must know whether the first noun in the sentence is more likely to be the

subject or the object of the verb in that sentence.

(4)   They must learn the meanings of the many thousands of words that people use routinely, even in fairly ordinary conversations.

Consider the second problem just mentioned, for three different types of words which the child must learn to use correctly. The first kind of word to consider is proper nouns--words like *Sam*, *Jill*, *Mommy*, *Daddy*. In order to use the word *Daddy* correctly, the child must learn to recognize certain invariances and to ignore certain variances. Name some of the things about the named object (Daddy) which can

34   vary without changing the applicability of the term. _____

_____

A second type of word which children must learn how to use is the common noun. *Banana*, *shoe*, and *dog* are examples of common nouns. There can be even more variation in the objects to which a common noun can be applied than is possible for proper nouns. Name some of the things about a named object (such as *dog*) that can vary without changing the applicability of the term. Mention types of things that

35   cannot vary for proper nouns. _____

_____

Do you think that a child could appropriately use a common noun without having some sort of primary node "definition" (in the sense of Chapter 10) for that noun in

36   memory? _____ Explain. _____
37
_____

A third type of word which children must learn how to use is the verb--a name for an event. Here the child's problem must be even more complex. List some

38   special problems that must be part of the task of learning verbs. _____

_____

Despite the above-mentioned problems, Piaget feels that most of children's early vocabulary is essentially verbal or action-oriented in concept. If this were so, what might a child "really mean" when it squeals "Ball!" upon seeings its

39   favorite toy? _____

_____

One important feature of human language use is the fact that the speaker of an utterance always presupposes some shared knowledge with his hearer. It has been claimed that young children learning to speak often make the mistake of presupposing

too much knowledge on the part of the listener. In fact, to judge by their speech, some children think that the person they are addressing knows everything they do, right down to what they mean by some pronoun which has no clear referent in the context. Such speech is called *egocentric speech*. Give an example of egocentric
40 speech. _____

_____

There is a stage in the acquisition of language for most children in which they can only produce two-word, but not three- or more-word sentences. There are **six** possible two-word pairs which can be made out of this three-word sentence: *Mommy like banana.*

41 What are they? _____

_____

_____

_____

_____

_____

Which three of the above pairs will probably not be used to convey "Mommy like banana"
42 in the speech of a child learning English? _____
What does this fact imply about the child's knowledge of English grammar at this
43 point in its development? _____

_____

_____

It is generally believed that children have a great advantage over adults in language learning. Children transplanted to cultures in which totally foreign tongues are spoken usually seem to adapt fairly quickly and to learn the language with native fluency if they are immersed in the culture that uses it. Adults (at least adults raised in our culture) have a great deal more difficulty when transferred to a foreign country. Even after some years, they are likely to still have a foreign accent and to not feel completely comfortable in their adopted tongue.

Two theories have been proposed to account for this. The first we will call the "imprinting" theory. It states that there is a biological predisposition to learn a language natively only in immature members of the species. After the critical period has passed, certain cognitive links have been "frozen" or "imprinted" in certain patterns, and a language cannot be used in the same way.

The second theory could be called the "motivational" theory. According to this theory, only children have the time and energy to learn anything, including a language, very well. After a certain age has been passed, people are too busy making a living or learning how to make a living to spend the tremendous amounts of time that are required to really learn a language well.

Use the space below to propose an experiment to distinguish between these

44   theories. Comment on the feasibility of your experiment. _____

_____

_____

_____

_____

14 Problem solving and decision making

1. There tends to be little external evidence of thought processes. An experimental method that helps to overcome this is _____.

2. This method, however, generates data that are difficult to analyze and visualize. A representation for these data, which is more easily interpretable, is a _____.

3. _____ is a group of letters in the form of an arithmetic problem. Each different letter represents a different digit.

4. In the Restle puzzle problem, substituting "Puzzle A" for a phrase in the sentence is an example of the use of a _____.

5. An _____ is a guaranteed method for solving a problem, whereas a _____ often, but not always, helps in finding a solution.

6. In making decisions, people tend to assign a psychological worth to various components of the decision. A term used for this worth in decision theory is _____.

7. Rather than make an extensive decision analysis, a person makes a spur-of-the-moment choice. This may appear to be irrational, but if one adds in the utility of _____ the course of action may very well be reasonable.

8. A $5 bill would probably not influence you in deciding between two different but equally fabulous around-the-world trips. What is the principle behind this?

_____

_____

9. A friend is using a biased coin which comes up heads 60% of the time. He offers to give you $20 if the coin comes up tails, but you must give him $15 if it comes up heads. What is the expected value of this bet for you? _____

_____

10. A series of choices are offered in HIP, from 10 cents or a 1/10 chance for $1, to $1,000,000 or a 1/10 chance for $10,000,000. Most people will begin by taking the gambles but choose the "sure thing" at higher values of money. Can you explain why this is reasonable, simply in terms of utility for money? _____

_____

_____

1. verbal protocols; 2. problem behavior graph; 3. Crypto-arithmetic; 4. label; 5. algorithm, heuristic; 6. utility; 7. the effort needed to analyze the choices and make the decision; 8. Utilities depend upon the context in which they appear: The utility of the $5 bill is insignificant in comparison to the utilities of the trips; 9. EV = (=$20) x (.4) = (-$15) x (.6) = -$1; 10. To accept the 1 in 10 gamble, one is saying that the "chance money" has more than 10 times the utility of the "sure money." For greater monetary amounts the utility will usually increase slower than the money, and thus eventually one will not accept the gamble.

INTRODUCTION

This chapter theorizes about how people solve problems, play games, gamble, do math, decide which car to buy, and determine where to go on a trip. Because human behavior at this level is so complex and variable, many of the theories tend to be more descriptive than explanatory. For example, this chapter considers how people solve problems such as crypto-arithmetic. Information about the problem-solving process is obtained through *protocols*, that is, by having the subject "think out loud" while solving the problem. The most successful work done in this **area** involves using a *problem behavior graph*. This simply proposes that a person goes through *states* in solving a problem. It does not explain how or why the person solves the problem.

Similarly, the *Subjective Expected Utility (SEU)* theory concerns how people make decisions about money, including which bets are the most attractive. This model is again largely descriptive, allowing each person to have his own utility for different amounts of money and his own set of perceived probabilities.

Descriptive psychological theories serve a useful purpose. In describing a situation, one often finds that a few features and operations can be used to depict a large number of situations--that is, one begins to observe useful patterns in the data. For instance, in a problem behavior graph, one finds that there are usually a quite limited number of types of states that a person solving the problem passes through. Furthermore, the step or operation that a person uses to get from one state to another may be one of just a handful of possible operations. These patterns in the data can trigger a theory that goes beyond description to actually explaining what happens. For example, humans may have only a limited number of "tricks" that they have learned to use for solving problems. Second, these patterns can be used

to predict new behavior. An example is in SEU theory, where once a person's
"utility curve" for money and subjective probabilities are found, one can
predict how that person will react to future gambles and decisions.

This process of going from description to patterns to the beginning of an
explanation is repeated several times in Chapter 14. In this study guide chapter,
you will get a chance to work through this process a couple of times yourself.

PROBLEM SOLVING AND PROTOCOLS

You give a person a problem to solve and 10 minutes later she comes back with the
correct solution. How did she do it? You could perhaps ask her to write the steps
she used in computing the answer, much as teachers often ask for your "work" for
each problem on a math test. But such a list of steps surely will not include all
the false starts and backtracks taken along the way, or even all the small steps
taken toward the correct solution. The basic assumption the solver is making is
that you do not want incorrect paths, nor do you want to hear all the tiny, very
obvious steps. Furthermore, the solver may not even be consciously aware of some of
these last steps. However, if we really want to find out how humans solve problems--
exactly how they are able to move from one mental step to the next--then somehow we
need to get a complete list of mental states, correct or incorrect, that the solver
went through in attempting to solve the problem.

A somewhat more successful way of doing this is by having a solver think aloud
when working on the problem, naming each mental state. Although this *verbal
protocol* is a great improvement over a written list of steps, there are at least two
problems that can still cause a protocol to differ from an ideal list of all mental
states passed through: *(i)* limits of self-awareness, and *(ii)* what the solver
assumes about your knowledge of the problem and of his knowledge. Think about
exactly what these men and then try to describe how they would affect verbal proto-

1   cols. *(i)* _____

_____

_____

2   *(ii)* _____

_____

_____

As a consequence of these problems, collecting protocols has become almost an art,
inducing subjects to say as much as they can about each mental state without
bogging down, getting them to be conscious of their thinking processes, and, as

experimenter, learning to say as little as possible so as not to "jar" the thinking process in any direction than where it would not have gone without interference. In addition, subjects learn to give better protocols over several attempts, gradually reducing the number of "long pauses," where thinking is going on, of which you will know little about.

Let us take a problem to solve and a protocol collected on a solution to it in order to have an example to work with. Although the "Missionary and Cannibal problem" has many forms, one version can be stated as below:

> Three missionaries and three cannibals have banded together in an uneasy alliance in order to traverse a difficult region of jungle. Halfway through this region they reach a wide river they must cross. Luckily they find a small abandoned boat with a capacity of two people, which all six in the group find easy to operate. They decide to use this boat to ferry themselves across the river. However, here a problem arises, for they all know that if cannibals outnumber missionaries on either side of the river, then those cannibals will become uncontrollable and kill and eat those missionaries. How are they to arrange the boat crossings so that everyone remains intact for the rest of the journey? Note that dropping a passanger off to swim the last few feet in order to avoid a confrontation will not work because of the crocodiles in the river.

You will probably find that you will appreciate the protocol and subsequent analysis more if you spend some time trying to solve the problem (if you have not seen it recently), before looking at the protocol.

The protocol that follows is from a subject who was presented with a sketch of the problem and worked on it for about 8 minutes. It has been edited somewhat to make it of manageable length.

> *O.K. Take two missionaries over...*
> *No, we can't take two missionaries over...because there are three cannibals on the other side.*
> *O.K. We'll take a missionary and a cannibal over...and bring a missionary back.*
> *Then take two cannibals over. Then one of them comes back. Then you take...*
> (long pause)
> Exptr: *What are you thinking about here?*
> *I'm thinking that if I take a missionary and cannibal over then the missionaries will be swamped...*
> *O.K. We'll take two missionaries over and have one of the cannibals bring back the boat...(pause)...then you'll have a problem!* (laughs)
> (begins problem again)
> *I don't think I want the two cannibals over on the other side.*
> *We'll take a missionary and cannibal over...bring a missionary back...*
> (long pause)
> *O.K., we'll take the two missionaries over...no, that won't work...*

> *So, let's take two cannibals over and let a cannibal take the boat back...*
> *Let's see, we have three missionaries and a cannibal to go and two*
> *cannibals on the other side...were's the boat?*
> (long pause)
> *Oh!...O.K., we'll take two missionaries over, and missionary and a*
> *cannibal back...*
> Exptr: *Why did you decide to do that?*
> *Because if I took either a missionary or cannibal alone back, then it*
> *would be unbalanced either on one side or the other. So I brought a mission-*
> *ary and cannibal back, which left a missionary and cannibal...and two*
> *missionaries and two cannibals back on the original side....*
> *So I bring...um...(long pause). So I bring a missionary and a cannibal*
> *over...*
> (realizes this won't work)
> *O.K. So I bring two missionaries over....I'm stuck again.*
> Exptr: *No, you're not....*
> (decides to take back the last move anyway)
> *Take a missionary and cannibal over....This won't work--I can't do*
> *anything...*
> (takes back the last move again)
> *O.K., take two missionaries over; that's the only thing I can do...*
> *and then...Oh!...I can take a cannibal back over....*
> *And then he can pick up another one, take him across, and then go back*
> *for the last one, and then they're all across.*

Suppose you have a protocol. Where do you go then? Even if you explain what you
think is going on in the protocol, it is difficult to convince anyone of a theory, using
a protocol as evidence. First, it is amazing how many different ways one can take a
protocol and interpret some mental process which is occurring. Second, numbers are
against you--it is a tremendous amount of work to collect and analyze even a few
protocols, and yet someone could argue, "How can you conclude anything about human
problem solving from just a couple people?" Finally, a protocol is simply an
indication of how a problem was solved, and provides little hint of why it was
solved in that manner, or how similar problems would be solved.

It is clear that some further analysis of the protocol needs to be done in order
to make it really presentable as evidence. One quite useful way to represent the
protocol in another form is by using a *problem behavior graph*, by which you infer
from a subject's words what mental states the subject is going through, and what
operations or processes are being used to go from one mental state to the next. You
might argue that different experimenters can sometimes make quite different inferences
about the same states (and you would be right), but the graph is often a good start and
quite valuable for beginning to see patterns in the solution.

From the preceding paragraph you can see that, in order to get a problem behavior
graph, you need a set of *possible mental states* and *operations* to go between these

states. How does one derive these in the first place? Usually they are suggested
by the structure of the problem to be solved and the protocol, but sometimes finding
a set of states is a monumental problem in itself. One good example of this is
studying how chess masters play chess. One might think that the mental states
are the positions of the pieces on the board after each move, but after reading a
couple of protocols or talking to a grandmaster it becomes clear that his mental
states are not in this form at all; they are composed more of pathways and dynamic
balances and dependencies between pieces.

In our Missionary and Cannibal example, however, a possible set of states is
much more obvious (although certainly not unique--after reading the protocol, can
you think of a couple ways of representing the mental states and operations?). In
order that our problem behavior graphs look alike, a set of possible states and
operations will be described below, and from these you will try to construct the
graph.

Suppose that each mental state is represented by the number of missionaries and
cannibals on each side. Thus a condition of having one missionary and one cannibal
on the original side of the river with the rest on the far side would be represented
as shown in Figure 14.1.

```
┌─────────┐
│ M 1 : 2 │
│ C 1 : 2 │
└─────────┘
```

Figure 14.1

In this same notation, how would you represent the original state at the beginning
of the problem?

3

In addition, a state can be either possible or impossible (that is, undesirable because
some number of missionaries will be eaten). This undesirable imbalance of cannibals
over missionaries on either side will be noted by an "I" in the bottom corner of the
box, on that side of the river, e.g., a missionary and two cannibals on the original
side of the river would be drawn as shown in Figure 14.2.

Figure 14.2

Think of and draw an impossible state on the far side of the river:

4

What are the operations to use to get in between states? There are two possible
types of operations to use, depending on the location of the boat. If the boat is on
the original side of the river, then the operation will be called a "ferrying action,"
and depicted as F(M,M), F(M,C), F(C), etc. An example is drawn in Figure 14.3.

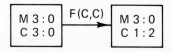

Figure 14.3

Similarly, if the boat is carrying people from the far side to the original side,
then the operation is called a "returning action" and designated R(C,C), etc.
Draw an example:

5

Is it true that, given an initial state and a particular operation such as F(M,C),
6   that you can always infer the next state? _____ Why? _____
7   _____

_____
_____ Do you think that your answer
8   is always true of all problem behavior graphs? _____
One last thing is needed in order to construct a problem behavior graph--
developing a way to depict what happens when a solver *backtracks* to an earlier state
to continue. In this case an unlabeled arrow is drawn down from the state which she
backed up to and this state is redrawn identically. For example, the first backtrack

in the protocol:

> *O.K. Take two missionaries over....*
> *No, we can't take two missionaries over....*

would be depicted as shown in Figure 14.4.

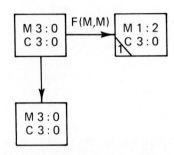

Figure 14.4

What conditions in the mental states would normally cause a solver to backtrack in a

9   protocol? _____

_____ Suppose there were no

cases of backtracking in a protocol. What could you say about the problem solution?

10   _____

_____

    You should now be armed with everything you need in order to construct a problem

behavior graph for our protocol. Try to build this problem behavior graph on

page 212. The protocol is typed again in order to make it easier to refer to

A few hints: It is easiest to build this graph by taking one statement from the

protocol at a time, inferring the operation that has been carried out, and applying

this to the last state you have drawn to get the next state. It is useful to draw

fairly small so that you don't run out of room on the right-hand side. Remember

that each arrow except those which point downward must be labeled with an operation,

and that states which are impossible should be appropriately marked with an "I."

Number each state or box that you use in the order that they are constructed, so that

they can be referred to later. There should be 31 states in all. Finally, statements

which are just further comment by the subject or experimenter are marked with an

asterisk ("*"). These should not be translated into states, but may be of help

in constructing the graph. Good luck!

O.K. Take two missionaries over...

No, we can't take two missionaries over...because there are three cannibals on the other side.

O.K. We'll take a missionary and a cannibal over...and bring a missionary back.

Then take two cannibals over. Then one of them comes back. Then you take...

*(long pause)

Exptr: What are you thinking about here?

I'm thinking that if I take a missionary and cannibal over then the missionaries will be swamped...

O.K. We'll take two missionaries over and have one of the cannibals bring back the boat...(pause)...then you'll have a problem! (laughs)

*(begins problem again)

I don't think I want the two cannibals over on the other side.

We'll take a missionary and cannibal over...bring a missionary back...

*(long pause)

O.K., we'll take the two missionaries over...no, that won't work...

So, let's take two cannibals over and let a cannibal take the boat back....

Let's see, we have three missionaries and a cannibal to go and two cannibals on the other side...where's the boat?

*(long pause)

Oh!...O.K., we'll take two missionaries over, and missionary and a cannibal back....

Exptr: Why did you decide to do that?

Because if I took either a missionary or cannibal alone back, then it would be unbalanced either on one side or the other. So I brought a missionary and cannibal back, which left a missionary and cannibal...and two missionaries and two cannibals back on the original side...

So I bring...um...(long pause). So I bring a missionary and a cannibal over....

*(realizes this won't work)

O.K. So I bring two missionaries over...I'm stuck again.

Exptr: No, you're not....

*(decides to take back the last move anyway)

Take a missionary and cannibal over....This won't work--I can't do anything...

*(takes back the last move again)

O.K., take two missionaries over; that's the only thing I can do...and then...Oh!...I can take a cannibal back over...

And then he can pick up another one, take him across, and then go back for the last one, and then they're all across.

11

Some questions about this example:

Note that the information as to which side of the river the boat is on is not part of the state at any particular step in the solution, yet this information can

12   be inferred from the state diagrams and the operations between them.   How? _____

_____

_____

One statement that the subject makes provides a small piece of evidence that information about the location of the boat is not explicitly contained in the mental states of the subject either. Can you find that statement? _____

13

_____

Of course, in order to prove that the subject does not explicitly store boat location, one would need to provide further evidence. Consider, without writing anything down, how you might set up an experiment to further test this.

    How many backtracks were made by the subject during the solution of the

14 problem? _____ What is the reason for the first four of these backtracks?

15 _____

_____

    The backtracks after states 21 and 25, however, are not because of impossible conditions, yet the subject knew not to go on. How might you explain what's

16 happening here? (<u>Hint</u>: Do there implicitly exist other states?) _____

_____

_____

_____

Note also that states 24 and 25 are exact repeats of states 20 and 21--that is, the subject, after realizing that she could go nowhere after 21, tried the same sequence just a couple of states later. This type of behavior is very uncharacteristic of computer programs which have been written to solve problems such as these--the computer has perfect memory of what paths it has tried. Behavior of this sort has advantages as well as disadvantages, given the way humans solve problems. Sometimes it is simply a waste of time; however, in other cases, a new, undiscovered path will be found. Another example of this is a chess player who will go over a seemingly faulty combination of moves several times and finally notice a new move variation which wins. Thus the advantage of this behavior is that humans are imperfect in another sense--they do not always see all possible operations to apply to a particular state.

    A vivid example of this last process is with state 19, which was actually

17 reached once considerably earlier (When? _____). What operation was

18 missed in this earlier state which would have led to the solution? _____

19 Can you speculate as to why it might have been missed? _____

_____

_____

_____

This missed operation and the unnecessary backtracking which it will cause, occurs in almost every protocol of a solution to this problem (by someone who doesn't know the solution), and the reason for missing it is the subject of considerable controversy in psychology. You may have noticed that, after you drew the problem behavior graph, the necessity of trying R(M,C) was much more apparent than when you were originally working on the problem. This is another common occurrence when one formally writes out a graph to a problem--it is as though the problem were better structured and you can see all the possibilities. Finally, we note that "GPS," a program that can solve this problem, has no diffi- culty at all at this point, but stumbles at other parts that humans find easy.

20
21
   When in state 23, the subject backtracks even though there is an obvious operation that could be applied to that state, which is _____. What might the subject be thinking about which could have caused this to be overlooked? _____

_____

_____

_____

   Finally, it is clear that in the preceding question we would be only speculating. Similarly, it is almost certain that something is happening to the subject's mental state during the "long pauses," yet again we can only speculate. What other kinds of information could we obtain to help confirm our hypotheses? One such method collects eye movements of the subject as the problem is being solved. The problem was presented to the subject as a river and a set of M's and C's drawn on a sheet of paper, and during most of the solution as well as the long pauses the subject's eyes could be seen shifting from one side of the river to the next. One way that these eye movements can be collected is using a television camera which continually photographs her eyes and tracks the dark centers (pupils).

   A second method involves collecting evoked potentials by attaching electrodes to the scalp and measuring electrical activity. Characteristic electrical waves will occur each time the subject makes a decision. Analysis of these waves, however, is extremely complex, and their use in this fashion is just beginning in psychology.

DECISION MAKING AND UTILITY FUNCTIONS

   In a sense the process of making a decision can be simply defined as follows: you have a set of alternatives, each of which has a certain value or *utility* to you. If you make the decision rationally, you will simply choose the alternative with the highest utility. You might argue that many times humans do not seem to decide rationally, but this irrationality is often not in the choosing step but in the assigning of utilities to different alternatives. Thus a major question both in making a decision and in analyzing how other people make them is how utilities are assigned.

Suppose we first take an example where assigning utilities would appear to be easier than most, that is, money. It is clear here that a larger amount of money will never have less utility than a smaller amount, no matter what quantities are involved. (For example, a million and one dollars is no less useful than a million dollars, although it may be very little more useful.) The question thus becomes: Exactly what is the relationship between utility and money? They could be *linearly related*, i.e., for each dollar that you increase any amount by, utility is also increased by one unit. Or the relationship could be *accelerating*--small amounts of money have very little utility whereas larger amounts have increasingly significant importance. Similarly, it could be *decelerating*--small amounts of money have relatively large importance, while for larger amounts, although they have greater utility, the increases tend to flatten out.

Which of the three types of relationships would you say is characteristic of

22   most people? _____ How might you show this is true? One way is to ask people to rate (with some number greater than 0) how "happy" they would be if you gave them $10, then rate how "happy" they would be if you gave them $20, $30, $40, etc. If the relationship is decelerating, the $20 should have a "happy rating" of less than twice $10, $30 less than three times $10, etc. There are a couple of problems with this method. One is that it is difficult to rate how happy you would be for many different amounts--how many degrees of happiness can you feel, one right after another? The second reason involves the unreality of the situation--it is often difficult to imagine how you would really feel, since you are not really getting the money. This problem pervades much of the psychological study of utility, decision theory, and gambling--either the subject must <u>imagine</u> that he is taking the gamble or making the decision, or the gambles are real but the amounts must be small enough (typically a tenth of a cent for each trial) that the experimenter will not go broke running several subjects. The subject can always sit back and remember, "In reality, I'm really gaining or losing nothing." Despite these problems, evidence and intuition both say that greater amounts of money have less and less effect on

happiness and hence on utility. If you interpret utility in terms of buying power

23   for desirable things, can you give another reason why this might be true? _____

_____

_____

_____

Where would <u>your</u> utility curve really level off, that is, where would increasing the

24   dollar amount any further increase utility by very little? _____

_____

     The last sentence alluded to a *utility curve*, which is a convenient way of
expressing the relationship between utility and amounts of some other commodity,
usually money. For example, if utility "levels off" or decelerates with respect to
money, the relationship could be described by a curve such as any one of the three
in Figure 14.5.

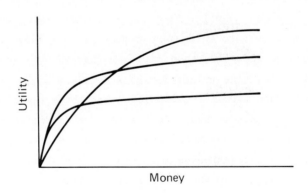

Figure 14.5

In Figure 14.6, draw two curves, one that would express the relationship if utility
were linearly related to money, and, remembering the definitions in the first
paragraph of this section, one showing a positively accelerating relationship:

25

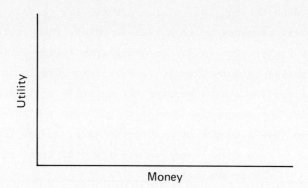

Figure 14.6

Which of the curve or curves above do you think would be a miser's utility curve

26   toward   money? _____ Why? _____
27
_____
_____

Suppose this curve were continued below 0, i.e., as shown in Figure 14.7.

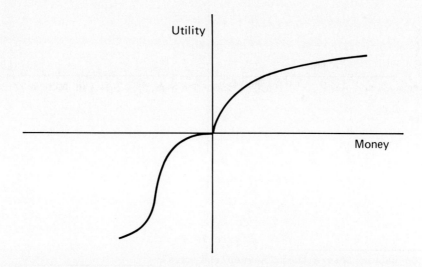

Figure 14.7

28   What could the bottom half of the curve represent? _____

_____

This half, which is called *negative utility*, is not necessarily (and in fact, not usually) symmetrical with the top half of the curve. For example, with money, as you lose greater amounts of money up to a certain point, the negative utility is increasing at an even faster rate (e.g., in going from losing \$5 to losing \$50, the negative utility increases by more than 10 times). One example is that you would be willing to play poker for low stakes because the negative utility of losing a couple of dollars is very low, but you wouldn't want to get into a high stakes game because you couldn't afford to lose a couple of hundred dollars, and so the negative utility of this is very high. Do you think negative utility will level off eventually?

29 _____ Why or why not? _____
30
_____

_____

Using the preceding information and what you know about your own utility for money, draw your full utility curve for money in Figure 14.8, labeling parts where the curve changes.

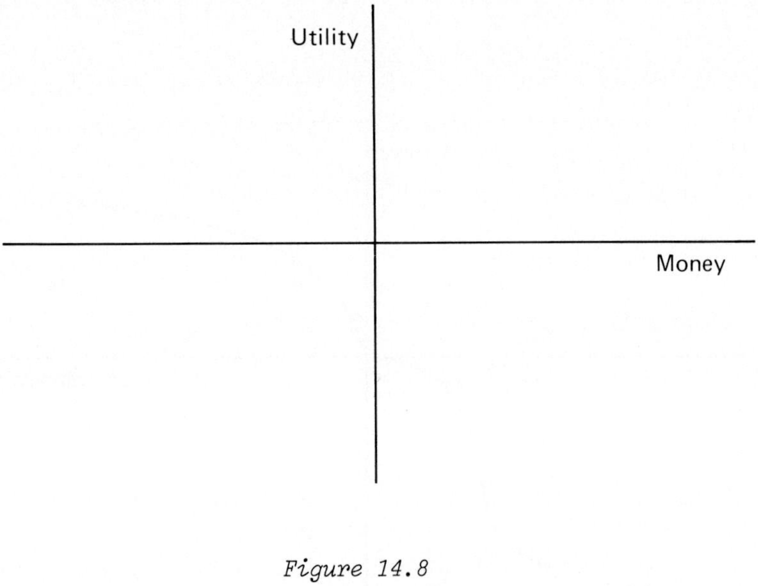

Figure 14.8

31   Why do people insure their houses and cars? _____

_____

And yet they are losing money through the money they are paying for insurance, since insurance companies must be making money (and lots of it). Explain why insurance is

32   still a reasonable proposition from what you know now about utility curves. _____

_____

_____

_____

          Why do people play in state lotteries, for again they must be losing money since
33   the states are making money? _____

_____

_____

_____

      Suppose you increase the amount needed to place a bet in a lottery from 50 cents to
34    $5. What do you think this would do to the state lottery and why? _____

_____

_____

_____

UTILITY OF NONMONETARY COMMODITIES

      Decisions will almost never involve simply choosing between two dollar amounts--
usually a decision involves at least one object or situation that is considerably
more complex than money. Thus one needs to consider how to determine the utilities of
these nonmonetary choices. This analysis will generally involve three tasks: *(i)*
breaking the situation or object into less complex components for which utilities can
be judged individually, *(ii)* determining the utilities of each of these parts, and
(iii) adding these utilities together to get the total utility. The first two steps
are not necessarily easy, or even possible. For example, consider the utility of going
out for a pizza dinner tonight. Possible components are the utility of the pleasure
of eating pizza for dinner, the utility of the work saved in not having to prepare
dinner and clean up afterward, the pleasure of just going out and simply of a
change, the cost of the meal, the cost of the gas for driving there, the cost of
possibly running into another car and losing your life....But some of these utilities
may be very hard to judge, e.g., what is the utility of the pleasure of eating pizza
for dinner? And do you want to even consider the last component, the possibility of
losing your life? Yet it is certainly a possibility (admittedly quite small)
whenever you drive. If you do consider it, how can you assign any finite utility to
it--certainly you would not trade any amount of money for death. This would argue
that you should never go anywhere because the cost is too high. This argument

might sound ludicrous, but in fact is a genuine concern of a person studying decision

35   theory. How might you explain a way out of this dilemma? (difficult) _____

_____

_____

_____

In a surprisingly large number of cases, however, it is possible to break down a choice or situation into components for which utilities can be fairly easily assigned, as in the example in HIP, "Choosing a mate." Another example follows for which you will be given utilities, and you must make an eventual decision from them.

A rich uncle has finally allowed you to use the money in the trust account he set up for you, and you have concluded that the first priority is getting a car. You have decided that the component dimensions along which you will base your decision are: safety, style (panache!), gas economy, frequency and cost of repair, price, and the pleasure you get out of driving it. Using these criteria, you have narrowed down your choices to two cars, a Volkswagen and a Porsche. You rate each car for each of the dimensions on a -10 to +10 scale (0 is average, 10 is fantastic, -10 is as bad as possible). These ratings are listed in Table 14.1.

	Porsche	VW
Safety	-1	+1
Style	+8	-6
Gas economy	+2	+8
Repair	-3	+5
Price	-5	+5
Pleasure to drive	+9	-2

Table 14.1

A decision strategy described in HIP that would compare each component separately

36   is called _____. Using this strategy, which

37   car would you choose? _____ If one judges each car as a whole

38   and then compares these judgments, this strategy is called _____

39   _____, which would pick the _____ here.

Note that the two strategies will often not differ on their choices, as is the case here.

Now all these dimensions are not necessarily equally important to you--for example, a high rating in price should probably carry more weight than the same rating in style (your uncle's trust account isn't unlimited and there are other things which you would like to get). Thus your ratings in this case aren't actually true utilities--if they were you could simply add them up for each car as you have just done, and choose the one with the highest utility. These ratings should be

multiplied by the weight you feel each dimension is worth, with the larger the
weight the greater the worth. Another way of looking at this is that if one were to
determine the utilities of the components directly, then the possible utilities you
would assign to an unimportant dimension would have a much smaller range than an
important dimension. For example, style might range from -3 to +3 rather than the
-10 to +10 of price. Therefore we need to know the weights of each of the
dimensions. These are listed in Table 14.2.

	Weight
Safety	2
Style	2
Gas Economy	2
Repair	1
Price	4
Pleasure to drive	3

Table 14.2

Thus, for example, the utility of the Volkswagen along the style dimension is
2 x (-3) = -6. Fill in the utilities in Table 14.3.

40

| | Utilities | |
	Porsche	VW
Safety		
Style		
Gas economy		
Repair		
Price		
Pleasure to drive		
Total		

Table 14.3

By this decision rule, based upon strict utility, which car would you choose?

41 _____

     Most people don't make decisions like this; instead they fall prey to a *focusing
problem*, vacillating between the two cars, first focusing on one dimension ("But the
Porsche has such great lines!") and then on another ("Think how much gas I'd be
saving with the Volkswagen!") until they finally make a decision, perhaps half on
impulse. Why does this happen? First there are memory limitations. Explain why

42   this might cause focusing._____

_____

_____

Second, when you focus on one dimension for a moment, the subjective weight or
importance of that dimension seems to get temporarily larger, making it hard to
compute utilities rationally. In fact, to be completely impartial with the weights,
43   one should decide upon the sizes before making any of the ratings. Why? _____

_____

_____

_____

There are some decisions where a strict decision rule based upon utility is not
the most reasonable way to decide. For example, in choosing which people to train
to be astronauts, a better decision rule might be: "Reject anyone whose rating is
below some criterion level on <u>any</u> dimension." Can you explain why such a rule might
44   be important here? _____

_____

_____

RISKY DECISIONS

In most decisions that have to be made, you are not really sure of exactly what's
going to happen in the first place; that is, there is a certain chance or *probability*
that one alternative will happen, and some chance that another alternative will
happen. On example is the chance of running into an accident while you are going
out to dinner--you are certainly fairly sure that it won't happen, but to be cold-
blooded, there is some chance that this could occur--accidents happen to a few people
every night. A second instance is a dimension you might have considered in choosing
a car--the chance of having several major repairs during the first couple of years
that you own it. In both of these cases, how can you assign a utility if you don't
know it is going to happen?

Suppose you have an idea of the chances of either of two alternatives occurring--
say half the time you think the first alternative with utility u_1 will occur, while
the other half of the time the second alternative with utility u_2 will occur. Then it
seems intuitively reasonable that one should take half the utility u_1 of the first
alternative and half of u_2 and add them to get the total utility of the two alterna-
tives. The quantities "$\frac{1}{2} \times u_1$" and "$\frac{1}{2} \times u_2$" are called the *expected utilities* of the
first and second alternatives respectively, and their sum is the *total expected*

utility. For example, at a particular restaurant suppose that half the time the pizza will be superb (utility = 10, the maximum), whereas the other half of the time the pizza is definitely average (utility = 0), depending upon the mood of the chef. Then, when computing the utility of going out to dinner, it would seem reasonable to have the utility of the pleasure of the food to be half of the utilities of each of the two alternatives, or 5, which would then be added to the utilities of the cost of the dinner, etc. Similarly, if the chance or probability were 1/5 that the pizza will be superb and 4/5 that it will be average, then we would multiply 1/5 times the utility of a superb pizza and 4/5 times the utility of an average pizza and add them together to get our overall expected utility of pizza

45
46   there on any given night, or 1/5 x _____ + 4/5 x _____ = _____.
47   In general, if we have a set of events, any one of which can happen to the exclusion of the others, and we know the probability or chance that each event can occur along with the utility of each event, then the total expected utility of the set of events is:

$$u(\text{total}) = \text{prob}(E1) \times u(E1) + \text{prob}(E2) \times u(E2) + \text{prob}(E3) \times u(E3) + \cdots$$

Note that the probability of all the events added together should equal 1, since we assume that the probability is 1 (or a "sure thing") that something is going to happen. Thus in our pizza example, either we will get a superb pizza or an average one, with the probabilities of one or the other adding up to 1. Finally, there may be cases where probabilities don't seem to add up to 1, but that is because the event, "nothing happens," is not mentioned and is assumed to happen the rest of the time.

48   What then will be its probability? _____

_____

   To provide a more flexible expected utility rule, one can allow people to estimate the probabilities themselves, instead of having them done objectively, such as gotten from a weatherman. Using subjective probabilities, the rule above becomes that used by *Subjective Expected Utility (SEU)* theory, perhaps one of the most general models of decision making. However, in the problems that follow we will assume that the probabilities have been objectively specified, and that the rule described before can be used.

   From the preceding paragraph, how would you describe the difference between

49   utility and expected utility? _____

_____

In order to become familiar with computing utility of uncertain or risky situations, try computing the total expected utility in each of the following problems:

A. You have planned a fine day in the mountains for Saturday ($u = 16$). However, you won't much like hiking and lunching in the rain ($u = -10$). The weatherman has given the probability of rain to be 40% (or .4). If you base your decision to go on the hike upon whether it has a positive expected utility, and you trust the
50 weatherman, what is your total expected utility and should you go? _____

Suppose the chance of rain is 60%. If you use the same decision rule, should you
51 go? _____
Yet surely most people, on hearing such a weather report would say, "It's going to
52 rain on Saturday, we better not go." Can you suggest any explanation for this? ____

B. Suppose you have planned a weekend camping trip, and this time the weather report is, "20% chance of rain, 40% chance of snow." Now you would enjoy a sunny day ($u = 18$), and snow would certainly be a variety and not too bad ($u = 4$), but
53 rain would again make the trip miserable ($u = -30$). What's your decision? _____

C. As a result of winning a lottery, you are guaranteed to win a prize; however, which prize you will get depends upon one roll of a fair die, with each of the six possible numbers signifying a certain prize. If the utilities of the prizes (named by the same six numbers) are: $u(1) = 1$, $u(2) = 2$, $u(3) = 3$, $u(4) = 4$, $u(5) = 5$, $u(6) = 6$, what is the total expected utility of your prize? _____

Suppose that you did not know the utilities of the prizes, but instead that they consisted of dollar amounts of $1 through $6. If the utility of $1 is 1 and monetary utility curves are decelerating, will the total expected utility of the
55 dollar prizes be greater or less than the previous prizes? (difficult) _____
56 _____ Why? _____

D. You are considering whether to apply to one more medical school in addition to the 15 you have already written applications to. To be simple, we'll say that there are two factors in favor of applying: (i) You may get accepted by this school and rejected by all the other schools which you would consider to be higher choices. Certainly this has a very high utility--it's the only way to become a doctor (although you could perhaps wait a year and reapply)--let's give it a utility of 600. However, the probability is quite small that you'll be accepted without a scholarship and also that you won't be accepted by a higher choice-- say .005. (ii) In addition, you might be accepted with a scholarship. Suppose this has a slightly higher utility of 670 and also a probability of .005. These two factors have to be balanced against the cost and work of applying to another medical school--another $25 and several hours of work. Let's say this has a utility

57 of -7.0. What is the total expected utility and your decision? _____

_____

In practice, at least one of the utilities we just used might be very hard to

58 estimate. Which one? _____

59 Why? _____

_____ Note that you are applying

to 15 other medical schools. How and why might this affect the negative utility

of applying to this school? (Hint: Remember the example in HIP about adding options

60 to a sports car.) _____

_____

_____

You might ask whether such a pure decision rule based upon expected utility is ever really used in practical decisions. In fact, its use is probably quite rare by individuals. However, corporations often make use of this cold-blooded analytical rule in many important decisions about products and internal structure--anything from whether to open a plant in another state to whether to reorganize management positions.

To take an example, suppose an orange company is considering branching out into marketing tangerines. Some of the factors they would have to consider are the effect of competition of other companies on their chances of succeeding, the cost of setting up harvesting and shipping operations, the cost of advertising to establish a new brand name, the probability of a coup and takeover of foreign businesses in the South American country where they would be getting the tangerines, the probabilities and effects of weather changes, the probabilities and utilities of writing off possible losses through taxes. Each of these probabilities and utilities have to be estimated and combined into a total expected utility. Although this example is more complex, the process is very similar to the problems you have just worked out.

Among the possible events in the preceding example are a few situations where the company might suffer a severe loss, say by a coup and takeover of a newly finished expensive plant. Although the negative utility is large, the probability is quite small, and suppose the total expected utility comes out a little positive. Why might the corporation still decide not to take the venture? (<u>Hint</u>: Consider insurance again.) _____

61

_____

_____

_____

HUMAN DECISION MAKING

It can be proven mathematically that if the principle of expected utility is followed over a long series of decisions, then overall utility or "happiness" will be maximized. Yet most of the time humans pay little attention to such a formal rule in making their decisions. Many times, whatever process they use will suggest the same choice as expected utility, but often these other processes will name other choices, or will leave the human in a state of vacillating indecision. Of these cases where differing choices are made, there are a few times where expected utility is actually wrong or at least useless--times when interactions among components makes assigning utilities impossible. One example is if a new basketball franchise tried to build a team by assigning utilities to all players and drafting those with the highest utilities. The franchise may very well end up with a group of talented players but a poor team. A related problem with expected utility concerns any case where people are being judged--a breakdown into components is bound to miss parts of the total character.

However, in the majority of the cases where decision rules differ, expected utility would probably have given the best decision. Why do humans still use these other rules? Several examples of human decision making are given below. In each case there is at least a reasonable chance that the same decision would not have been made if the formal decision rules described above were used. The reasons for these "nonrational" decisions are mentioned in either HIP or the workbook. Find and briefly explain the appropriate reason in each case:

"Deciding whether to get married has just too much involved to think about. So
62 let's not think about it and just get married." _____

_____

_____

"The University of Michigan has a great law school and several times I've made
63 up my mind to go there. Then I think about the weather some more...." _____

_____

_____

"The store in the town we just left gave us a slightly better deal on this bike
than this store, but it's almost five o'clock and I've just got to get a ride in
64 before dinner." _____

_____

_____

"A '7' hasn't come up in the last 15 rolls, so one has got to come up now. Let's
put the rest of our money on "any seven." Besides, all the times I remember making
65 a big gamble like this, it's worked out." (two problems) (i) _____

_____

66 (ii) _____

_____

So perhaps one could argue that expected utility theory and mathematical models
like it are of little use in psychology, because they don't even describe how most
real decisions are made. However, they do in fact serve a very useful purpose,
for since they are ideal decision rules, the points at which human decisions differ
provide clues to unraveling the human decision process. An analogy can be drawn to
the study of perception, where our knowledge of the rules governing how the real
visual world is constructed helps point out where and how the human visual system
stumbles--visual illusions thus play a similar role to nonideal decision rules.
However, in the study of decision processes, we have barely reached the stage of
pointing out the visual illusions; to put it another way, our knowledge in this area
is still largely descriptive, and the hard task of explaining is still ahead.

15 The mechanisms of thought

PRETEST

1. Tasks that have been practiced for very long periods of time appear to become _____.

2. The three major components of an information-processing system are _____, _____, and _____. These concepts are utilized in an analogy of the human brain as a computer.

3. The _____ does the actual executing of sequences of commands, called _____.

4. That some strategies have high memory loads but small amounts to learn, whereas other strategies have just the opposite situation is called the _____ _____ between processing and memory.

5. A procedure in which a processor will alternate work on two or more different programs is called _____.

6. In a dual processor system, unless the tasks done by the two processors are totally different, a _____ is needed to resolve conflicts.

7. An altered state in which the Supervisor is given something irrelevant to do is called _____. The irrelevant task that is given is _____.

8. A mental state in which you believe that what you are seeing comes from memory is _____.

9. By placing electrodes on the scalp, one can measure the overall electrical activity of the cortex. The waves obtained, called _____, appear to reflect a large proportion of the neurons in the cortex firing in synchrony.

10. The state of sleep characterized by rapid eye movements is called the _____ state. Most _____ appear to occur during these times.

1. automated; 2. processing unit, memory, IO mechanisms; 3. processing unit, programs; 4. trade-off; 5. time sharing; 6. supervisor; 7. meditation, repeating a mantra; 8. deja vu; 9. alpha waves; 10. REM, dreams

---

INTRODUCTION

One strategy for understanding complex behavior is to draw an analogy between the object of study and some other model or object that is much better known. Thus, this chapter makes extensive use of a comparison of the human brain to a computer. Terms such as *processing unit, supervisor, modifiable programs,* and *interrupts* help provide an overall pattern to complex behavior. It is important to remember that this approach is only as useful as the analogy is valid. In other words, the point of comparing the human brain to a computer is <u>not</u> to explain human behavior. Rather, it provides a way to organize our experimental knowledge, and to suggest new ways of testing the patterns we see.

A second strategy is based upon the fact that information processing systems have some general properties that hold true--no matter what the elements are made out of, whether neurons, flip-flop switches, or even little men running around inside of the head. Thus, for example, any such system, including the human brain, needs a controlling executive to resolve conflicts between interacting parts, and a way of stopping or interrupting ongoing processes should something important occur outside the organism. These properties can then be applied specifically to the human brain.

Chapter 16 of HIP and this study guide will utilize these approaches in examining processes underlying problem solving strategies, learning, and other conscious mental activity.

COMPUTER PROGRAMS

In order to understand fully the human-brain-as-computer analogy, and especially the interpretation of human thinking as the execution of programs, it is very useful to have worked with computer programs and even to have written a few. For those of you who have had some computer programming, this next section should be fairly easy, although the approach may be different from what you are used to. For those of you who have not, computer programming is not nearly as foreboding as it might seem, and can even be fun.

Let's consider a simple computer analogy of how people might recognize objects in the external world. Given an object, suppose your senses analyzed it, perhaps using the feature detectors developed in Chapter 6 of HIP. After your senses have processed the image of this object, the rest of your brain is presented with a list of features of the object, such as its color, texture, size, and shape. In order to identify an object as being of a particular kind or species, such as a man or zebra or mountain or chair, your brain runs a *program,* which takes that list of features and analyzes it to see whether it has the appropriate ones.

What would a program be like that could do this task? A program can be considered to be a list of *commands* that are usually executed in order one after another. Thus our question could be asked another way: What commands do we need to carry out the task? Surely one useful command would be one in charge of finding a particular feature on a list. Let's assume we had such a command, like

    FIND GR

where GR stands for "green." If we apply this command to a list such as

    fuzzy

    green

    round

then it would notice that there was the feature "green" on the list.

Similar commands could be used to find any other feature; in fact, only the second word would have to be changed. In computer terms, there is actually only one command, FIND, which has an *argument* that tells it what it should be looking for.

To be of any use, this command has to have a way of communicating with other commands, to tell them whether it found the feature it was looking for or not. Suppose that there is a central message box (called MBOX) into which it can drop the message SUCCESS if it finds the feature and FAIL otherwise.

With this one command and by varying the arguments we have almost enough to identify whether an object with some feature list belongs to a particular species. If some species consists of a certain set of features, we check to see whether each of the features is there using FIND commands, and if they are all there, then we have identified the object. But how could we determine whether each of the FIND commands has

1   succeeded? _____

_____

_____   Thus we need a command which checks the message box:

    IF NOFAIL THEN SAY __ __ __ __ __ OTHERWISE SAY NOMATCH.

In the blank we would put the name of the species to be identified. To paraphrase this command: Check to see whether there are any FAIL's in the message box. If not, then each of the FIND commands must have put a SUCCESS into the message box, and the (until now) unidentified object has all the same features as our species. Therefore, identify the feature list with the name of the species. Otherwise, there is at least one FAIL in the message box, and the command says NOMATCH between the feature lists, i.e., the object is not of the species that this program can identify.

You are visiting Venus and have been exploring the countryside for a few days now. From the travel guides and what you have seen you have some idea of what the things you encounter are called. For example, you are fairly sure now that anything that is red, fur-covered and square is a Venusian dog. Some of the features you have noticed in other objects are:

red (RD)	round (RN)
blue (BL)	square (SQ)
brown (BR)	irregular-shaped (IR)
green (GR)	long (LN)
yellow (YL)	
fuzzy (FZ)	1 leg (L1)
fur-covered (FR)	2 legs (L2), etc.
smooth (SM)	1 arm (AR1)
hard (HD)	1 antenna (AN1)

You have noticed that, in general, Venusian rocks are blue, round, and hard. A program that would test whether an object (represented by its feature list) is a Venusian rock would be:

PROGRAM: Venusian Rock

```
10   FIND BL
20   FIND RN
30   FIND HD
40   IF NOFAIL THEN SAY ROCK OTHERWISE SAY NOMATCH
```

Notice that each of the commands are numbered. Although this is unnecessary now, it will be very important later when we begin to modify programs.

You have also noticed that the Venusians themselves tend to be red, furry, have one leg and four arms. On the next page write a program which will recognize Venusian people. Remember to title it and number the commands.

2

Easy, right? Unfortunately, the real world doesn't let everything be so simple.
Often a species doesn't necessarily have to have a particular feature--it may perhaps
have one of several. For example, flowers can be red, blue, yellow, etc. (or even
combinations, but we won't consider this). Suppose Venusian people could be either
red or green in addition to the other features. How could you write one program to
recognize either type? You'll need other commands. One is:

    CLEAR MBOX

which clears and throws away all messages in the central message box. The other
two are:

    IF NOFAIL THEN GO ON OTHERWISE SAY NOMATCH

    IF NOFAIL THEN SAY __ __ __ __ __ OTHERWISE GO ON

The first of these commands will either go on to the next command or else say NOMATCH
and stop. The second command will say what you put in the blank and then stop, or else
say nothing and go on to the next command. Try writing this program. Remember,
Venusians can be red or green but not both.

3

    We have been assuming so far that the programs that you have been writing are
already "inside" of your head, i.e., you can already recognize these objects. How
might you have acquired these programs in the first place? And suppose your programs

were not entirely accurate--how might you go about changing the program to be correct?
Suppose for example that you have miscounted the number of arms on Venusian people,
that there are actually five instead of four arms. We need a command that locates
a particular statement or command in a program and tells us where it is, and
another command that allows us to modify commands in a program. The following
command does the first job:

    LOCATE AR4

This command will find the statement in your program that uses the feature AR4,
which was probably "30 FIND AR4," and places the number of the command in the
message box, in this case, "30." Just as with the FIND command, you can vary the
argument in the LOCATE command to be any word in a program.

    The second command:

    CHANGE AR4 AR5

takes the statement number that you have just placed in the message box, goes to that
statement in the program, and changes the AR4 to AR5. Using these two commands, a
program that would fix the Venusian-Person-recognizing program would be:

    PROGRAM: Fix Person Program

    10   CLEAR MBOX

    20   LOCATE AR4

    30   CHANGE AR4 TO AR5

    You may have noticed that the command LOCATE has very much the same function as
FIND, for the first one looks for a feature in a list of features while the second
looks for a word in a list of commands (i.e., a program). In computer terms, any
command "operates" on "data"; for example, the data the FIND command operates on is
the list of features, whereas LOCATE's data are the words in a list of commands. But
LOCATE itself is also a command: In fact, LOCATE could operate on a program with
itself in it. Having commands that can treat other commands like data is crucial to
a system that is ever going to learn or change. It is worthwhile to consider exactly
why for a moment--from what you know about why LOCATE and CHANGE were created in the
4   first place, can you explain why such commands are necessary? _____

_____

_____

_____

_____

    You have discovered to your dismay that what you thought were Venusian rocks were
actually Venusian turtles, and that the rocks are actually brown, fuzzy, and round.

Write a program to fix up the Rock-recognizing program. Remember that the CHANGE command only works if there is exactly one number in the message box:

5

   There are a few other interesting points concerning this method for recognizing objects. Suppose one species has all of the features of another species and in addition has one more? For example, suppose Venusian mushrooms are brown, fuzzy, and round, but also have one antenna. Given that you have recognizers for both

6   these species, what problem would occur? _____

_____

_____

It would be possible to get around this problem by using the notion of having no features left over in the feature list to be recognized. One needs to use the command:

     DELETE YL

which will delete a feature (in this case, "yellow") from a feature list. Also:

     IF EMPTYLIST THEN SAY _ _ _ _ OTHERWISE SAY NOMATCH

which checks to see whether a list has any features remaining on it. Using these commands (with other arguments) and other commands you know, try writing a Rock-recognizer program which identifies only rocks, and no mushrooms, as rocks:

7

Instead of using the above method, one might purposefully notice that a particular object does not have an antenna and therefore can't be a mushroom. This use of *negative features*, or checking to make sure that an important feature is not there (as with an antenna in the case of a rock versus a mushroom) provides an alternative solution to the above problem. Can you write a Rock-Recognizer program using this method instead?

8

Finally, back in Chapter 7 of HIP the "specialist demon" model of pattern recognition was discussed. In a sense, this recognizer model and that model are quite similar. Each of the FIND commands is like a demon that searches for a particular feature and announces when it finds it. One difference is that here each demon does not start working until the last demon is done, whereas in the

9   specialist demon model _____

What in this computer model corresponds to the "blackboard" in that model?

10   _____

FROG VERSUS CAT

At the beginning of Chapter 6 of HIP the work of Lettvin, Matunara, McCulloch, and Pitts was discussed, concerning the first thorough exploration of the visual receptive fields of neurons in the frog. It was found that there were only four or five different types, and that each responded only to a very specific stimulus. For example, the "bug detector" neurons responded only to small, dark, concave moving objects. It was as though the important object-recognizing programs were already "wired-in" to the ganglia. On the other hand, when Hubel and Wiesel did a

similar study of receptive fields in a cat, they found that ganglia tested at the
same level as in the frog (at the LGN) had receptive fields resembling much more
basic features--concentric on-center, off-surround cells or simple edge detectors.
At higher levels, these simpler receptive fields _perhaps_ combined together to form
more complex feature detectors, such as lines, lines moving in a particular direction,
edges of a specific length, all of which they found in the visual cortex. If we
were to apply a computer analogy much like the one used in the last section, what would

11   the basic feature detectors at the LGN correspond to? _____

What term could be applied to the more complex feature detectors in the

12   visual cortex? _____   Given that the frog's feature detectors can
be compared to wired-in programs, while the cat's feature detection system might
operate like the computer programs in the last section, what advantage might the

13   cat have in coping with new situations? _____

_____

_____

The cat is higher on the evolutionary scale than the frog, and thus its brain
is presumably more like the human brain. This ability of higher evolutionary
animals to adjust their internal information processing system to better deal with
the outside world has been interpreted as one of the major signs, and even as a
definition of intelligence.

TIME SHARING

You have been asked to compute mentally the answer to the following problem:

$$9643$$
$$\times\ 757$$

At the same time you have been asked to count mentally the number of stoplights one
would pass through taking the shortest route by car going from the roller coaster
on Coney Island to the corner in front of Macy's in Manhattan (you have lived in
New York City for most of your life). Assume you are being paid enough to make such
a simultaneous task worthwhile. In addition you have been warned that you may be
tested at any point during the time you are solving, on your progress up to that
point in either task. Thus you have decided that the only way to survive is to
work a little while on one problem, then switch to the other and work a while, then

14   switch back, etc. In computer terms, what is this procedure called? _____

_____.

15   Unfortunately, this strategy has a problem, which is _____

_____

What information would one have to store in switching from the multiplication problem

16   to the stoplight problem? _____

_____ What two facts would one have to store in

17   switching back? (i) _____

18   (ii) _____

19   Which switch do you think would cause the greater problems? _____

_____ Why would these tasks be easier if one were

20   allowed to use paper? _____

_____

_____ This is one area in which the

human-brain-as-computer analogy is not particularly good, for whereas a major

problem in human thinking and problem solving is storing intermediate results (why?

21   _____

_____

_____), computers generally have large memories into which

results can be stored and retrieved without problem. However, this is only a

matter of degree, for if there is enough time sharing, computers will also be much

slowed by the time taken to store and retrieve intermediate results.

MORE THAN ONE COOK....

     One way that the dilemma outlined in the preceding section could be solved would

be if a different processor could work on each of the tasks simultaneously. What

22   term is used for this? _____ Why is it unlikely

that such a solution would work in humans for these two tasks? (Hint: How are the

23   two tasks related?) _____

_____

_____

     There are some tasks that humans seem capable of performing simultaneously,

though. Choose either of the tasks above and try to think of another task that could

24   be performed at the same time. _____

_____

     In both humans and computers, even in cases where two or more processes can

operate simultaneously, several serious problems can arise. One major type can occur

when both processes are using the same memory and changing information in that memory

In this case it is possible for one process to erase or modify some piece of
data in the memory which the other process was about ready to use and was counting
on not being changed. For example, if two processes both used the commands introduced
in the first section, two of these commands could cause just that problem. Which

25 two? (*i*)_____ (*ii*)_____

26   Another possible problem occurs quite strikingly in human thought. One has a
list of words--all names of colors--printed in different colors of ink. Sometimes
the color names agree with the color of ink they are printed in and sometimes they
disagree. You are asked to say just the colors of the inks going down the list.
People find this task very difficult, often saying the color name instead of the
ink color when the two disagree. This phenomenon is called the "Stroop effect"
(as described in Chapter 11 of HIP). What are the two simultaneous processes here?

27 (*i*)_____

28 (*ii*)_____
The problem in the last paragraph occurs when two processes try to use the same data.

29 How would you describe the problem underlying the Stroop effect? _____

_____

_____

_____

30 This problem is one of the major reasons given in HIP for needing a _____
around to resolve conflicting outputs. Unfortunately, in the case of the Stroop
effect, this mechanism seems unable to suppress the unwanted output.

LEFT AND RIGHT

    Dr. James Jamison is studying the differential abilities of the right and left
hemispheres of the human brain and wants to run an experiment giving evidence that
further supports differential abilities. He has two auditory tasks: the first one
is either a low tone followed by a high tone (ascending) or vice versa (descending).
A subject must press one button if the tone pair is ascending and another button
otherwise. Reaction times are taken on how fast the subject decides and presses a
button. In the second task a list of nouns and verbs mixed together are presented
one at a time, and the subject must press one button if the current word is a noun
and another if verb. Again reaction times are taken. It is known that one of
these tasks favors the left hemisphere and the other the right hemisphere in right-

31 handed people. Which one favors which? _____

_____ Dr. Jamison needs a way
of testing each of the hemispheres separately on each of the tasks. So he uses
earphones and sends a single task to only one ear for any particular set of trials.
32   Why does this procedure tend to test each hemisphere separately? _____

_____ Thus he has four tasks for which he runs a set of trials for
each subject, collecting reaction times for each task. Which pairs of these reaction
33   times will he compare? _____

_____

34   What results do you predict should happen? _____

_____

     Dr. Jamison unfortunately finds no differences. That is, each ear is equally
fast at each task. There is something he didn't do, which is crucial to an
35   experiment like this succeeding. What did he need to do? _____

_____ Why is this necessary? (Hint: What is
36   the communication link between the two hemispheres? _____)
37   _____

_____

     Suppose Dr. Jamison had used patients who had their corpus callosa cut as subjects
in the same experiment that he had just run. What do you think might have happened?
38   _____

_____ Why were the results the
39   same or why were they different? _____

_____

WHAT'S IN CONTROL?

     The *supervisor* in an information processing system can let its next action be
determined by various sources of information. First, its actions can be dependent
upon what input it receives from the outside world, in which case it is under
40   _____. Or, it can decide to run one of the
procedures it has in memory, perhaps like the ones considered in the first section.
During the time the system is moving through the list of commands (such as a FIND

command), executing them one after another, the supervisor has given up the reins

41 and the system is under _____. It is possible for the supervisor to get back control before the program is done, through the use of an

42 _____. Finally, the supervisor can let its actions be determined by one of a set of general goals which are stored in memory; then the

43 system is under _____. Since in this last case the supervisor itself is acting or "in charge," one might also call this last condition "supervisor-driven" control.

In most situations the human information processing system encounters, there are elements of all three types of control at some time during the situation, but it can sometimes be said that control is primarily of one type. A few such events are described below. Give the primary source of control for each:

A. You are considering various alternatives after graduation from college.

44 _____

45 B. You are running 1500 meters as part of a workout. _____

C. You have match point and an easy lob to put away in a tennis match against an opponent you have been itching to beat for the past year. You "choke" and hit

46 the lob out by 10 feet. _____

47 D. You are mentally computing the answer to 37 times 23. _____

_____

E. Later in the same tennis match, your opponent is at the net waiting for the same crosscourt shot that you have made the past six opportunities. You decide to

48 hit the ball down the line to pass him. _____

F. You are asleep and somebody calls your name softly and it wakes you.

49 _____

50 G. You are computing the answer to 6 times 4. _____

H. You are attempting to reach a meditative state using a mantra. You are having

51 trouble relaxing and hence are unable to change mental states. _____

I. You are attempting to learn how to juggle, remembering to watch until one

52 ball is at the peak of its arc before tossing another ball. _____

J. You are juggling and talking to a friend at the same time. The juggling is

53 under _____. Your conversation is under _____

54 _____ .

16 Social interactions

PRETEST

    1. The term for a mental representation of an average or typical member of some class (of people, social situations, or whatever) is _____ .

    2. A special kind of representation of typical sequences of events in social situations is called a _____ .

    3. Causes that are perceived to be due to the situation are called *situational* or _____ *causes*.

    4. Causes that are perceived to be due to an actor in the situation are called personality traits or _____ *causes*.

    5. The theory of how people assign causal responsibility for events or situations is called _____ *theory* .

    6. When information about a person is acquired in the form of a series of adjectives descriptive of that person's personality, does the information from successive adjectives seem to be *averaged* or *added*? _____

    7. When information about personality traits is acquired through a list of adjectives, words from which portion of the list seem to contribute <u>least</u> to one's overall impression of the person described? _____

    8. In transactional analysis theory, if I speak to you in an adult ego state, expecting an adult response, and you instead respond in a parent role, then a _____ transaction has occurred.

    9. How likely are subjects to change their reports of a fairly simple visual detection on the basis of the conflicting perceptions reported by others? _____

    10. Will subjects in a psychological experiment risk killing other subjects merely because they are told that the experiment must continue? _____

*1. prototype (or schema or stereotype); 2. script; 3. conditional or external or
extrinsic or situation-specific; 4. dispositional or internal or intrinsic or
person-specific; 5. attribution; 6. averaged; 7. the middle; 8. crossed; 9.
very likely (75% of subjects do); 10. yes, many will.*

INTRODUCTION

The topic matter of this chapter is how people understand social interactions.
The core concept which underlies most of the ideas presented in Chapter 16 of HIP is
that people understand social interactions by means of the *models* they have previously
constructed. People have models for prototypical behavior in certain types of
situations. They also have models for how certain people and certain types of people
behave in general. This latter kind of model includes the model each person has of
his or her own behavior and motivations. Topics of interest to us are the nature
of these models, how they are used, and how they are acquired in the first place.

PROTOTYPES

Let us begin by considering models or prototypes for types of people. The
informal definitions that follow are meant to represent someone's concepts for the
meanings of the terms "widow," "husband," and "married." These definitions are
English-language versions of the mental definitions which this person has associated
with the primary nodes WIDOW, HUSBAND, and MARRIED.

WIDOW: a woman whose husband has died

HUSBAND: a man to whom a woman is married

MARRIED: descriptive of the state that holds between a man and a woman who
have entered into a one-to-one contractual relationship. The
relationship is typically voluntary and has advantages for both
participants. The duration of the relationship is until the death
of one participant or until divorce.

Let's take the sum of these definitions as constituting a portion of the meaning of
the WIDOW prototype. (HUSBAND and MARRIED are included because the meaning of the
WIDOW prototype includes these concepts.) Following are four examples of uses of
the term "widow" (A-D), each of which is in some sense odd because it violates an
aspect of the WIDOW prototype.

A. *Poor Inge is now a widow. Fortunately, however, only one of her husbands was killed in the crash.*

B. *Poor Princess Juanita is now a widow, and she's only 7 years old.*

C. *Poor Diana is now a widow. She was married 1 minute, and then a piece of the church ceiling fell on the groom.*

D. *Poor Maxine is now a widow. Her husband Herbert, whom she divorced sixteen years ago, passed away yesterday.*

1 What aspect of the WIDOW prototype is violated in A? _____

_____

2 What aspect of the WIDOW prototype is violated in B? _____

_____

3 What aspect of the WIDOW prototype is violated in C? _____

_____

4 What aspect of the WIDOW prototype is violated in D? _____

_____

Are any of the above aspects of the WIDOW prototype not made explicit by the

5 definitions of WIDOW, HUSBAND, and MARRIED? _____ If so,

which? How could the definitions be improved? _____

_____

People have prototypes for many classes of people, including thereotypical views of national, racial, and ethnic groups. These prototypes play a role in people's perceptions of individual members of these groups. Suppose, for example, that, as a result of reading science fiction novels or comic books, people have a certain stereotypical view of Martians. Naturally this concept of Martians can be represented in the memory with the sort of structural descriptions introduced in Chapter 10 of HIP. Figure 16.1 shows such a representation. In a sentence or two, describe

6 this prototype of Martians. _____

_____

_____

One day a group of people having a picnic are surprised to see a large silver-colored globe descend from the sky into their midst. From it emerges a 3-foot tall yellowish-green humanoid creature, who says in a pleasant alto voice, "After coming all the way from Mars, I could sure use a beer. Let me take a liter." The people are frozen in astonishment, and the Martian is impatient, so it shrugs, jumps back in the space ship, and flies away.

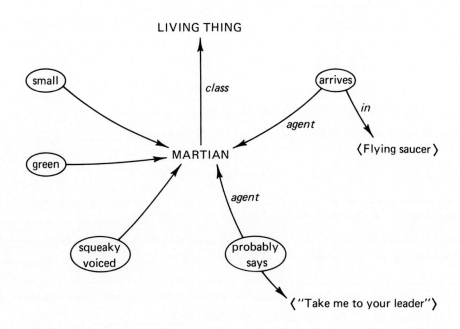

Figure 16.1

Which aspects of the prototype shown in Figure 16.1 were a good match for the

7   actual facts about this Martian? _____

When they were questioned later by the authorities, many of the picnickers are

discovered to have been so stunned by the appearance of the Martian that they

completely failed to process the first sentence that it spoke. These people often

misheard the second sentence. What you do think they were most likely to hear it as?

8   _____ Why? _____

_____

Many people did not report the shape of the space ship as completely spherical. How

9   are they likely to report it? _____

What sort of errors are people most likely to make when describing the Martian's

10   voice? _____

One advantage to having prototypes is that they help us to process new instances

of general classes. When we are busy perceiving many things, we don't have resources

(time) to check every detail of each object to be perceived. It is convenient to

assume that most of the details of the prototype are present in the instance being

perceived, and to avoid checking every detail. Is this role of prototypes in
perception an example of data-driven processing or of conceptually driven

11 processing?_____ Observers who make this sort of
use of prototypes in perceptual processing will find that, when they later try to
remember the instance, the details of the instance that came from the prototype in
memory are indistinguishable from the details that were completely determined by the
incoming sensory information. In view of the Martian example just discussed, how can

12 this use of prototypes sometimes be a disadvantage?_____

_____

   Racial, national, and religious stereotypes can be maintained for similar reasons.
That is, because the stereotype exists, features of individual members of the racial,
national, or religious group are not in accord with the stereotype may never be
noticed. Yet the presence of some of these features in certain other individual
members of these groups is quite likely to be noticed, since they are expected.

13 Give an example of this sort of robustness in some stereotype. _____

_____

STEREOTYPED INTERACTIONS

   The previous section discussed prototypes for classes of people. In this section
we will deal with prototypes for situations. People seem to have models for certain
types of common occurring social interactions. We call these models situation-
schemas or *scripts*. A very simple type of script is the one for the greeting ritual.

   Person 1 and Person 2 GREET each other:
   1: *Hi.*
   2. *Hi, how are you?*
   1. *Fine, you?*
   2. *Fine.*

Scripts like this one consist only of form. No content or purpose are included, and
the interaction is almost completely prescribed in every detail.

   Many other highly constrained social interactions can be represented by simple
scripts. Some of these situations involve more content, despite the constraints on
the form of the interactions. One example of constrained social interaction is game
playing. In a game like Monopoly, for example, the goals of the players are clearly
set out and are the same for all. There are also fixed rules which determine, to a
large extent, the nature and sequence of actions possible in the situation. Give

14   another example of this sort of constrained situation. _____

_____

     Other, less highly constrained types of situations can also be represented by
scripts. Consider the form of a script for dining at a restaurant. The actors in
such a script are the one(s) eating out and the waiter. Use the space below to
list the typical sequence of actions involved in the restaurant-dining situation.

15

     Does your script for restaurant-dining include information about what the customer
16   is likely to do if the service is poor? _____ Does it include information
     about how the customer can obtain the check? _____What can you say about the
     relative size and complexity of a complete restaurant script as compared with a
17   complete greeting script? _____
     A very high-level, all-inclusive sort of script is the one which the theory of
transactional analysis (TA) proposes. In this script, the actors in a social interaction can each assume one of three roles. What are the names of these three roles?
18   _____ Consider a situation in which
     one person approaches another to ask for help in solving some problem. If the one who
     is asking for help has assumed an adult role, what are his or her goals in the inter-
19   action? _____
     If the one asking for help has assumed a child role, what are his or her goals? ____

_____

Consider the two conversations below

CONVERSATION A:

Speaker 1: *I seem to be having some trouble with my simulation of auditory Fourier analysis, Marlene. I wonder if you could help me.*

Speaker 2: *There, there, Samson. Don't you worry about it. I think you're very smart. I bet it'll all seem better in the morning.*

CONVERSATION B:

Speaker 1: *I think I'm just too stupid to be alive. I'll never understand this dumb Fourier analysis stuff, Marlene.*

Speaker 2: *OK, let's see what the problem is. Explain what you've done so far.*

20 In Conversation A, what role (in TA terms) has Speaker 1 assumed? _____
What role is Speaker 2 using in this conversation? _____ In Conversation
21 B, what role has Speaker 1 adopted? _____ What role does Speaker 2
play here? _____ . Is either or both of these two conversations
22 an example of a *crossed transaction*?_____ What is a *complementary*
23 *transaction*? _____

ATTRIBUTING CAUSES

In understanding social interactions, we make use of schemata for *people* (both schemata for particular individuals and schemata for types of people) and of schemata for *situations*. Suppose you have a landlord who, you believe, is stingy and acquisitive, but who is otherwise a nice person. One night you play Monopoly with your landlord, who plays very aggressively and wins by a large margin. To what will you attribute the outcome of the game if you use a <u>person</u>-based schema?

24 _____ If you use a <u>situation</u>-based
25 schema? _____

When people act in accordance with our expectations for normal behavior in a given situation, do we usually attribute their actions to the people or to the situation?

26 _____ What if their acts are inappropriate? _____

_____

Just as we find it necessary to attribute the causes of the behavior of others, so we apparently also feel a need to attribute causes to our own behavior. When our behavior is sensible and when it has good outcomes for ourselves or for others, are we more likely to attribute the behavior to the person (ourselves) or to the

27   situation? _____ When our behavior is less rational and shows

neither altruism nor enlightened self-interest, are we more likely to attribute it

28   to the person or the situation? _____

Suppose you are a psychology experimenter who is running a very dull list learning
experiment. The experiment will continue for some weeks, during which time you must
be able to keep recruiting new subjects. Naturally, you would like your subjects
from today's experiment not to discourage other subjects from participating next
week. You decide the best way to do this would be to trick them into thinking that
the experiment really wasn't so bad, after all. At the end of each experimental
session, you ask them to "tell the subject waiting in the next room that the experiment was really pretty interesting. I really need an alert subject, so I'll pay you
for doing this." (The "subject" waiting in the next room is really just another
experimenter helping you out.) If you want the real subject, whom you are attempting
to bribe, to decide later that the experiment was interesting, should you offer him

29   or her 25¢ or $10.00 to tell the lie? _____ Explain why, in light of your

answer to 28. _____

_____

_____

SOCIAL INFLUENCE

This chapter has centered on the notion that people make use of prototypes to
understand social interactions. One problem we have not fully addressed is how
people decide which prototypes or schemata are appropriate in particular interactions.
In those cases in which one must make use of a schema for a particular person, we
may assume it is usually not too difficult to decide which schema is appropriate--
we simply look to see who is involved. In those cases which call for a situation
schema as an aid to understanding what is going on, the choice of the appropriate
schema may not be so straightforward. Under conditions in which the choice of
situation schemata is difficult, a natural solution is to look about and try to
discover how other observers of the interaction are interpreting it. That is, one
can try to figure out what situation schema has been activated by others as an aid
to understanding what is going on.

Here is an example of what these principles mean. Let us suppose that an experimenter wants to do an experiment on whether people will try to stop a theft. Two
different conditions of the experiment are run.

CONDITION A:
     The experimenter goes to a beach with only two or three other people
on it. She selects one of these people as her subject by putting her beach
towel 10 or 15 feet away from his or hers. A few minutes later she walks a
short distance away, out of sight, leaving a transistor radio on her blanket.
At this point, a confederate of the experimenter appears on the scene. The
confederate approaches the blanket, looks around, and then picks up the radio
and begins to walk off with it.

CONDITION B:
     The experimenter goes to a beach with thousands of people on it. She
selects several people as her subjects by putting her beach towel in a
location about 10 or 15 feet away from each of them. As in Condition A,
she then leaves her radio, and a confederate comes and picks it up.

     Under which condition do you think subjects are more likely to question the

30   confederate about his actions? _____ Imagine that you are one of

the subjects in Condition B. What kinds of things would you take into consideration

when you were trying to decide what to do after seeing the confederate pick up the

31   radio? _____

_____

Give an example of a schema that might apply to this situation, which would make

32   intervention on your part inappropriate. _____

_____

     Consider a new condition for this experiment.

CONDITION C:
     This is very similar to Condition B, except that the experimenter selects
one of the people near her on the crowded beach as a subject. She asks this
person, I'll be gone for a couple of minutes. Could you watch my radio?"
If the subject consents, she leaves, as in the other conditions, and the
confederate again tries to take the radio.

     Do you think that subjects are more likely to intervene in this condition than

33   in Condition B? _____ Explain why in terms of the problem of finding the

appropriate situation-schema for interpreting events. _____

_____

People seem to use the behavior of others as a cue to the nature of a situation.

34   Under what circumstances is "bystander apathy" most likely? _____

_____

     In experimental psychology, there are many ethical issues in the use of human

subjects. Do you think that any ethical issues are raised by the experiments just

35   discussed? _____ In particular, do you think it is ethical to make use of

people as psychological subjects without obtaining their permission? _____
If so, under what conditions? If not, why not? _____

_____
_____

WHERE DO PROTOTYPES COME FROM?

     Thus far we have treated prototypes and situation-schemas are preexisting concepts
in memory which could be applied to the interpretation of particular social interactions. In fact, of course, each prototype had to be acquired at some point. Some
prototypes are acquired simply through many exposures to similar social interactions.
Most people probably learn the greeting script in this way. Other schemas are
learned without any personal experiences with events or people that can be understood in terms of those schemas--for example the Martian prototype shown in Figure
16.1. Such schemata are acquired by being told about or by reading about the
persons or situations in question. Some prototypes are acquired through a combination
of description and actual experience. How do you suppose someone acquires the

36   relevant situation-schema for a game, such as Monopoly? _____

_____

    The means by which we may build up a prototype through exposure to instances
of the prototype is discussed briefly in Chapter 10 of HIP, in the subsection called
Generalization. In that section, it was pointed out that if all the people that
someone knows are short and have red hair, then that person may generalize this
information, deciding that it must be a characteristic of the PERSON prototype
that all people are short and have red hair.

    Let's consider some of what must be involved in the other means of acquiring
a prototype--by having it described. In particular, imagine the way in which a
very limited, simple prototype for a particular person might be acquired through a
description. Suppose that a subject is first told that Person X (whose prototype
is being acquired here) is *sincere*. Then the subject learns that Person X is
orderly. Assume that each of these terms (sincere and orderly) carry with them a
large number of inferences. For example, because the subject knows that Person X is
orderly, he or she also assumes that X is likely to be *neat* and *clean* and *uptight*
as well. Let's assume that part of the meaning of "sincere" in the mind of the
subject is "probably extremely likeable," and that part of the meaning of "orderly"
is "probably somewhat likeable." If this is the case, about how likeable is Person

37   X, according to the subject? _____ Did the subject *add*

38   the likeability ratings, or *average* them? _____

Do you think the subject would have found Person X *more* or *less* likeable if he
39   or she first learned that Person X was orderly and then sincere? _____
This difference is called an *order effect*. The order in which information is learned
about a person seems to have an affect on how the information is integrated. There
are two different types of explanations for the difference due to order. According
to the first model, new information is encoded in memory in such a way that it is
40   compatible with prior information. This is called the _____ model.
According to the other theory, more processing resources are allocated to the first
things one learns (and perhaps to the last), and thus accounts for their greater
41   impact on the prototype. This is the _____ model.

BARGAINING

Part of what is happening in a normal bargaining situation is that each participant is trying to build up his schemas for the other. One aspect of the prototype
for the other which a participant tries to understand is what the other's expectations
and goals are in the bargaining situation. The term for a bargainer's expected goal
42   is _____.

This is true only in a prototypical bargaining situation, one in which each
participant has incomplete knowledge of the other's potential profits and losses.
If one participant has such knowledge, a basic premise of the situation-schema of
43   the other is violated. What is that premise? _____

_____

The participant who has such information is capable of adopting an unfair strategy.
44   What is that strategy? _____

_____

Remembering that the other participant does not know that a premise of his
45   bargaining-schema is being violated, explain why the unfair strategy can work. _____

_____

_____

_____

17 Stress and emotion

1. When an individual is under stress, as for example, in a situation of impending danger, he or she may try to escape. If the attempt fails, what is the most likely subsequent response? _____

2. What is the name of the neural subsystem in the midbrain which functions to interact with cognitive processes, monitoring critical processing, and alerting the organism to high-priority signals which need attention? _____

3. Are biochemical responses to stress dependent on the source (physical or psychological) of the stress? _____

4. The first stage of the general adaptation syndrome (the biochemical response to stress) is called _____.

5. What are the chances of reversing the stage of exhaustion (the third stage of the general adaptation syndrome)? _____

6. According to the Juke Box Theory of Emotion, is arousal nonspecific or does it vary according to which of a variety of underlying events instigated it? _____

_____

7. Is it the sympathetic or the parasympathetic nervous system which is responsible for a reaction of tenseness and arousal? _____

8. The technique by which one learns to control some bodily function which is not normally under conscious control (because one is ordinarily not aware of it) is called _____.

9. In the experiment in which subjects were injected with epinephrine, which subjects imitated the emotional models provided by their "partners" (actually confederates of the experimenter)? _____

10. In the model of emotional arousal, are emotions the result of data-driven processing or of conceptually-driven processing? _____

1. to repeat the attempt, harder; 2. the reticular activating system; 3. no; 4.
the alarm reaction; 5. none; 6. nonspecific; 7. sympathetic; 8. biofeedback;
9. those uninformed of the physical effects of the drug; 10. both (or both and
physiological changes)

STRESS

    Stress can result from any of a number of quite different types of inputs to an
organism. Physical injuries or exposure to extremes of temperature can produce
stress. Not being able to cope with a situation can lead to stress. As we saw in
Chapter 16, people have a collection of situation-schemata that they use in interpreting what goes on in the world. When one finds oneself in a situation for which
there is no appropriate schema in memory, stress can result. Give an example of

1   this. _____

_____

Explain how the stress associated with learned helplessness can be attributed to

2   the absence of an appropriate situation-schema. _____

_____

    Subjects in psychological experiments are not ordinarily entirely unaware of the
sorts of things that might happen in this type of situation. They have at least
partial schemata for participation in experiments. What is it about a subject's

3   expectations that makes it difficult to produce stress in the laboratory? _____

_____

If an experimenter claims that an experimental procedure places them in mortal danger,

4   how likely are subjects to believe it?_____ Explain. _____

_____

    Another source of stress can be conflicting sources of information about the
same topic. Remember the experiment in Chapter 16 of HIP in which subjects were
asked to make judgments about the lengths of lines in a situation in which they were
able to hear the judgments made by confederates of the experimenter who were posing
as subjects. What were the conflicting sources of information in this experiment?

5   _____

_____

    Suppose that you have entered a room in a "fun house" at a carnival. Suddenly
you find yourself rising off the floor, apparently falling <u>up</u> toward the skylight

6   in the room. Do you think this situation is likely to produce stress?_____
If so, which of the causes of stress that we have discussed seems to be the most
likely one here? If not, why not? _____

_____

    Another source of stress is the anticipation of a negative result which is beyond
one's control. Having control over a situation is so important to some people that
they would rather follow some course of action which is more risky than another
simply because they feel more in control in the risky situation than in the safer
one. Give an example of two such courses of action, one of which is safer but less

7   under the control of the individual, who therefore prefers it over the other. _____

_____

_____

    Consider the biochemical response to stress. It seems to be controlled by

8   three neural and biochemical centers of the brain. These are _____

_____. The *general*

adaptation syndrome has three stages. Explain what each involves

9   (1) The alarm reaction. _____

          _____

10   (2) The stage of resistance. _____

          _____

11   (3) The stage of exhaustion. _____

          _____

To what extent does the form of this sequence depend on the source of stress (for

12   example, whether it is due to extreme cold, extreme frustration, etc.)? _____

_____

STRESS AND PERFORMANCE

    What effect does stress have on problem solving porcesses? Does it make thinking

13   clearer, or are people under stress more likely to become confused? _____

_____.

    Imagine that you have just devised a short manual for operating a special military
communications system. The operation of the system is moderately complex, but your
instructions, you have discovered, are clear enough that the average military
trainee can successfully operate the device after studying them for only 3 to 4
minutes. This level of performance is consistent within the relaxed conditions of

your office or laboratory, but you are concerned about the soldiers' ability to use your instructions under stressful battle conditions. You therefore perform the following experiment.

One member of a squad (14 men) of troops is picked out "for a soft job this afternoon," and is told that the rest of his squad will have to practice mine-detection in the mine field. He is put in front of a table in an isolated sentry box, which, he is told, is about half a mile from the mine field. On the table are a yellow light, a red button, and a green button. The subject is told, "Whenever the yellow light goes on, we're just checking that you're still alert at your post. Respond immediately by pressing the red button, which will let us know you're still here. Whatever you do, don't press the other button; that will blow up every mine in the field your buddies are working in right now. OK? If anything goes wrong, you can get in touch with us by using that new piece of communications equipment over there in the corner. The instructions on how to operate it are right next to it."

The subject is then left alone at his post. About half an hour later, the yellow light goes on. He dutifully presses the red button and immediately hears the huge roar of an explosion from the direction in which, he has been told, the mine field is located.

14   Do you think the subject will experience stress? _____ Since the subject believes that something has gone very wrong indeed, he wants to use the communications device. Do you think that his performance will be as good under

15   these conditions as in the lab or office? _____ Explain. _____

_____

Suppose the subject had been shown briefly how the device operated just before he was

16   left alone. How well would he do? _____
What if the subject had been drilled in the operation of the device for months, practicing until the use of the device was overlearned? How well would he do under

17   these conditions? _____ What ethical issues do

18   you see in this experiment? _____

_____

One theory has it that stress has a beneficial function for the organism in a stress-producing situation. According to this theory, stress reduces the number of cues to which processing resources are devoted. If this were true, under what

19   conditions would this reduction in attended cues be adaptive or useful? _____

_____

20   Under what conditions would this reduction in cues be maladaptive or harmful? _____

_____

A related theory of stress claims that it works to reduce processing resources available. The reduction of cues is a byproduct of the fact that the physical symptoms of stress demands attentional resources which could better be applied to external stimuli, according to this theory.

A frequently observed aspect of performance under stress is the tendency of many organisms to repeat and intensify efforts which their experience has already shown to be ineffective. Explain these results in terms of the theories just presented.

21   _____

_____

Because of the performance decrements which are attendant on stress, there are many circumstances in which society wants to place safeguards on the direction which behavior can take under stress. There are two general ways in which safeguards can be implemented in situations where behavior under stress could have important or dangerous consequences: either the environment can be designed to reduce the hazardous effects on behavior or the person who may be placed in a stressful situation can be thoroughly trained on how to behave in that situation. Environmental safeguards usually take advantage of the most likely responses of individuals to a stress-producing situation. Give an example of this type of

22   safeguard. _____

What role does overlearning have in safeguarding individuals from performance

23   decrements when under stress? _____

_____ Give examples of

professions other than acting and music which call for overlearning to avoid such

24   decrements in performance. _____

THE RETICULAR ACTIVATING SYSTEM (R.A.S.)

Apparently it is the function of the reticular activating system to control the deployment of cognitive and attentional resources to stimuli in need of processing. Are the R.A.S.'s neural connections spread out or confined to local areas of the

25   midbrain? _____ If electrical activity is applied to the

R.A.S. at the same time that an incoming stimulus is being processed, is the

26   response of the R.A.S. boosted or depressed? _____

The lower part of the R.A.S. is apparently responsible for maintaining a level of background activity. The upper part of the R.A.S. is called the *diffuse thalamic*

27   *projection system.* What is its apparent function? _____

_____

_____

INTERPRETING EMOTIONAL AROUSAL

      Does the basic physiological evidence suggest that at the <u>physical</u> level there

28   are one, two, or more types of emotion? _____ What physical symptoms accompany

29   the activation of the sympathetic nervous system? _____

_____

What are the symptoms of the activation of the parasympathetic nervous system?

30   _____

_____

      For the time being, let's ignore the parasympathetic nervous system and the

emotions which might be associated with its activation. Suppose that comprehensive

measurements show that there are some physical differences between anger and fright,

both of which are associated with the activation of the sympathetic nervous system.

For example, the first emotion might result in a clenched jaw, while the second

could cause trembling. Is it possible that these responses might be learned, and

31   thus be directed by higher, cognitive processes? _____ Explain. _____

_____

_____

      In the experiment by Schachter and Singer, described in Chapter 17 of HIP, subjects

were injected with epinephrine. Which nervous system does epinephrine activate?

32   _____ Of those subjects who were in-

formed what their physical symptoms would be as a result of the injection of the

33   drug, what did those who were placed in the Euphoric condition do? _____

_____ What about those in the

Anger condition? _____

Of those subjects who were <u>uninformed</u> of the physical effects of the drug, what

34   happened to those in the Euphoric condition? _____

_____Those in the Anger condition? _____

_____Explain the significance of these results. _____

_____

_____

Answers

CHAPTER 1

1   the five cardboard sheets

2   the groups of receptors on the retina in the shapes of the patterns

3   the black shapes printed on white paper

6   all patterns are matched simultaneously

7   Correct patterns which don't match the template exactly in size are not recognized.

8   Correct patterns which are not in the same orientation as the template will not be recognized.

10   patterns must be in the correct location on the retina to match the templates

14   The number of templates which would need to be kept for different variations of each pattern would be enormous.

18   With some letters a partial set of their features is enough to distinguish them from other letters.

19   TIE, TEE, TOE

20   We assume the presented word was English.

21   We assume the word had 3 letters.

22   One might have higher a priori expectations for a very common word than a less common one.

23   We expect the phrase to make sense; thus conceptually driven processing will even rule out some 3-letter words, e.g. TOE or TIE.

31   that the pattern is an English word, that it contains 3 letters

32   that the word makes sense in context

33   Figure 1-14 or 1-15 of HIP

34   red light receptors, green light receptors, white background will appear greenish

35   downward motion receptors, upward motion receptors, a textured background (such as a cliff) will appear to move upwards

36   vertical yellow stripe detectors, vertical blue stripe detectors, the white stripes in a vertical black and white stripe pattern will look blue

37   blue light receptors, yellow light receptors, white background will appear yellow

38   horizontal upward-moving green stripe detectors,

horizontal upward-moving red stripe detectors,

the white stripes of horizontal black and white stripes moving upward will appear
red

39   inward motion (or contracting spiral) detectors, outward motion detectors, textured
background will appear to expand

40   vertical green stripe detectors, vertical red stripe detectors, the white stripes of
vertical black and white stripes will appear red

41   Equal brightnesses of complementary colors will appear white since the antagonistic
systems will respond equally.

42   The green patch will appear greener (or more "saturated") than before.

43   The combination of two complementary colors is white, of two opposite motions is no
motion. But what can be the combination of horizontal and vertical?

44   *vertical* black and white lines would appear red

CHAPTER 2

1   candela/meter^2

2 10^{11} (100 billion times longer)

3   0 (Figure 2-2 is long enough)

4   -1, 0, 10, 20, 30, 40, 50, 60, 70, 80, 90, 100, 110, 120.

5   cornea

6   aquaeous humor

7   pupil

8   lens

9   vitreous humor

10   fovea

11   optic nerve

12   the cornea; the lens

13   chromatic aberration, spherical aberration, deterioration of lens with age (loss
of flexibility)

14   120

15   No; pupil change accounts for only 12 of the 120 dB range

16   Eyes point toward same target; extrinsic eye muscles

17   Changing thickness of lens; intrinsic eye muscles

18   visual purple

19   Turns yellow (retinene), then white or colorless (Vitamin A)

20   Different extents

21   Retinene is the first biproduct of the bleaching of rhodopsin; Vitamin A is the
       biproduct of more extreme bleaching. Rhodopsin can be regenerated from either.

22   The eye would be very much less sensitive.

	A	B
23		x
24	x	
25	x	
26		x
27	x	x
28		x
29	x	x
30		x
31	x	

32   bipolar cells; ganglion cells

33   amacrine cells; horizontal cells

34   ganglion

35   at the retina

36   there are no receptor cells at the point where the optic nerve and associated
       blood vessels leaves/enters the eye.

37   ganglion cells

38   ganglion cells

39   left; left

40   left

41   saccades

42   ballistic

43   Useful to successively apply the most powerful analytic portion of the retina to
       those portions of the scene which require analysis.

44   superior colliculus

45   lateral geniculate nucleus

46   confirm

47   No, some information must flow between the pattern analysis system (C and D) and
       the spatial location system (A and B).

CHAPTER 3

2   Mach band

3   **Yes**; conditions of brightness contrast

4   Give it a black border

5   Wyen the object is surrounded by a darker surround--get brightness contrast

6   brightness contrast

7   it appears darker than the other objects

8   put a stick behind the upright object

9   The patient with Curve 1 may not have any rod vision.
     The patient with Curve 2 may not have any cone vision.

10   The Curve 1 patient may have excellent color vision. Curve 2, none at all.

11   Curve 1 - red; Curve 2 - blue

12   Curve 1 - fovea; Curve 2 - periphery (or peripheral to fovea, anyway)

13   Rod vision is activated at dusk; rods more sensitive to shorter wavelengths than
     cones.

14   Both involve shift from cone to rod sensitivity with decreasing illumination.

15   Subjects are ordinarily "adapted" to bright light first. In this case, the dim
     room light permitted partial restoration of cone pigment.

16   As a series of "stills." Like a moving scene illuminated by a flashing strobe
     light.

17   15 to 50 times as many

18   Reduce intensity

19   Flash each frame several times

20   about 580 nm

21   yes; no

22   A fully saturated green of about 510 nm

23   highest B intermediate A lowest C

24   highest C intermediate A lowest B

25   induced color contrast

26   Use a green border for the red test patch, and a red border for the green test patch.

27   Give it a blue border.

28   He has red-green colorblindness.

CHAPTER 4

3   eardrum

5   malleus, incus, stapes

7   oval window

9   liquid within the cochlea, cochlea itself

11   basilar membrane, (liquid within the cochlea)

13   the nonuniform stiffness, width, and mass of the basilar membrane

15   hair cells, basilar membrane, (tympanic membrane)

17   hair cells, ganglia in the auditory nerve

18   It would then be very difficult to vibrate and thus extremely insensitive to sound
     waves.

21   The nonuniform width and stiffness cause the traveling wave to have a maximum bulge
     with location depending upon frequency, instead of the wave having approximately
     the same height all along the basilar membrane.

22   all frequencies would sound the same

23   If one plays a group of tones, humans can pick out the individual ones.

24   Poke a microelectrode into a ganglion in the auditory nerve and vary the frequency
     of a tone until you find one that the ganglion responds to. Then the ganglion is
     also likely to respond to that tone played in a chord.

25   With a microelectrode in any ganglion in the auditory nerve, vary the frequency of
     a tone from 20 Hz to 20,000 Hz. There should be only one frequency which the
     ganglion responds maximally to.

26   Same as 25, but now there should be several frequencies which a ganglion responds
     maximally to.

29   The tones would all sound the same.

30   Play a high frequency tone and poke a microelectrode around in the auditory nerve.
     There should be no neurons responding to this high frequency tone.

32   moves up

33   With higher frequencies the time between upward movements of the basilar membrane
     would be shorter.

35   yes

36   no

37   no

38   Since for a 500 Hz tone there are only 500 upward movements of the basilar membrane
     each second, there is nothing to cause the hair cell to fire 1000 times each second.

39   125 Hz

40   less than 2 milliseconds or .002 seconds

41 600 Hz

43 3 different sets

45 frequency of inward movements of the eardrum

46 frequency of vibrations of the middle ear bones

47 frequency of inward movements of the oval window

48 frequency of vibrations (upward movements) of the basilar membrane

49 frequency of firings on groups of hair cells

50 4 "10 times"

51 7

52 10 dB

53 30 dB

54 50 dB

55 90 dB

56 between 20 and 30 dB

57 between 40 and 50 dB

58 between 50 and 60 dB

59 20,000 dynes/cm^2

60 2,000,000 dynes/cm^2

61 .0002 dynes/cm^2

62 .01 dynes/cm^2

63 1000 dynes/cm^2

64 -20 dB

65 -50 dB

66 30 dB

67 .0000002 dynes/cm^2

68 .000000002 dynes/cm^2

69 .00001 dynes/cm^2

70 20,000 dynes/cm^2

71 that the base is the standard reference level of .0002 dynes/cm^2

72 100 times

73 10,000,000 times

74 The intensity of the noice will increase proportionately.

75 .00002 dynes/cm^2

76 no

77 It is below the minimum detectable sound of about .0002 dynes/cm^2.

78 2000 dynes/cm^2

79   40 dB

80   between a soft whisper and normal conversation

81   It is drowned out or "masked" by the intensity of the music.

82   2 layers

83   70 dB or 2000 dynes/cm^2

CHAPTER 5

2   B

3   B

4   B

5   A

6   B

7   A

8   A

9   B

10   nothing

13   the 1000 Hz tone is about 5 dB louder

14   the 1000 Hz tone is again slightly louder, and by almost the same amount as at 80 dB

15   softer

16   to make the frequencies in music have the same balance in intensities at home levels as at concert levels

17   20

18   40

19   increase

20   approximately correctly

21   lower frequency sounds are louder than they should be

22   It would decrease (or "attenuate") intensities of sounds of frequencies below 110 Hz.

23   The frequencies below 110 Hz would then not be loud enough for those sitting in the bleachers.

25   20 Hz

26   about 1050 to 6000 Hz

27   The traveling wave on the monkey's basilar membrane is square instead of rounded

28   The waves are symmetrical instead of steeper on the side nearer the apex of the cochlea as in humans.

31   the first pair

32   the 600 Hz (and 80 dB) tone

37   1 sone

38   2 sones

39   128 sones

40   .5 sones

41   .125 sones

42   21 sones

44   dynes/cm^2 or dB, Hertz

45   loudness, pitch

46   sones, mels

47   600 Hz

48   150 Hz

49   2 octaves

50   3 octaves

51   4 octaves

52   between 1 and 2 octaves

53   1

54   2

55   A

56   B

57   both have same number of octaves

58   Hertz

59   dynes/cm^2

61   The guesses in mels are going to correspond fairly well to the actual number of
        hertz until the higher frequencies, where the number of mels will be less than the
        actual number of hertz.

62   the basilar membrane

63   The nonuniform shape, stiffness, and mass of the basilar membrane causes the traveling
        waves to peak at different locations along the membrane depending upon the frequency,
        just as your friend picks a location depending upon frequency.

64   oval window

65   all three intervals cover exactly one octave

67   base

68   apex

69   B, same, B

70   B, same, B

71   B, same, B

72   A, A, A

73   same, A, A

74   the range will get larger

77   Take any two pokes on the back that can just be distinguished apart.   Then a "jnd"
     is the difference in mels between your two guesses.

79   fundamental

80   first harmonic

81   40

82   60

83   20 Hz (fundamental)

84   40 Hz

85   20 Hz

86   it is below the threshold of hearing curve

87   rise (to 40 Hz)

88   100

89   100 Hz

90   160 Hz

91   160 Hz, 940 Hz, 1100 Hz, 1260 Hz, 1420 Hz

92   yes

95   no

96   Figure 5-22 of HIP

97   Since 100 to 200 Hz is a full octave while 5100 to 5300 is a small fraction of one,
     the locations of the maximum peaks of the traveling waves on the basilar membrane
     are much further apart for 100 and 200 Hz than for 5100 and 5300 Hz.

98   The fundamentals of consecutive black and white keys are in the same critical band,
     while the fundamentals in a third or a fifth are not.

99   Various harmonics of the two notes in the chords may lie in the same critical band.

100 differences in arrival times of sound between two ears

102 20 to 1300 Hz

104 differences in sound intensities between two ears (sound shadows)

106 about 3500 Hz to 20,000 Hz

109 they would be worse than humans

110 In this range elephants would be using phase differences (as would humans), which
     depend upon there being less than one cycle being completed during the time the
     sound takes to go between the ears.   Since the elephant's eardrums are further apart
     than human's, for these frequencies more than one cycle would be completed and this

location method would be of much less use.

111 diplacus

112 relationship between pitch and frequency can be explained by distribution of hair cells along the basilar membrane

113 one can hear frequencies of higher than 4000 Hz

114 goldfish

115 the existence of beats

116 the case of the missing fundamental (actually closely related to the existence of beats)

CHAPTER 6

2 The dendrites of a neuron can have synapses from axons belonging to more than one other cell.

3 receptor (or transducer)

4 transducer (or receptor)

5 20, 20, 20, 10, 10, 10, 10, 20, 20, 20

6 The output response pattern will be the same as the input light pattern.

7 Such inputs are necessary for any features to be extracted from the input light pattern--if no such connections are allowed, no analysis can be done of the input pattern.

8 lateral inhibition

9 Output of neurons from left to right: 6, 6, 6, 6, 4, 14, 12, 12, 12, 10, 20, 18, 18, 18, 16, 26, 24, 24

12 4, 4, 4, 4, 4, 4, 4, 3, 1, 11, 9, 8, 8, 8, 8, 8, 8, 8

14 1, 1, 1, 1, 1, 0, -2, -5, -1, 4, 8, 5, 3, 2, 2, 2, 2, 2

15 The peaks are becoming more rounded and the line between them is becoming less steep.

16 The gains or inhibitions of any one connection are less, and there are more connections per neuron.

17 Continue the trend in 16.

18 That synapse is not functioning, or an axon or dendrite is broken or non-functional.

19 The neuron would think that there was an edge at that point in the pattern.

20 There would be large changes in the output patterns.

23 Change the inhibitory connections to excitatory and vice versa.

24 a bright spot of light just covering the on-center with darkness elsewhere

25 a doughnut-shaped spot of light just covering the off-surround with darkness elsewhere

26   off-center, on-surround

27   More of the surround field is covered by the light pattern.

31   This is a color light detector sensitive only to red light.

33   changes in light intensity

34   34, 14, 18, 18, 14, 34

35   90 units

36   30 units

37   62, 2, 14, 14, 2, 62

38   The response level is lower.

39   first

40   second

41   brightness contrast

42   lateral inhibition

43   62, 2, 14, 26, 26, 26, 26, 14, 2, 62

44   The middle part is brighter than that of the first pattern. (Note: It would still
     be brighter if the dark area of the first pattern were also widened.)

45   The dark patches were so narrow that the inhibitions from the bright areas affected
     the responses of each neuron in the dark area. (This is no longer the case when the
     patch is sufficiently wide.)

46   The receptors inhibiting any one ganglion cover a much wider area than the 5 cells
     here.

47   440 nm

48   blue

49   the blue-yellow channel

50   high

51   decrease

54   Since it fires at below background rate to blue light it can't be fatigued by it.

55   blue

56   yellow

57   at a completely desaturated blue or yellow

58   Answer will probably be negative but will depend upon the exact curve drawn for
     Figure 6.23.

59   a somewhat desaturated yellow

60   Answer should be negative, but the magnitude will depend upon both Figure 6.23 and the
     second curve drawn in Figure 6.22.

61   a more saturated yellow than before

62   induced contrast

63   like a somewhat desaturated yellow

65   The outside blue field will inhibit the third-level neurons in the yellow area, much
       as the outside bright field inhibited the neurons in the dark field in brightness
       contrast.

66   brightness contrast

67   the stripes will be wider

68   The edges of the letters are sharp like the square wave, and thus contain high
       frequency components like the square wave does.

69   the lowest frequency component is much higher for the letters

70   the higher frequency ones

71   The stripes should look narrower than if you had not stared at the previous pattern.

72   (Distinguishing Characteristics only) location specific, orientation specific, not
       size specific, simply-shaped receptive fields, often have preferred direction

73   orientation specific, not size or location specific, often have preferred direction

74   orientation and size specific, not location specific, can sometimes respond to
       movement in two directions, receptive fields sometimes more complex

CHAPTER 7

2   Suppose that at any given time a word is entering on each channel, and a person
      must decide which of the two words to analyze and which word to discard. Since the
      person must make the choice before any information is known about either word, the
      choice will be right only about half the time. Thus a person could never separate
      out one message to listen to from two or more messages, which is clearly false.

3   She can't.

4   A person could extract the tone level of words from each channel as they come in,
      and listen only to those words in a high pitched tone.

5   Since the same person reads both passages, basic features of each of the channels
      will be the same, and the subject has nothing to base a choice on.

6   Since the subject understands only English, he or she will be able to identify only
      the sounds in the English passage as words, and can thus choose to attend to only
      the English passage on the basis of this.

7   "feature" under the first stage, "cognitive" and "decision" under second stage

8   The "decision" in decision demons refers to deciding what letter best fits the
      features extracted, and not to deciding which channel to attend to further, as
      indicated by the switch.

9   Missing features are: vertical lines, slant lines, curves. Numbers in each line
      below refer to features from left to right across the table.

      a: 1, 3, 6, 1, 0

      b: 3, 3, 8, 0, 1

      v: 3, 4, 10, 0, 0

      g: 2, 0, 0, 3, 2

      d: 4, 4, 11, 0, 0

      e: 1, 0, 0, 0, 1

      x: 3, 4, 10, 0, 2

      z: 3, 3, 10, 10, 0

      tz: 4, 4, 15, 0, 0

      i-1: 4, 4, 16, 0, 0

      i-2: 2, 0, 4 (or 0), 2, 0

      y: 2, 3, 15, 1, 0

      k: 1, 0, 1, 4, 0

      1:   4, 4, 16, 0, 0

      m: 0, 1, 0, 0, 2

      n: 2, 1, 4, 1, 0

      o: 0, 1, 0 (or 2), 0, 2

      p: 3, 3, 9, 0, 0

      r: 2, 1, 3, 1, 0

      s: 1, 2, 4, 0, 1

      t: 1, 2, 4, 0, 2

      u: 1, 1, 4, 2, 2

      ph: 2, 1, 4, 0, 1

      ch: 1, 2, 1, 4, 0

10   the right angle feature demon

11   The template for "g" is the following feature list: 2 horizontal lines, 3 slant
       lines, 2 curves.

12   a list of features that the letter contains

13   They would all take the same amount of time.

14   the number of occurrences of its most numerous feature

15   "i-1" and "1"

16   They have very similar lists of features.

17   very small

18   "x"

19   "v", "d", "z", "tz", "i-l", "l"

20   "i-l" and "l", (since their feature lists are the most dissimilar to the list of extracted features)

21   yes

22   no

23   Since "g" contains no right angles, and there is at least one right angle in the character presented, that character cannot be a "g".

24   The box marked "K" contains the number of times that both the letter "tz" was presented and the subject guessed "tz".

25   In addition to the errors, the response matrix records the correct responses to the boxes along the diagonal (A, F, K, etc.). The confusion matrix records only errors, i.e., the diagonal is left blank.

26   A, F, K, P, S, U

27   These six boxes record correct responses; all other boxes record errors. Since no errors were made, all these other boxes should have "0"'s in them.

28   no

29   The predictions one can make of a matrix like this concerning a pandemonium model and its feature set are about whether a box should contain more errors than another box (depending upon how similar the features are in the letters involved). If there are no errors then none of these predictions can be tested.

30   greater

31   less

32   less

33   no prediction

34   greater

35   no prediction

36   less

37   no

38   Suppose one letter has all the features of a second letter plus one more. Let Case I be that the first letter is presented and the second letter is guessed, and Case II be that the second letter is presented and the first letter guessed. In Case I, if that extra feature is extracted, then one can't guess the second letter (since it doesn't contain that feature). However, in Case II, all the features that can be extracted are consistent with both letters, and thus either could be guessed. Thus II should be greater than I. (It is useful to try this rule on C and G in the

Roman alphabet.)

39 no prediction

40 no prediction

41 greater

42 greater

43 greater

44 According to the pandemonium system, one must recognize a letter using only the list of features extracted from it. If only the features mentioned here are used, then "i-1" and "1" have the same features, and there is no way to use this list of features extracted to distinguish between them.

45 C and G, D and H, E and I, A and B, B and F, A and F

46 One that works is extracting the number of squares and rectangles.

47 segmentation problem

48 Pick any two characters which differ only in the presence or absence of the feature in question. If a subject can distinguish between the two, then the feature is being used, otherwise not.

49 Two phonemes are distinct if, when substituted for each other in a word, two words of different meanings are formed.

50 No way has been found for analyzing and extracting phonemes from a speech waveform.

51 less

52 no prediction

53 greater

54 greater

55 same

56 features: operations used in generating sounds

57 phonemes

58 spoken words

59 context

60 redundant

61 contextual demons

62 In order to take advantage of context one must know what it means (e.g. to expect a word based upon the rest of the sentence requires knowledge of what the rest of the sentence means), and this knowledge must be stored in memory. Thus if there is no memory then context is of no use.

63 supervisor

64 to organize the activities of the demons such that they do not conflict with each other

65   to make sure the blackboard does not get so crowded that relevant information is lost

66   C

67   C

68   D

69   C

70   D

71   C

72   D

73   C

74   D

75   C

76   D

77   C

78   C

79   D

80   D

81   C

82   C

83   C

CHAPTER 8

2   maintenance rehearsal

3   short term memory

4   tachistoscope

5   4 or 5

6   No. The information will probably be available for 90 msec longer, but in either
     case SIS preserves the information for more than 150.

8   4 or 5 times

9   As long as it takes to respond. Several seconds, at least.

10   Ignores the fact that time is required to answer.

11   critic

12   About the same number of letters would be recalled, because in both cases recall is
     limited by the same factors: size of STM or transfer from SIS to STM.

13   about 100%

15   9 items or more. Possibly very large.

16   Yes.

17   150-500 msec

19   Report-All

20   STM or capacity for rapid transfer from SIS to STM.

21   Probe

22   Pattern recognition can take place during the duration of information in SIS.

23   50%

24   higher than

25   The letters in Display A look more like 'T' than 'S'; those in Display B look more
       like 'S' than 'T'.

26   Yes. Make guess based on fragments or features of letters remembered.

27   straight lines, right angles; curved lines.

28   At the offset of the display, expose in the location of the target character a
       circle which would have just enclosed the character.

29   about 150-500 msec.

30   about 10 msec.

31   counting backwards by threes

32   more; easier task--does not interrupt rehearsal as much.

33   STM follows pattern recognition.

34   speaking and hearing

35   acoustic/articulatory

36   All have the same final sound "-ee" when their names are pronounced.

37   very few, if any.

38   very few, if any.

39   straight lines and right angles

40   Group 1.

41   Group 1; Group 1

42   Rehearsal seems to put all the information in an auditory form.

43   1 out of 16; or 06.2%

44   50%

45   more features remembered, higher probability of correct reconstruction.

46   more alternatives possible, lower probability of correct reconstruction.

48   List 2

49   List 2 words more complicated or less familiar than those of List 1

50   perfect recall

52   decay of information in memory

53   probably not

54 Saying a sequence of 'yeses' and 'nos' to report whether the successive words of a remembered sentence are nouns or not.

55 Pointing to 'Y's and 'N's to report whether the successive words of a remembered sentence are nouns or not.

56 the visual/spatial task

CHAPTER 9

2 positions 1–14, approximately

3 positions 15–20, approximately

5 The effect due to STM has been eliminated.

7 The words from the center of the list (#7–15) are better remembered than in the above experiments

8 LTM (and probably STM as well);

9 reconstruction

11 recognition

12 They devote all processing resources to these stimuli. Also, the course of a cocktail party conversation is often easy to predict; therefore, expectations can help guide processing.

13 Yes, probably.

14 Yes, probably.

15 Apparently not all resources are devoted to the attended conversation. Other input must be partially attended to.

16 0 (none); apparently not enough resources allocated to get any of the unattended words into memory.

21 organizational factors

22 slow (or impossible)

23 The more time spent mentally organizing academic material, the more retrievable the information will be later.

24 Relating more previously learned information to new information will help improve chances of retrieval.

25 repeating over and over.

26 3, 1, 4, 2

27 Task 3

28 metaknowledge

29 repeated over and over

31 method of places

32   probably not;

33   probably not;

34   key words

35   relate new items to each other.   relate new items to old organization.

36   the interpreter

37   the monitor

38   the data base

39   very appropriate

40   inappropriate; it probably does not provide new information

41   "In the United States."

42   world

43   Hwy 17

44   Black Hills

45   Hwy 24

46   United States

47   South Dakota; fairly appropriate

48   Mt. Rushmore

49   Whenever Q-node is the same as the answer by the above rule, give explicit directions
       on how to get to the questioned location.

50   "In the United States."

51   The questioner has already made it clear that he knows the answer at this level.

52   "In South Dakota" or "In the Midwest"

53   The rule is too inflexible. It does not make use of enough cues to the appropriate
       level of response.

54   It would consult a more complete model of the questioner's knowledge to decide on
       an appropriate level of specificity for the answer.

55   the appropriateness of the "recalled" name; new contexts which will lead to new
       candidates for "recall."

CHAPTER 10

1   *500; *501

2   generic

3   ANIMAL; thinking

5   *499; *500

6   name

7   thinking

8   sensory; motor

9   sensorimotor

12 No; the same meaning is conveyed by either phrasing.

13 that they are animals and that they are thinking.

14 generic; specific

15 Three little pigs

19 In *17*, the proposition *large* applies to the generic concept ELEPHANT. In *18, large* applies to the concept of a specific individual elephant.

23 two; one

26 Martha owns the car she washed.

28 Sam's car

29 Joan

30 two

31 No; no

32 Yes. Knowledge about the typical sizes of houses and forests--part of generic representations of HOUSE and FOREST.

33 the girl who wears a cloak.

34 Yes; no

35 There is a girl who lives in a cottage. She lives in a dark large forest. There is another girl, who is little, who wears a cloak that has a little red hood.

39 episodic

40 semantic

41 On the average, semantic memory retrieval is faster than episodic, but there are exceptions.

42 word-identification (37) - semantic; window-recall - episodic.

43 STM

44 The more information in the data base "excited" by the interpreter, the more <u>details</u> are available in the image.

45 That it moves.

CHAPTER 11

1   If a stimulus causes a particular behavior in an animal, then habituation occurs when, after repeated application of that stimulus, it no longer causes that behavior.

2   touching or squirting the siphon

3   touching the purple gland

4   retraction of the gills

6   The Aplysia will no longer retract its gills.

7   A and C

8   habituation

9   There is none--more information is needed.

10 B and C

11 A

12 If neuron C held all or part of the memory, then the response to poking the purple gland would be less than on a fresh Aplysia.

13 no (Since A supposedly holds the first memory, neither of the possible candidates B and C could have been affected by our experiment, and thus either or both could contain the memory of the second behavior.)

14 Do the reverse experiment, i.e. habituate the response to poking the purple gland, and test whether the response to poking the siphon is the same as on a fresh Aplysia.

15 C

16 no

17 In either case dishabituation would then affect habituation to only one of the two stimuli.

18 yes

20 no

21 Since the memory for the behaviors is stored in neurons A and B, dishabituating C will not affect either of these behaviors.

22 If the memory were solely in neuron A, then the second behavior should not be affected at all. However, it might be in both A and C or C alone, either of which could partially affect the response to the second stimuli (since neuron C is part of the other pathway).

23 motion in a particular direction, shown to the right eye; same shown to the left eye

24 perception of that motion

25 the apparent "perception" of motion in the opposite direction

27 Cover one eye of a subject and present a moving pattern to the other eye. Then move the eye patch to the other eye and show the originally covered eye a textured background. If a motion aftereffect is observed, then part C of the network stores the memory or aftereffect. If there is no transfer of the aftereffect then parts A and B store the memory.

28 Part C is implicated

29 When one applies the stimulus to the first eye, either part A or part C must store

the aftereffect. If part A holds the aftereffect then the other eye should not be
affected. But since the aftereffect transfers to the other eye, part C must store
the aftereffect.

30   Each time the rat is placed in the room will be like the first time--the rat will act
as though it does not know about the food in the other room.

31   no

32   The rat could be interpreting the ECS as punishment for going into the room with food.
Thus the fact that the rat does not go into the food room on the next trial could be
explained by this as well as by the rat's memory of the food in the room being wiped
out by the ECS.

33   If the animal is learning to do something pleasant, then the effect of the ECS is
ambiguous: either memory for the learning is being erased or the animal is being
discouraged from doing the task by the possible pain of the ECS.

34   On each new trial the rat will jump into the dark room as though it has remembered
nothing from the previous trials.

35   yes

36   If the rat were interpreting the ECS as punishment for jumping into the dark room,
then it would not do so on the next trial. Since the rat does jump, this explanation
can't be right.

37   The rat needs to be learning that it must do one distasteful task (e.g. staying
in an intensely lit room, on top of a small pedestal, etc.), in order to avoid an
even more distasteful situation (e.g. an electrified floor).

39   The second experiment provides evidence that ECS is not an aversive stimulus and
instead erases short-term memory. Since the shocks from accidents that cause
retrograde amnesia appear to have the same effect as ECS, it is likely that these
shocks are also not aversive stimuli.

40   Perhaps older memories are less accessible and thus have less chance of being reached
by the shock which caused the amnesia.

41   It is difficult to determine what the victim knew before the accident.

42   Patients may not be aware of or remember all the things which are still in their memory.
Also, what they do remember may not be a representative sample of what's in their
memory.

43   If one waited an hour or so after taking the rat out of the dark room and then gave
the rat the ECS before placing it in the lighted room again, the memory of the
electrified floor in the dark room will not be disrupted and the rat will remain in

the lighted room. Since the ECS will disrupt any electrical form of memory, the
memory must have been encoded in some other form.

44   consolidation

45   immediately

46   If one waits a while before injecting, the animal will have had a chance to begin
       encoding the memory in terms of proteins, and a partial permanent memory will have
       formed.

47   1

50   N.A. appears not to be able to encode new information in long-term memory.

51   The tip of a sword poked through his nose and slightly into his brain.

52   Perhaps N.A. is not able to retrieve information from long-term memory.

53   N.A. is not able to accomplish the retrieval step needed for recall when dealing with
       new information.

55   corpus callosum

56   a large number of axons from neurons in either hemisphere

57   It is simply a redistribution of fibers from the two optic nerves: fibers from the
       left visual field of each eye are now channeled to the left hemisphere and right
       visual field to right hemisphere.

58   axons from ganglia in the retina

59   The cat will go through the maze about as well as it has learned to go through with
       a patch over its other eye.

60   nothing as far as whether memories are transferred to both hemispheres

61   Since the optic chiasma is uncut, information about the task being learned is going
       to both hemispheres even with a patch over one eye. Thus this experiment provides
       no evidence concerning transferring of memories between hemispheres.

62   One would conclude that memory for the task is stored in one hemisphere only, and
       is not transferred to the other hemisphere even during performance of the task.

63   The cat is able to perform the task as well as it has learned to do so with a
       patch over the other eye.

64   Memory is either transferred to the other hemisphere during learning, or is trans-
       ferred to the other hemisphere when needed for performance.

65   The cat will not know the path through the maze.

66   From the results of an experiment described in HIP, it is shown that memory for a
       task is transferred *during* learning. Since the other hemisphere was "asleep," this
       was not possible in our experiment; thus no memory is stored in the other hemisphere.
       Since the corpus callosum is also cut before testing, the hemisphere that was

"asleep" also can't find out about the task by communicating with the other hemisphere.

67   yes

68   Even though information in this case will go to both hemispheres, the hemisphere that is "asleep" will not record the information; thus this experiment will have the same result as the previous one.

69   The cat will be unable to see.

70   Since the right eye is covered the right hemisphere sees nothing. Since the left hemisphere is "asleep" it can also see nothing.

71   Instead of injecting the potassium chloride before the experiment, inject it into the left hemisphere at various times during the learning: right after beginning, after some learning, after considerable learning. Then, after completing learning, put the right hemisphere to sleep and let the left one wake up, and test the left hemisphere on how well it knows the task (i.e. its memory strength for the task). This could be done by seeing how many trials it takes to relearn the task.

72   Learning is transferred rapidly at the beginning, and transfer levels off after a while.

73   Learning could be transferred immediately, and the shape of the curve could be due instead to the gradual encoding of the learning in long-term memory. This is reasonable since this curve and the curve in Figure 11.7 have the same shape.

74   the right hand

75   Sensory input from the right hand goes to the left hemisphere, which takes care of speech production in a strongly right-handed person.

76   a hammer

77   no

78   In order to verbally identify the object, her left hemisphere must know about the object. However, only her right hemisphere knows about the hammer. (The right hemisphere directed the left hand to draw the hammer.)

79   yes

80   The right hemisphere is capable of speech understanding, which is all this task needs.

81   yes

82   Say the name of the object aloud, and the right hemisphere will listen to and under-stand the speech, and thus know what object to draw.

83   words

84   tones

85   As mentioned in HIP, most of the information from the right ear goes to the left hemisphere and left ear to right hemisphere. Therefore, since the left hemisphere is

better for verbal material, the right ear should be better for words. Similarly, since the right hemisphere is better at music, tones heard by the left ear should be better remembered.

86 In testing one hemisphere for words or tones it is necessary to keep the other hemisphere occupied (by listening to random clicks or some other irrelevant task), or else it will help in the processing of the stimulus by communicating across the corpus callosum. Thus the right hemisphere, which is better at tones, could help the left hemisphere in processing when the right ear is listening to tones, and vice versa for words. Thus little or no difference in error rates would probably be observed for the two conditions.

CHAPTER 12

1   In both cases, the incoming sentence must be analyzed for its meaning in context, using grammatical/syntactic knowledge, word-meaning, and knowledge about the world.

2   No;

3   The word order is wrong

4   Meaning structures probably don't involve the same order relationships that sentences do.

5   The cat chased the dog.

6   "the my" is not necessary because "my" is definite in English.

7   Whenever the translation includes a definite article immediately followed by a pronoun, delete the definite article.

8   No.

9   My younger sister was funny.

10 My great grandmother was funny.

11 People ordinarily use all the above sources of information.

12 It is phrased as a command rather than a question.

13 Yes; both sentences deny the worth of the cake. The command form implies that the cake is only eaten under duress, although both speaker and hearer recognize that this is not the case.

14 The hearer's previous knowledge about the topic. Plausibility. Grammatical knowledge. Semantic knowledge. Pragmatic/contextual knowledge.

15 Grammatical, semantic, and pragmatic/contextual knowledge.

16 1. The speaker knows the "answer."

    2. It is not obvious that the hearer would provide the information without being asked.

3. The speaker wants to know whether the hearer knows the "answer."

4. The speaker intends that, as a result of his utterance, the hearer will tell him the "answer."

5. The speaker bears a <u>teacher</u> relationship to the hearer.

17 Yes. 2, 4.

18 *B* needed to know more about *A*'s knowledge so as to be able to give the answer in a useful form.

19 The question-begets-question process outlined in *18* happened 3 times. Thus four answers were called for.

20 indefinite; definite

21 a. An aspect of the setting of the utterance identifies the referent.

b. unique referent

c. introduced earlier in conversation

d. introduced earlier in conversation

22 Check whether the definite noun phrase might refer to a *generic* concept (a primary node, in the terminology of HIP, Chapter 10).

23 1, 2, 5, 6, 7, 8; 3, 4

24 1 = 2; 3 = 6; 4 = 8

25 The context does not tell the hearer what the intended referents of "he" and "him" are.

26 Find a pre-existing referent; definite

27 No.

28 The meaning structures are the same, but the surface structures are different.

29 It can mean either: 1) It is boring to visit professors; or 2) Professors who visit are boring.

30 The sentence can be represented by more than one meaning structure.

	Produced by above rules?	Grammatical English?
31	Yes	Yes?
32	Yes	Yes
33	Yes	No
34	Yes	No
35	Yes	Yes
36	Yes	No?
37	Yes	No
38	No	Yes
39	Yes	No

40   Yes, both.

41   No. People must begin with meanings they would like to convey, otherwise language
       isn't functional.

       EQUI applied?   Condition(s) not met?

42   Yes   --

43   No   3

44   No   1 (However, you could argue that there was a
       lower sentential idea as in "Eloise wants
       Eloise to _have_ a soft drink," in which case
       EQUI could apply.)

45   No   1

46   Yes   --

47   No   3

48   No   2

49   They are the same.

50   d-f?

51 NP_1-V-Part-$NP_2 \rightarrow$ NP_1-V-NP_2-Part, when NP_2 is not large. (Notice the oddity of
       "The realtor pointed the large yellow house with green shutters out.")

52   It moves the particle around the second Noun phrase. Notice that it does _not_ move
       to the end of the sentence: "The realtor pointed the house out to us."

53   Those who are old must man the boats.

CHAPTER 13

1   Whenever in the context of a small red round light and an unlit (?) where there is
      also a small red square and a tray, then if one pecks the square, food appears in the
      tray.

2   A predisposition to peck at things.

3   The _If PECK then_ structure expresses a causal relation.

4   If the experiment is being performed on human subjects, then the _aware_ group could
      have the contingency verbally explained to them. No such explanation would be made
      to the _unaware_ group. Or the experimenter could interview the subjects after the
      experiment to see which ones were aware and which were unaware of the contingency.

5   Group 2; one who was not listening, did not understand the explanation, or did not
      believe the experimenter.

6   Yes;

7   No;

8   Group 2; they learn the contingencies before any of the experimental trials begin.

9   Superstitious behavior.

10 Group 1

11 Not knowing the true contingency, a subject from this group is more likely to develop an erroneous explanation of the relationship between his behavior and the shocks.

12 Subjects in the unaware group might develop erroneous impressions of the <u>purpose</u> of the experiment, perhaps deciding that it is a test of patience rather than a learning test.

13 Learned helplessness; Group 2

14 Make the escape contingency much more difficult to discover (or make escape impossible)

16 10%

17 Those who gave certain answers would be more likely to condition.

18 c, d, f, g, h, j.

19 Yes.

20 Hypotheses c, d, g, h, and j are all incorrect but give the appearance of conditioning.

21 Yes.

23 Their hypothesis keeps getting confirmed so long as they use this restricted rule.

24 The animals form the hypothesis that the novel food was the <u>cause</u> of the illness.

25 concrete operations

26 formal operations

27 sensorimotor learning

28 preoperational thought

29 formal operations

30 preoperational thought

31 formal operations

32 sensorimotor schemata

33 Development is restricted with respect to the <u>order</u> in which various cognitive skills develop.

34 The named object can have different clothes, can wear or not wear sunglasses, have shaving cream on its face, and so on.

35 The basic identity of the object cannot change. Ordinarily, sex, height, color, and so forth cannot change.

36 No.

37 The "definition" specifies the range of items to which the term applies.

38 Verbs ordinarily do not name things which can be pointed to. Verbs which name actions

usually have brief referents. Verbs like <u>know</u>, <u>believe</u> and so on have invisible
referents.

39 The child might really mean "Rolling and bouncing."

40 "At nap-time today, Mommy, he hit him on the ear."

41 *Mommy like; Mommy banana; Like banana; Like Mommy; Banana Mommy; Banana like.*

42 *Like Mommy, Banana Mommy, Banana like.*

43 The child is aware of basic subject-verb-object word order in English, even though
no sentences longer than two words are spoken.

CHAPTER 14

1 Parts of the problem solving process which the solver is not aware of will not show
up in the protocol.

2 Solvers may not include steps or stages they go through in the solution that they
think are obvious to you or too trivial to mention. Nevertheless these steps may be
important parts of the problem solving process.

6 yes

7 Simply apply that operation to the initial state to get the next state. Operations
must be so defined that when they are applied to any given state it produces a
unique next state.

8 yes

9 The solver is in an impossible state, or thinks so.

10 The solver reached no "dead-ends" and probably applied the correct operation at each
point in the solution.

11 Problem behavior graph drawn on next page

12 If the last operation was a FERRYing operation, then the boat is on the far side. If
it was a RETURN then the boat is on the original side.

13 "Let's see, we have three missionaries and a cannibal to go and two cannibals on the
other side...where's the boat?"

14 seven

15 The solver has reached an impossible state in the problem.

16 The solver probably looked ahead a state or two without saying anything, and noticed
that an impossible state would soon arise. (Another possibility is that the solver
realizes a state has been reached that had been reached before, and thus no progress
is being made.)

17 state 10

18 R(M,C)

19 It probably seemed that returning with a full boat isn't any progress toward a solution. Also, the state you end up with after applying this operation (2 missionaries, 2 cannibals, and the boat on the original side) is similar to a state reached at the very beginning of the solution. The crucial difference, which is probably not noticed, is that the boat is on the original instead of the far side.

20 R(C)

21 R(C) puts all the cannibals back in their original state, which may <u>seem</u> to be going backward. The solver may also have considered R(M), but this returns to an earlier state. (<u>Note</u>: This is only speculation.)

22 decelerating

23 There is probably only a limited number of things which you could buy which would really make you much happier; after these have been bought, money to buy other things would not affect your happiness much.

26 probably linear or accelerating

27 Usually misers are thought of as people who get much happiness from more money, no matter how much money they already have, i.e. their utility curve for money does not decelerate.

28 how unhappy losing various amounts of money would make you

29 yes

30 If you have lost all that you own, losing any more money can't change your unhappiness too much more (e.g. you could always declare bankruptcy, etc.).

31 They spend small amounts of money in place of possibly losing large amounts.

32 Since negative utility accelerates for a while, losing small amounts of money (i.e. paying for insurance) has a very small negative utility, in comparison to the very large negative utility of losing a greater amount of money (losing a house or car). Thus, although insurance is a bad deal from a money standpoint, it is often a good deal if one considers utility.

33 Paying the small amount for the lottery ticket has almost a negligible negative utility, while the chance (although quite small) of winning a large amount, has a high positive utility. A second reason that we will consider later is that people tend to overestimate their chances of winning.

34 People would probably not buy nearly as many tickets. Whereas the negative utility of 50 cents is negligible, the negative utility of $5 is significant.

35 There is no really satisfactory answer here. One possibility is that, if the chance of death is small enough, it should not be considered in making a decision.

36 dimensional comparison

Answer to Question 11, Chapter 14

37   the Volkswagen

38   overall impression

39   the Volkswagen

40   Porsche: -2, +16, +4, -3, -20, +27, total = +22

Volkswagen: +2, -12, +16, +5, +20, -6, total = +25

41   Volkswagen

42   When there are many components to a decision it is difficult to keep all the
relevent dimensions in short-term memory at once.

43   If you have an initial preference for one of the choices, and you make your ratings
before deciding upon the weights, then you may unconsciously or consciously bias the
weights to favor your preference (i.e. give large weights to dimensions where your
preference has high ratings).

44   In situations where everything must go right, it is important that no person has one
"fatal flaw" which could ruin a project.

45   10

46   0

47   2

48   1 minus the sum of the probabilities of all of the other events

49   With simple utility the value of the choice you make is definite, whereas with
expected utility the value of your choice is not known until it happens, and the
utility of your choice is just the average of the utilities of the events which could
possibly happen.

50   (+16) x (.6) + (-10) x (.4) = +5.6, yes

51   (+16) x (.4) + (-10) x (.6) = +.4, yes

52   If the chance of rain is higher than about 20%, people tend to overestimate its
occurence, assuming that it will rain most or all of the time.

53   (+18) x (.4) + (+4) x (.4) + (-30) x (.2) = +2.8, go on the trip

54   1 x (1/6) + 2 x (1/6) + 3 x (1/6) + 4 x (1/6) + 5 x (1/6) + 6 x (1/6) = 21/6 = 3.5

55   less

56   Since we have been given that the utility of $1 is 1, and we know that the utility
for money is decelerating, then the utilities for $2, $3, $4, $5, and $6 must be less
than 2, 3, 4, 5, and 6 respectively. Since these were the utilities used in
question 54 above, the total utility here must be less than in that question.

57   (600) x (.005) + (670) x (.005) + (-7.0) x (.99) = -.58, don't apply to one more
medical school

58   the utility of becoming a doctor and being one for the rest of your life

59   This utility will involve your attitudes, which may change over your life. Also,
       there are many possibilities and it is very difficult to consider or even think
       of them all.

60   Applying to one more medical school may seem insignificant after having already
       applied to 15 others.

61   The company may not want to risk the huge negative utility of possible bankruptcy
       when something catastrophic happens (e.g. a coup) for a small, although positive,
       expected utility gain, or even a chance at a large gain (for example, if business
       goes very well). A company that felt it was in trouble anyway would probably be
       more willing to take such a risk.

62   There are often too many components in a decision to fit simultaneously into short-
       term memory. This can make analysis of the best choice quite difficult. Also,
       the utility of the effort of doing an analysis of the choices is sometimes a factor
       in making a decision.

63   Focusing on a particular dimension will often appear to increase its importance.

64   Human decisions often must include factors other than price and quality of each
       choice. Considerations such as time needed to take particular choices, effort
       needed to make the decision itself, etc., must be taken into account in analyzing
       or explaining a decision.

65   gambler's fallacy

66   availability: One of the determiners of the subjective probability of an event is
       what examples of the event in the past are best remembered.

CHAPTER 15

1   If a FIND command finds the feature it is searching for, it has to generate some
       signal which can be noticed by the rest of the program.

2   This program and the other programs below are not the only solutions to the problems.
       In particular, the order of many of the commands in the programs can be changed.
       PROGRAM: Venusian Person

```
10   FIND RD
20   FIND FR
30   FIND L1
40   FIND AR4
50   IF NOFAIL THEN SAY PERSON OTHERWISE SAY NOMATCH
```

3   PROGRAM: Venusian Person

```
10   FIND FR
```

```
    20  FIND L1
    30  FIND AR4
    40  IF NOFAIL THEN GO ON OTHERWISE SAY NOMATCH
    50  CLEAR MBOX
    60  FIND RD
    70  IF NOFAIL THEN SAY PERSON OTHERWISE GO ON
    80  CLEAR MBOX
    90  FIND GR
   100  IF NOFAIL THEN SAY PERSON OTHERWISE SAY NOMATCH
```

4   In order for a system to learn by changing it must modify the programs it has to
    reflect these changes. Thus it needs commands to treat these programs as data--to
    locate commands and change, delete, or replace them.

5   PROGRAM: Fix Rock Program

```
    10  CLEAR MBOX
    20  LOCATE BL
    30  CHANGE BL TO BR
    40  CLEAR MBOX
    50  LOCATE HD
    60  CHANGE HD TO FZ
```

6   If the system ran the rock recognizing program on the list of features for a
    Venusian mushroom, it would mistakenly recognize the list as being a Venusian rock.

7   PROGRAM: Venusian Rock

```
    10  FIND BR
    20  FIND FZ
    30  FIND RN
    40  IF NOFAIL THEN GO ON OTHERWISE SAY NOMATCH
    50  DELETE BR
    60  DELETE FZ
    70  DELETE RN
    80  IF EMPTYLIST THEN SAY ROCK OTHERWISE SAY NOMATCH
```

8   PROGRAM: Venusian Rock

```
    10  FIND BR
    20  FIND FZ
    30  FIND RN
    40  IF NOFAIL THEN GO ON OTHERWISE SAY NOMATCH
    50  FIND AN1
```

60 IF NOFAIL THEN SAY NOMATCH OTHERWISE SAY ROCK

9   the demons are working simultaneously

10 the message box

11 single commands

12 programs

13 In order to recognize a new object it might be able to combine these basic feature detectors in new ways, much as one would construct a new program or modify an old one.

14 time sharing

15 the problems involved with switching between tasks, i.e. saving the current information in short-term memory (partial results, etc.) and remembering where you are in the task

16 all the partial products that you had already multiplied out

17 the number of stoplights that you had counted so far

18 where you were along the route from Coney Island to Macy's

19 from the multiplication problem to the stoplight problem

20 This information which must be remembered before each switch could be written down on paper instead. Also, even when you were not switching, the multiplication would be easier if you could write down the numbers as you computed them.

21 The size of short-term memory is so small.

22 dual (or multiple) processors

23 Both tasks involve counting and numbers; thus even if two processors could be utilized, they would be constantly conflicting and wanting the same resources.

24 one example: one could walk while doing either of the tasks

25 CHANGE

26 DELETE

27 identifying the color of ink that the word is printed in

28 identifying the word itself

29 In the Stroop effect the two processes will sometimes give conflicting results. Since identifying the word itself is the usual response when reading print, the result of this process is more available. However, one is supposed to output the result of the other process instead, and thus there is a problem.

30 supervisor

31 word task favors left hemisphere, tone task favors right

32 Most of the sensory input from the left ear goes to the right hemisphere and vice versa.

33   He should compare the reaction times to the noun-verb tasks to each ear, and he should also compare the reaction times to the tone tasks for each ear.

34   Left hemisphere should be faster for word task, right hemisphere for tone task.

35   He needed to include an irrelevant auditory task to the ear which was not being tested in each of the four conditions.

36   corpus callosum

37   Otherwise the hemisphere which is not being tested can help the hemisphere which is by communicating across the corpus callosum. This is particularly useful when the untested hemisphere is better at the task than the tested one.

38   The results should come out as predicted earlier, even without using an irrelevant task.

39   The hemispheres can't help each other since they can't communicate across the corpus callosum.

40   data-driven control

41   program control

42   interrupt

43   conceptually guided control

44   conceptually guided

45   program

46   conceptually guided

47   conceptually guided

48   conceptually guided

49   data-driven

50   program

51   data-driven (or possibly conceptually guided)

52   conceptually guided

53   data-driven control

54   conceptually guided control

CHAPTER 16

1   "one-to-one" feature of prototypical marriage.

2   "woman" feature of one participant in marriage usually applied only to adults or near-adults.

3   No clear violation according to the prototypes stated above. Presumably more information about durations of marriages is needed in the MARRIED prototype.

4   Marriage is usually considered terminated at the time of the divorce.

5   Yes; see answer to 3, above

6   Martians are little green living things who arrive in flying saucers. They should
     say "Take me to your leader," in a squeaky voice.

7   green, small, living thing

8   "Take me to your leader"; the actual sentence spoken has some sound similarities
     to this sentence and the witnesses' expectations directed their perception/under-
     standing.

9   As saucer-like

10   They will probably report it as higher-pitched than it was.

11   Conceptually-driven processing

12   Perception will be biased toward expectations. This can lead to inaccuracies.

15   Purpose of customer: have enjoyable meal

     Purpose of waiter: get good tip

     Scene 1: Entering

          Customer: Select restaurant

                     Enter restaurant

          Hostess: Guide customer to table; give customer menu

          Customer: If no hostess, find table

          Waiter: If no hostess, give customer menu

     Scene 2: Ordering

          Waiter: Ask customer for order

          Customer: place order

     Scene 3: Eating

          Waiter: Bring food to customer

          Customer: Eat

     Scene 4: Paying

          Customer: Request check from waiter

          Waiter: Provide check

          Customer: Leave tip

                     Pay cashier

                     Leave restaurant

18   Parent, Child, Adult

19   Obtaining assistance so as to solve the problem; obtaining comfort and reassurance or
     punishment from a Parent.

20   Adult; Parent

21   Child; Adult

22   Yes, both.

23   One in which the participants are in complementary ego states, such as Adult-Adult
      or Child-Parent.

24   Greed, stinginess, acquisitiveness

25   The goals of the game

26   The situation; the person

27   The person

28   The situation

29   25¢. Those who accept a mere 25¢ bribe will not be able to attribute their lies to
      great benefit for themselves, thus they will attribute their statements to the nature
      of the experiment, which, they will come to feel, is not so boring after all.

30   Condition A.

31   What other people who are witnessing the event are doing--do they seem to be perceiving
      it as a theft or as something else.

32   The apparent thief might actually be a friend of the owner, bringing the radio to her.

33   Yes, the alternative explanation presented in 32 is not nearly as plausible.

34   When the observer is uncertain whether action is called for and notices that other
      people in his situation are doing nothing.

36   Through explanation and experience with the game.

37   quite likeable

38   Average

39   less

40   assimilation

41   attentional

42   level of aspiration

43   That both participants have approximately equal knowledge of each other's.

44   Make small concessions in return for large concessions, punish small concessions
      with very unfavorable offers.

      CHAPTER 17

2   Once the hypothesis of learned helplessness has been adopted, one has admitted to
      oneself that one does not possess an appropriate situation-schema.

3   Subjects believe that experimenters would not really allow subjects to be seriously
      injured.

4   Not very. Their schema for the laboratory experiment includes the concept of basic
      safeguards for the subject.

5   The visual perceptions of the subject; the reports of the other subjects, presumably based on their perceptions.

7   Flying on a commercial airline is safer than driving, but less under the control of the individual passenger.

8   hypothalamus, pituitary, and adrenal systems.

9   Adrenaline discharge, increased heart rate, reduced temperature and muscle tone, anemia, increased blood sugar and stomach activity.

10   Defense reactions, increased metabolic rate

11   Depletion of adaptation reserves

12   Not at all

13   Confusion is more likely

14   Yes.

15   No; the stress should result in confusion

16   Possibly, but not necessarily, better

17   very much better

19   If only unimportant cues were lost.

20   If some important cues were lost.

21   Possible alternative actions are not noticed because the relevant cues are not available or are not attended to.

22   (Fire doors open <u>outwards</u>)

23   The relevant situation schema is certain to be available.

25   spread out

26   boosted

27   Alerting organism to changing environmental conditions and modulating the flow of sensory traffic in response to changing environmental demands.

28   two

29   Muscular tenseness, faster heartbeat, increased blood pressure

30   slower heartbeat, dilated blood vessels, reduced blood pressure

31   Yes

32   the sympathetic nervous system

33   Nothing--they behaved in a normal fashion.

Nothing--they behaved in a normal fashion.

34   They acted giddy and happy.

They acted enraged.

Part of emotion seems to involve the need to attribute a cause for the physical sensations of arousal.